order to arrive at the final 150 names a number factors were taken into account. For example, ears of service to the Lions and the number of ppearances; the number of tries and goals ored; leadership qualities; and the presentative honours secured whilst each man as a Swinton player. Particularly in respect of ore recent times (when playing contracts have ten been shorter and the club less successful), e player may have made an outstanding ntribution under difficult circumstances. And ccasionally you might see a player chosen simply s a "cult hero".

evitably there are players who missed out on the nal cut in marginal circumstances, and perhaps ome honourable mentions are worthy here. From e club's Rugby Union days there was Tom lallam who played almost 250 games as a orward; and also Tom Coulthwaite, who not only on a Lancashire cap, but went on to train race-orses and won the Grand National three times. ack Johnson, was a towering forward who was apped by Lancashire under both rugby codes hilst playing for Swinton; Evan Vigors was nother forward and county cap from the same ra; David (D.B.) Davies who won three Welsh caps rior to the Great War; Jack Pearson, the full-back f the great 1920s team missed out on inclusion imply due to the large number of worthy

candida forward lads and Critchley, t Moses and ...st spring to mind who helped inspire Cliff Evans' emerging team; then into the glory years of the 1960s there's Malcolm "Midge" Cummings and Derek Whitehead from Folly Lane, plus forwards Harold Bate, Ken Halliwell and Graham Rees. Finally, inevitably over the past 30 years or so everyone will have their own recollections and favourites, too numerous to list here, but all of them remembered as "Lions of Swinton".

You will find sections elsewhere in this book which set out the unique Heritage Number and brief playing record of every single player that is known to have played for the Lions. From the first recorded game against the Number One Company of the 46th Lancashire Rifle Volunteers on 2nd January 1869, right up to the last day of the 2016 season. This remarkable piece of work contains a virtually complete record from 1877 onwards, representing research probably unequalled anywhere in the sporting world. We hope that you enjoy this book, and continue to support Swinton Lions as the club embarks on its next 150 years!

Acknowledgements

his book has largely been written, compiled and edited by Stephen Wild, with valued input from Martin McDonough, Ian Jackson and Stephen Johnson. Credit also goes to the Swinton Lions club photographer, Pete Green, who is responsible for the Chris Atkin cover picture as well as others within this book. However, the exceptional detail of statistical information concerning players' career records, owes everything to the painstaking research over many years of Les Smith and John Edwards. The Swinton club and its fans owes a debt of gratitude to Les and John for their efforts, and for making the fruits of their research available to all via this book. Grateful thanks also go to the Swinton Supporters' Trust, which has partially funded the printing of the book.

The foundation of Swinton Rugby Club can be traced back to 1866. It was on 20th October of that year that members of Swinton Cricket Club (which had just completed its first season) decided to keep themselves amused during the winter months by playing "football". This was decided at a meeting held in the old school rooms of St Peter's, and the club immediately established its headquarters at the Bull's Head. But other than an annual challenge against the local rifle volunteers which began in January 1869, the only games played in those early days were amongst the club's own well-to-do membership. These games were played just off Burying Lane (now Station Road), on a field now roughly covered by Buchanan Street. However, in October 1871, the club decided to join the recently formed Rugby Football Union under the title "Swinton and Pendlebury Football Club".

Swinton's first official match took place on 4th November 1871 against a club called Standard from Eccles, and within a few short years the team became virtually unbeatable in the Manchester area. This meteoric rise in stature was made all the more remarkable by the fact that Swinton at this time was nothing more than a tiny colliery village with a few cotton mills. However, what it also had was a staggering number of local junior teams from which the club drew its talent.

An 1873 move from their Burying Lane pitch to another at Stoneacre (close to the White Lion pub where the club now moved its headquarters and the players got changed), gave rise to the famous "Lions" nickname. This nickname is undoubtedly one of the oldest in world sport. Then, having gone three years undefeated in the mid-1870s, culminating in a ground-breaking victory over the great northern "establishment" club, Manchester, the Lions gradually sought a tougher fixture list.

In 1878 came the club's first ventures into Yorkshire, and fairly soon the club was travelling the length of breadth of the country taking c such illustrious opponents as Oxford Universit Cardiff and Edinburgh Institution. Such was th Lions' success that by the mid-1880s Swinton ha become recognised as a national force ar unquestionably they were the strongest team i Lancashire.

A short move to the more palatial Chorley Roa ground in 1886 enabled the club to develo further. The new ground could accommodat much larger crowds and the staging of a couple c Lancashire County matches added to Swinton growing reputation. During their Rugby Union er the Lions produced five England internationals the first being Ted Beswick as early as 1882. I addition, some 40 Lions gained RU representativ recognition wearing the red rose of Lancashire. I 1888 the first ever representative British tourin team to Australasia included four Swinton players of whom Robert Seddon was named captair Sadly, whilst on that tour Seddon would drown i a boating accident on the River Hunter in Ne South Wales. Later that same year, the firs overseas tourists to reach these shores, a team o New Zealand Maoris, was defeated at Chorle Road.

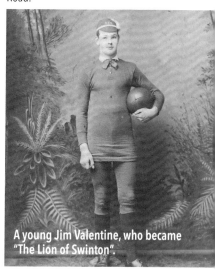

A young Jim Valentine, who became "The Lion of Swinton".

he most famous of the Lions' Victorian sportsmen as Jim Valentine, still arguably the most famous Lion" that ever lived and who served Swinton for 1 years from 1883. Valentine's finest hour came hen he led his Lions to a Challenge Cup Final uccess over bitter rivals Salford at Fallowfield in 900. By then Swinton had reluctantly joined the edgling Northern Union, albeit a year after the ew code's formation in 1895.

nly a financial crisis had enforced Swinton's efection from the Rugby Union to which they had itherto been staunchly loyal. As for Valentine, he vas incredibly killed by lightning whilst on oliday at Barmouth in 1904. Amazingly his all-ime club record haul of 301 tries still to this day eats his nearest challenger by over a hundred, nd is unlikely ever to be beaten.

he period leading up to the Great War was not a articularly auspicious time for the Lions. Financial risis followed financial crisis and only the sale of he popular side stand saved the club from closure uring 1917. The war took the lives of an stonishing 13 Swinton players, but back home he Lions played on in a desperate attempt to stay float.

Peacetime brought about the shrewdest of gambles by the Lions' directors who had managed to reign in the support of local businessmen. The signings of Hector Halsall from Wigan, a centre and future inspirational captain, and Albert Jenkins, a brilliant Welsh half-back, provided the catalyst. Throughout the 1920s the Lions got better and better until at last they won their first Lancashire Cup in 1925 before recapturing the Challenge Cup in 1926. They followed this with their first-ever Championship in 1927, and then in 1928 the team reached its zenith securing all five available trophies - a feat unique in the history of the sport. Crowds in excess of 20,000 were commonplace at Chorley Road where the fans marvelled at the skills of Welsh half-back Billo Rees, and the brothers Bryn and Jack Evans, all of them Great Britain internationals.

A rent dispute in 1928 caused the club to search for pastures new so they reluctantly vacated Chorley Road and built a new stadium just off Station Road on former allotments, taking the old stands with them. In March 1929, a 20,875 crowd saw the Lions defeat Wigan 9-3 in the first match on their new turf.

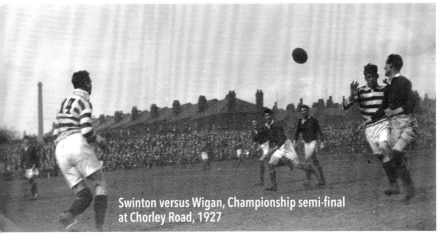

Swinton versus Wigan, Championship semi-final at Chorley Road, 1927

If the 1928 team was built around brilliant backs, the next great Swinton side relied on awesome forward power. International front-men Fred Butters, Joe Wright and Tommy Armitt, not to mention the legendary Martin Hodgson who had now emerged as one of the finest second-row forwards the game had ever seen, guaranteed that further Championships were won in 1931 and 1935. Hodgson would terrorise the Australians on the 1932 and 1936 Ashes tours, and in 1940 he kicked a world record penalty kick from 77.75 yards at Rochdale Hornets.

Swinton won the Lancashire Cup again in dramatic style against Widnes in 1940, but thereafter the Second World War curtailed the promise of further progress. Station Road was requisitioned by the Home Guard and the Ministry of Works, and consequently no rugby was played by the Lions in the three years up to 1945. By the time Britain emerged from the storm clouds Swinton had apparently lost their way, whilst the conflict itself had claimed the lives of scrum-half Tommy Holland and centre Dick Green.

Throughout the late 1940s and early 1950s the Lions strove unsuccessfully to repeat former glories and often flattered to deceive, but the appointment of Welshman Cliff Evans in 1954 as coach signalled a renaissance. Concentrating on youth policy and training methods beyond his era, Evans, recruited from California of all places, began to model a young exciting Swinton team.

It all became to fruition in 1963 when, under the shrewd captaincy of Albert Blan, the Lions completed the final 18 games of a 30 match league calendar undefeated to walk away with the Championship. To complete two remarkable seasons, Swinton's 6th title was retained in style 12 months later.

The Lions' backline of the early 1960s still rolls off the tongues of those who witnessed them in full flow. Ken Gowers, John Speed, Bob Fleet, Alan Buckley, John Stopford, George Parkinson and Graham Williams. Even in an era where the unlimited tackle rule ensured much tighter matches, these players could create a try from any position on the field. The only sad aspect being that this team never received the credit it deserved simply because ill-fortune ensured that they never appeared at Wembley. A 1965 semi-final defeat to Wigan proving the closest Swinton came.

John Stopford in action for GB against Australia at a packed Station Road, 1963

tation Road itself was also recognised as one of the finest grounds in the Rugby League. In its heyday it boasted a capacity of 60,000, although with a record attendance of 44,621 for a cup semi-nal in 1951 this was never really tested. A club ecord crowd of 26,891 witnessed the Lions defeat Vigan in a Challenge Cup tie in 1964. In all, 19 nternationals, 5 Championship finals, 17 Lancashire cup finals, 4 Premiership finals and 30 Challenge Cup semi-finals were played on the amous Station Road turf. But then came a emarkable decline in fortunes, due perhaps to complacency and a lack of foresight. Although the Lions won a fourth and final Lancashire Cup in 1969 the die was cast, and by the time two divisions were introduced in 1973, Swinton found themselves out of the top flight. By the end of the 1970s the club had hit rock-bottom, even though Station Road continued to host semi-finals and finals.

initially under Frank Myler, and then under Jim Crellin, the Lions briefly threatened a revival during the 1980s. Players such as Les Holliday and the sublimely talented Danny Wilson offered great hope for the future.

But despite a Second Division title in 1985, and a Second Division Premiership success in 1987, three separate promotions to the top flight simply brought about three immediate relegations.

The highly controversial sale of Station Road because of bad debts and the move to Gigg Lane, Bury, in 1992, did not prove as successful as the club management had hoped. Supporters meanwhile felt that their heritage had been betrayed in the darkest of secretive deals and they certainly had a point. Although Peter Roe led the Lions to promotion to the middle tier in 1996, subsequent significant investment a year later by Bury FC owner, Hugh Eaves, achieved only a disappointing play-off defeat. Within a few years relationships had soured completely and the football club forced the Lions out in 2002. The resulting move from that expulsion brought the club back to within a mile of the Swinton and Pendlebury border, when home games were played at Moor Lane, home of the local non-league football club, Salford City.

Swinton versus Leigh, Lancashire
Cup Final, 1969

Unfortunately, Salford City FC would not grant Swinton the ten year lease which was required to enable much needed funding to bring the ground up to standard. However, the Lions struck a deal with Sedgley Park RUFC to play at Park Lane, Whitefield, which enabled the club to enjoy a semi-permanent home from 2004 to 2010. The highlight during this period was a run to the Championship One play-off final in 2006, following epic victories at Featherstone Rovers and Celtic Crusaders. But sadly Paul Kidd's team lost out to Sheffield Eagles in the final at Warrington. A brief one-year tenure at The Willows in 2011 saw the Lions pick-up their first silverware in 24 years when captain Lee Wingfield held aloft the Championship One winner's trophy. The Lions' step-up into the Championship proved as difficult as imagined, but many creditable performances under Steve McCormack and later Gary Chambers kept the club in the middle tier between seasons 2012 and 2014.

A further financial crisis at the end of 2013 saw the departure of chairman, John Kidd, and the club was rescued by a new consortium which initially comprised of director David Jones and the Supporters' Trust.

Although RFL re-structuring then left the Lions in the third tier for season 2015, there was at last clear evidence that under the stewardship of former Leigh Chairman, John Roddy, long-standing director David Jones, and a new board comprising of Stephen Wild, Alan Marshall, Richard Ralphson and Peter Aaronson, that the club was heading in a transparent direction to a much brighter future.

Under new head coach John Duffy, the club relocated to Sedgley Park for season 2015, and a promising start saw the Lions reach the inaugural iPro League 1 Cup Final, which took place at Bloomfield Road on the same weekend as the new Championship "Summer Bash". However, after racing into an early 8-0 lead, the Lions eventually went down in searing heat to North Wales Crusaders by 14-8.

The set-back of losing that final knocked the Lions off their stride for a while, but happily Swinton regained their form and shape to finish their league campaign with 10 wins from 11 matches. The southern teams in particular came in for some severe punishment, and Ian Mort created a club record of 48 individual points in an annihilation of Oxford.

Swinton eventually finished in 3rd place which meant a home play-off semi-final against York, and the Lions looked to be heading for a one-point defeat until a Ben White drop-goal rescued the game with just 12 seconds left. Then in golden point extra-time, another drop-goal by Chris Atkin sent the Lions into ecstasy and a play-off final against Keighley at Widnes. In the final again it came down to fine margins, but the Lions held off the Cougars to win 29-28 in a dramatic match.
Having achieved promotion, the Lions set about the difficult task of consolidating in the Championship, a league of wide variance in terms of central funding and resources.

The club's planning was not helped by another forced move following the failure to get permission from Bury Council to bring Sedgley Park up to Championship standard. The first two home games of the 2016 season had to be taken to Salford and Widnes, but the Lions then found a friend in Sale RUFC and were able to switch operations to their homely Heywood Road ground.

On the field, and against the predictions of many "experts", Swinton then performed with great credit and eventually finished the campaign in ninth place, with three other clubs below them in the Championship table. Victories away against high-flying Batley and Halifax, and a double over full-time Sheffield Eagles provided the highlights, not to mention an epic 28-26 home win over Halifax which secured the team's status. At the time of going to print the club has just confirmed a deal with Sale FC to remain at Heywood Road until season 2019, but the Lions still retain the long-term ambition to return to a new ground in the M27 post code area.

In the summer of 2016 the club launched its own charitable arm in the shape of the Swinton Lions Community Sports Foundation, through which it is intended to greatly enhance the club's community presence and reputation, as well as help create a new generation of supporters. Former Super League player Rob Parker then arrived as General Manager in late 2016 having cut his cloth as a successful commercial operator at Bradford Bulls. So with the club modernising its strategy at all key strategic levels, the plan now is to kick on towards a successful new era, having completed an astonishing 150 years of proud history.

Swinton Lions in their 150th Anniversary Kit, 2016

Reverend Henry Robinson Heywood

Born 18 August 1833 (Claremont House, Pendleton);
Died 12 March 1895 (aged 61).

Reverend Henry Robinson Heywood was the vicar of St Peter's Parish Church, Swinton, from 1864 to 1895, and oversaw the construction of the present church in 1868/1869. He was married to Ella Sophia Gibson and had eight children. He was also the first President of Swinton Cricket Club (formed in 1866), and was in the Chair on 20 October 1866 when the cricketers met at the old St Peter's School and decided to play "football" in the winter. The Parish magazine of the time noting that, "We mention also that it was agreed to have football on Saturday afternoons. Play to commence at 3 o'clock." This was the founding moment of Swinton Rugby Football Club.

The Reverend Heywood was a much loved parish vicar and now lies buried in the graveyard of the Church he helped build.

Although not a former player of course, he is included in this list as a significant figure in the club's origins.

Radcliffe Dorning

Born 1849 (Swinton); Died 1888 (aged 39).

Debut : not known.
Last Match : not known.

Due to the sparsity of records from the early 1870s not much of Radcliffe's statistical history is known, although it's established that he scored at least one try. He also played against Swinton in the second of the annual challenge matches for the local Number One Company of the 46th Lancashire Rifle Volunteers in December 1869. However, he gains his place here as one of the pioneers and prominent early members of the club.

Radcliffe was also a keen cricketer, and on 4 April 1867 he attended the club's first AGM and was elected to the committee.

John Owen

Born 1845 (Swinton); Died 1887 (aged 42).

Debut : v 46th Rifle Volunteers, 2 January 1869.
Last Match : v Chorley, 20 January 1883.

1871/72 to 1876/77 – Known Appearances 9, Tries 4, Goals 0.
1877/78 to 1882/83 – Appearances 65, Tries 11, Drop-Goals 1.

"Little" John Owen was elected to the Swinton Cricket Club committee in 1868 and served on it for many years. He played in the rugby club's inaugural "competitive" match on 2 January 1869 against the 46th Lancashire Rifle Volunteers. John then captained the Swinton team in their second game against the same opposition on 18 December 1869 and scored the only two goals of the game.

John was a small but very agile player. He is also the first Lion known to have scored a hat-trick of tries (against Patricroft Rangers in October 1876).

Born 1851 (Swinton); Died 1893 (aged 42).

Debut : v 46th Lancashire Rifle Volunteers, 2 January 1869.
Last match : v Manchester Athletic, 27 October 1877.

1871/72 to 1876/77 - Known Appearances 10, Tries 3, Goals 5.
1877/78 - Appearances 1, Tries 0, Goals 0.

John was a member of a prominent Swinton family, well known in the licensed and farming trades. He was a clever half-back who played in both the 1869 matches against the 46th Lancashire Rifle Volunteers, and indeed scored Swinton's first ever goal in the January encounter. John also scored the club's first try under Rugby Union rules, this coming against Eccles Standard in the opening game of the 1871/72 season.

Dorning was the club's first official secretary from 1871 to 1875, and produced the first printed fixture list for season 1874/75. Depicting a lion on its cover, this fixture list represents the first known use of a lion insignia in association with the club.

Born 1853 (Swinton); Died 1927 (aged 74).

Debut : v 46th Lancashire Rifle Volunteers, 18 December 1869.
Last match : v Salford, 29 October 1881.

1871/72 to 1876/77 – Known Appearances 7, Tries 1, Goals 0.
1877/78 to 1881/82 - Appearances 62, Tries 3, Goals 0.

Edmund or "Ted" Barker was another stalwart of the club's early days, and he made his debut in the December 1869 encounter with the 46th Lancashire Rifle Volunteers. Ted was a forward who played throughout the three undefeated seasons of 1875/76 to 1877/78.

He later captained the "A" team, and also served as a club committee member at various times. Upon retirement from the Lions, Ted assisted the Clifton junior club.

Born 1851 (Swinton); Died 1893 (aged 42).

Debut : v Eccles Standard, 4 November 1871.
Last match : not known.

1871/72 – Appearances not known.

Harry was the son of the club's first President, William Longshaw, and the brother of fellow Swinton player, Walter. This wealthy family resided at Swinton Hall and owned the Windmill public house as well as a cotton mill which stood alongside the pub. Harry was a member of the Swinton-based 46th Lancashire Rifle Volunteers and actually played against Swinton in the historic meetings of January and December, 1869. He was promoted from Ensign to Lieutenant in January 1869, and then to Captain at some point not long afterwards.

Harry was appointed as Swinton's first official captain under Rugby Union rules, a position he relinquished to his brother Walter partway through the 1871/72 season.

It's likely that his playing career was brief and we only hold records of him scoring a single try, but his important position in the club's history is nonetheless secured.

Edward Farr

Born 1854 (Swinton); Died 11 April 1905 (aged 51).

Debut : v 46th Lancashire Rifle Volunteers, 18 December 1869.
Last match : v Cheetham, 13 April 1878.

1871/72 to 1876/77 ; Known Appearances 11, Tries 3, Goals 0.
1877/78 : Appearances 17, Tries 0, Goals 1.

Edward or Ted was the eldest of the four Farr brothers, all sons of the local physician Doctor C Farr. Edward was the first of the brothers to play for the club, making his debut in the second of the challenge matches against the 46th Lancashire Rifle Volunteers in December 1869. Usually playing at full-back, he gave the club excellent service on and off the field.

In the 1871/72 season Edward was elected to the club's committee.

Born not known; Died not known.

Debut : not known.
Last match : v Cheetham, 3 November 1877.

1871/72 to 1876/77 : Known Appearances 8, Tries 0, Goals 0.
1877/78 : Appearances 3, Tries 0, Goals 0.

Although records for the first few seasons are sketchy, it is believed that George played regularly between 1871 and 1877 and occasionally deputised in the role of captain. Indeed he skippered Swinton on their first ever trip to Wigan in October 1873. George was elected as the club's first ever treasurer in 1871 and held the rank of Major in the military.

Born 1851 (Swinton); Died 1925 (aged 74).

Debut : c.1874.
Last match : v Birch, 19 February 1881.

1871/72 to 1876/77 : Known Appearances 4, Tries 0, Goals 2.
1877/78 to 1880/81 : Appearances 34, Tries 3, Goals 1.

Representative Honours :
Lancashire : 2 caps (1877/78 to 1878/79).

Henry was an excellent forward who is thought to have made his debut in 1874, and therefore he would have played throughout the Lions' three undefeated seasons of 1875/76 to 1877/78.

In February 1878, he became only the third Lion to be capped by Lancashire when he played against Cheshire at Whalley Range.

In March 1879, he gained a second county cap against the same opposition at Bowdon. Henry earned himself everlasting fame by scoring the winning try in the historic match against the mighty Manchester club in March 1878, a result which was pivotal in the annuls of the club. Sadly, he is the only player in this list for whom we have not been able to locate a photograph.

Born 1857 (Pendlebury); Died 1925 (aged 68).

Debut : not known.
Last match : v Bolton, 21 April 1883.

1871/72 to 1876/77 : Known Appearances 9, Tries 2, Goals 0.
1877/78 to 1882/83 : Appearances 108, Tries 5, Goals 0.

Bob was a strong forward with a great wit and no-nonsense attitude. He made his debut in around 1875 and played through to 1883. He was a coal miner by trade, but between 1899 and 1902 he was the landlord of the Bowling Green public house in Pendlebury. In October 1878, he scored the game's only try against Halifax in Swinton's first ever match against Yorkshire opposition. Bob liked to demonstrate his sense of humour by dressing in traditional kilt and garb on trips to the Scottish capital, where the Lions regularly played local clubs Edinburgh Royal High School and Edinburgh Institution. On another occasion, whilst playing in an away match against Oxford University in March 1883, he asked his dumfounded team mates at half time, "Who is this chap Varsity they keep shoutin' after? Show 'im ter me and I shall attend to 'im!". Bob became a gateman at the Lions' old Chorley Road ground in around 1900, a position he held until his death in

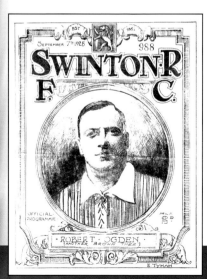

1925. He was in charge of the "Boys' Rush" turnstile, where the entrance fee was 2d. Quite often youngsters would offer only a penny, explaining that this was all the money they had, to which Bob's catchphrase response was always, "Another brown thee!" Or, in other words, 'Another penny if you don't mind!'. However, he had a heart of gold, and would always let the poorer children in for a penny. At the time of his death, Bob was the club's first, and only, Life Member.

Joe Mills

Born 1856 (Healey Stones, Rochdale); Died 8 March 1920 (aged 64 at Swinton).

Debut : v Birch, 17 March 1877.
Last match : v Manchester, 21 March 1891.

Appearances 267, Tries 85, Goals 26.

Representative Honours:
The North : 2 apps (1886/87 to 1887/88).
Lancashire : 29 caps (4 goals, 7 tries) (1881/82 to 1889/90).

Joe is perhaps second only to Jim Valentine in terms of contribution to the club under its famed Rugby Union era. On the field he formed a long standing half-back partnership with Walter Bumby in a Lions' career spanning 14 years. He was a brilliant player and a born leader, captaining the club as well as Lancashire for whom he played 29 times over nine seasons. Joe captained the Lions on 2 September 1886 when Manchester were defeated at the opening of the Lions' Chorley Road ground. He was twice named reserve for England in 1887, but was sadly never capped. He did, however, play twice for the North at Blackheath in the prestigious bi-annual matches against the South. Off the field Joe served the club as President, secretary, committeeman and county representative. He also served his local community in various roles including Local Councillor for 20 years as well as a Magistrate. Joe was a director of the Worsley Brewing Company and at different times was landlord of both the Bull's Head and Football Hotel. In his role as a local Councillor he was a prime mover behind the formation of the "Swinton Pals" during the Great War.

Walter Longshaw

Born 1855 (Swinton); Died 1888 (aged 33).

First match : v 46th Lancashire Rifle Volunteers, 2 January 1869.
Last match : v Halifax, 15 November 1879.

1871/72 to 1876/77 : Known Appearances 9, Tries, 2, Goals 1.
1877/78 to 1879/80 : Appearances 38, Tries 4, Goals 0.

Representative Honours :
Lancashire : 1 cap (1877/78).

The younger brother of Harry and son of the club President, William, Walter Longshaw was a powerful forward. He took over the club captaincy part way through the first official Rugby Union season of 1871/72 and kept the position until he retired in 1879. Walter played in both matches against the Rifle Volunteers in 1869, and at Hanson Lane, Halifax, on 19 January 1878 (alongside Herbert Farr) he became the first Lion to play for Lancashire. In November 1871, Walter played against Eccles Standard in Swinton's inaugural game under Rugby Union rules, a match in which he kicked the club's first ever official goal.

Herbert (HF) Farr

Born 1855 (Swinton); Died 1918 (aged 63)

Debut : not known.
Last match : v Broughton, 15 March 1879.

1871/72 to 1876/77 : Known Appearances 9; Tries 2, Goals 2.
1877/78 to 1878/79 : Appearances 29, Tries 14, Goals 4.

Representative Honours :
Lancashire : 2 caps (2 tries) (1877/78).

One of the four Farr brothers, Herbert was a very fast three-quarter who could turn opponents inside out with his dodging and side-stepping. Known as "Buck" or "Corkscrew", he was a great crowd favourite and was even seen to hurdle over the top of opponents.

In January 1878, he became the first Lion (along with Walter Longshaw) to be capped for Lancashire at a time when the county team was run by the Manchester club.

On 9 February 1878, Herbert scored five tries against Pendleton, a club record for a single match which was equalled but not beaten for another 118 years. "Buck" may well also have been the first ever Swinton player to be honoured with a rhyme or chant, "You'll oft hear their opponents call, beware of Herbert Farr. They know whene're he gets the ball he's like a shooting star."

Born 1855 (Swinton); Died 1944 (aged 89).

Debut : v Halifax, 26 October 1878.
Last match : v Rochdale St Clement's, 1 March 1890.

Appearances 112, Tries 16, Goals 0.

Representative Honours :
Lancashire : 3 caps (1882/83).

Albert, alongside his brother Harry, were long-standing stalwarts of the club and came from the Hazlehurst area of Swinton. He made his debut in the 1878/79 season and went on to serve the Lions for 12 seasons.

Albert was a very good forward who gained three Lancashire caps in 1882/83, and indeed the county team which faced Yorkshire that season at Whalley Range contained no less than eight Swinton players. His other two caps came against the Midlands at Whalley Range, and against Cheshire at New Brighton. Albert was elected to the club committee in 1880.

Born not known (Swinton); Died not known.

Debut : v Free Wanderers, 9 October 1880.
Last match : v Broughton Rangers, 15 November 1890

Appearances 123, Goals 110, Drop Goals 6.

Representative Honours :
Lancashire 1 cap (1882/83).

Billy was a diminutive but very effective full-back, and served the Lions throughout the successful decade of the 1880s. He was the club's first regular goal-kicker and became the first Lion to notch 100 goals. He played once for Lancashire in the autumn of 1882 against Yorkshire at Whalley Range.

Born 1858 (Pendleton); Died 1927 (aged 69).

Debut : v Birch, 24 September 1881.
Last match : v Barrow, 14 November 1885.

Appearances 75, Tries 1, Goals 0.

Representative Honours:
Lancashire 2 caps (1881/82 to 1882/83).

Walter was a very good forward who began his career with the Pendleton club. Together with Charlie Horley he is credited with persuading a young Jim Valentine to join the Lions from Pendleton in 1883. He played for Lancashire twice at a time when the county had many fine forwards, those occasions being against the Midlands at Coventry in March 1882, and against Yorkshire at Whalley Range eight months later. Walter's final appearance, which was against Barrow in 1885 at Stoneacre, coincided with the Lions' first home defeat in five years.

Ted Beswick

Born 1858 (Penrith); Died 23 January 1911 (aged 52).

Debut : v Chorley, 11 October 1879.
Last match : v Rochdale Hornets, 20 November 1886.

Appearances 105, Tries 49, Goals 15.

Representative Honours:
England 2 caps (1881/82); The North 1 app (1881/82); Northern England 1 app (1881/82); Lancashire 5 caps (4 tries) (1879/80 to 1882/83).

Edmund, Ted or Teddy Beswick, was a brilliant and inventive try scoring three-quarter, who was one of the leading lights of the Lions' early days. He was a clever tactician before anyone else in the game had heard of tactics. Although a Cumbrian by birth he played junior rugby for Weaste, Claremont and Seedley before joining the Lions in 1879. Within weeks he had been selected for Lancashire, and in 1880 he was appointed club captain. After impressing for the North in an international trial game, on 4 February 1882 Ted became the first-ever Lion to play for England. That was against Ireland at Dublin, and he retained his place against Scotland at Whalley Range a month later. A severe knee injury cut short Ted's career, after which he assisted the Lions in a coaching capacity.

He died at an early age of cancer, after which Swinton and Salford played a special veterans' benefit game under Rugby Union rules at The Willows for his family.

Born 1858 (Swinton); Died 1930 (aged 72).

Debut : v c.1875.
Last match : v Manchester, 10 November 1883.

1875/76 to 1876/77 : Known Appearances 1, Tries 1, Goals 0.
1877/78 to 1883/84 : Appearances 106, Tries 58, Goals 11.

Representative Honours:
Lancashire 5 caps (4 tries) (1882/83 to 1883/84).

Tom was a three-quarter and the youngest of the four remarkable Farr brothers who all played for Swinton. He was appointed captain for season 1879/80, and scored a very fine 20 tries in 19 appearances in season 1882/83. In November 1882, Tom scored two tries on his Lancashire debut against the Midlands Counties at Whalley Range.

For season 1883/84, he was re-elected club captain, and in November of that season he gained a fourth and final county cap against Northumberland. Tom was bitterly opposed to the club joining the Northern Union in 1896 and resigned his club membership
following the secession vote.

Joe Bagshaw

Born n/k; Died n/k.

Debut : v Wakefield Trinity, 15 October 1881.
Last match : v Halifax, 23 April 1887.

Appearances 116, Tries 5, Goals 0.

Representative Honours:
Lancashire : 4 caps (1883/84 to 1884/85).

Joe was a very good forward who played during an extremely successful period for the club. In season 1883/84, he gained three caps for Lancashire, against Cheshire, Yorkshire and the Midlands, and he added a final fourth cap when his county beat Cheshire at Liscard in November 1884. In 1886 Joe was one of 12 Lions to play in both Swinton's last game at Stoneacre, and the first at their new Chorley Road ground. Joe later played for the Manchester Athletic club from Old Trafford.

28

Charlie Horley

Born 1860 (Pendlebury); Died 10 May 1924 (aged 64).

Debut : v Manchester, 1 November 1879.
Last match : v Warrington, 8 April 1893.

Appearances 261, Tries 28, Goals 1, Drop-Goals 3.

Representative Honours:
England 1 cap (1884/85); The North 3 apps (1 try) (1884/85 to 1889/90); Northern England 1 app (1881/82); Lancashire 21 caps (2 tries) (1881/82 to 1889/90).

Charlie joined the Lions from the Pendlebury Rovers club and was one of the most brilliant forwards of his day, and arguably the club's finest forward of the Rugby Union era. He was a confident character and was known for his excessive chatter on the pitch, something which didn't endear him to opposition players and supporters.

Horley was a line-out specialist, and an accomplished footballer in the loose which was unusual for forwards at that time. After impressing regularly for Lancashire (for whom he would win an impressive 21 caps), and also for the North in the major international trial game, Charlie became the second Swinton player to be selected for England - his cap coming against Ireland in February 1885.

Charlie was also a regular member of the club committee, but he severed official connections with the Lions when they defected to the Northern Union in 1896.

1885 150 GREATEST

SWINTON LIONS 1866

Bob Seddon

Born n/k; Died n/k.

Debut : v Chorley, 11 October 1879.
Last match : v Stoke, 18 April 1887.

Appearances 121, Tries 10, Goals 0.

Representative Honours:
Lancashire 3 caps (1881/82 to 1882/83)

Bob was a fine forward whose consistent performances for the Lions earned him three Lancashire caps. His county debut came in a win over the Midlands at Coventry in March 1882, and further caps followed against Yorkshire at Whalley Range and Northumberland at Newcastle during season 1882/83. Bob then missed seasons 1883/84 and 1884/85 after moving away for work reasons, but he returned in 1885 to play for another couple of years.

Against Manchester on 2 October 1886, Bob became the first player ever to score a try on the Lions' new Chorley Road ground.

Born 1860 (Bury); Died 1927 (aged 67).

Debut : v Mossley, 26 December 1885.
Last match : v Moseley, 13 February 1892.

Appearances 93, Tries 13, Goals 23.

Representative Honours:
England 2 caps (1886/87); The North 1 app (1886/87); Lancashire 7 caps (7 goals) (1886/87 to 1888/89).

Accomplished full-back Sam came to Swinton from the lowly Bury club, and as such he was one of the few non-local players in the team at the time. After a meteoric rise in reputation, on 8 January 1887 Sam was selected for England and thus became only the third Lion to achieve international status – the game against Wales at Llanelly finishing scoreless.

Alongside Joe Mills and Jim Valentine, Roberts also played for Lancashire in a prestigious match at the Oval in March 1887. This was against Middlesex before the Prince of Wales, in a match played to mark Queen Victoria's Golden Jubilee.

Sam remained a keen supporter of the club up until his death in 1927.

Bob (RL) Seddon

Born 21 October 1860 (Broughton); Died 15 August 1888 (aged 27 at Maitland, Australia).

Debut : v Douglas, 3 September 1887.
Last match : v Aspull, 11 February 1888.

Appearances 14, Tries 4, Goals 0.

Representative Honours: British RU Tourist 19 apps (3 tries, 1 goal) (1888); The North 2 apps (1887/88); Lancashire 3 caps (1887/88).

Bob adopted his mother's maiden name "Lever" to create a middle initial and so avoid confusion with a couple of other Bob Seddons playing rugby in the Manchester area – including one at Swinton. He began his career with a junior outfit called Hightown, but became a founder member of Broughton Rangers and played in their first ever match on 13 October 1877. Ten years later it caused something of a stir in local rugby circles when following a disagreement with Rangers he defected to Swinton. By this time he had become an England international, so his arrival at Chorley Road was quite a coup for the Lions. Bob was a classy forward who only had a short spell at Swinton, but during that period he achieved a unique and personal representative honour. This was because by being named skipper of Shaw and Shrewsbury's rebel tour of New Zealand and Australia in 1888, he gained distinction as the first-ever ever captain of an overseas British touring team. Tragically, however, he drowned on that tour when his foot caught in the strap of a boat he was sculling on the Hunter River near Maitland, New South Wales. As a strong swimmer and expert rower there was total bewilderment at the calamity, which was felt across the entire rugby playing world. Bob's funeral was a huge public affair at Maitland Cemetery, attended by hundreds of people. Meanwhile there was controversy back home in Broughton, due to the insensitive manner in which news of his death was conveyed to his family via a London news agency. Ironically on the voyage out to New Zealand he was almost washed overboard in a storm. Following that escape he jokingly wrote back to his sister, "I don't think I was born to be drowned".

32

Arthur Paul

Born 24 July 1864 (Belfast); **Died** 14 January 1942 (aged 77 at Didsbury).

Debut : v Wakefield Trinity, 1 October 1887.
Last match : v Broughton Rangers, 4 February 1893.

Appearances 113, **Tries** 1, **Goals** 95, **Drop Goals** 1.

Representative Honours:
British RU Tourist 29 apps (15 goals) (1888); Lancashire 3 caps (5 goals) (1889/90).

Arthur was a brilliant all round sportsman, and as well as rugby he tried his hand at soccer as well as professional cricket with Lancashire. He came to Swinton's attention whilst playing for Douglas on the Isle of Man, a location where the Lions enjoyed regular pre-season matches. At Swinton he started out as a full-back and graduated to the forwards, but was equally adept in either role. In 1888, he was selected for the rebel tour of Australasia, although plans to remain in Melbourne and play professional cricket there did not materialise.

Arthur was an excellent goal-kicker, and in November 1889 he booted three on his county debut for Lancashire against Cheshire at Whalley Range. In early 1890, he won further county honours against Cumberland at Whitehaven, and against Ulster in his home city of Belfast. Arthur also later played for Salford.

1889 150 GREATEST

Walter Bumby

150 GREATEST 1890

Born 29 October 1861 (Pendlebury); Died 23 December 1936 (aged 75).

Debut : v Free Wanderers, 9 October 1880.
Last match : v Blackley, 30 March 1896.

Appearances 333, Tries 87, Goals 1, Drop-Goals 1.

Representative Honours:
British RU Tourist 23 apps (5 tries) (1888); The North 1 app (1889/90); Lancashire 23 caps (1 try) (1885/86 to 1892/93).

Walter was a local man who had played junior rugby with Newtown Wanderers and Pendlebury Blues. After joining the Lions he went on to forge a brilliant half-back partnership with Joe Mills, and was unlucky not to win international honours. He scored a then record 21 tries in the 1882/83 season, and his grand total of 87 is bettered only by Jim Valentine under Rugby Union rules. Alongside his close friend Tom Banks, Bumby was selected for the 1888 rebel tour of Australasia, one of four Swinton men to make the trip. In 1890 Walter played for the North versus the South, this being a major trial game ahead of the Home International matches.

After his retirement from rugby Walter became landlord of the Bridgewater Arms which stood on Worsley Street in Pendlebury. He filled that role for 30 years up to 1926, by which time the pub was known locally as "Bumby's".

Tom Banks

Born 17 August 1858 (Pendlebury); Died September 1915 (aged 57).

Debut : v Birch, 24 September 1881.
Last match : v Leicester, 14 March 1892.

Appearances 146, Tries 25, Drop Goals 2.

Representative Honours:
British RU Tourist 7 apps (1 try) (1888); Lancashire 6 caps (1 try) (1884/85 to 1887/88).

Pendlebury swimming champion Tom Banks was a versatile player who won Lancashire honours as a forward, but also played in the backs for his club. He made his Lancashire debut at the same time as Jim Valentine against Yorkshire in November 1884 at Whalley Range.

Although he had only just taken over as landlord of the Lord Nelson pub in Pendlebury, Tom accepted selection for the 1888 rebel tour of Australasia. However, a bad injury early on in the tour meant that he made only six appearances. The injury persisted and he managed only three more appearances for the Lions before being forced to retire in season 1891/92.

Tom resigned his club membership following the 1896 decision to join the Northern Union.

Jimmy Marsh

Born 1866; Died 1 August 1928 (aged 62).

Debut v Mossley, 26 December 1885.
Last match v Walkden, 18 April 1896.

Appearances 103, Tries 21, Goals 2, Drop Goals 8.

Representative Honours:
England 1 cap (1891/92); Scotland 2 caps (1888/89); The North 2 apps (1890/91 to 1892/93); Lancashire 14 caps (6 tries) (1887/88 to 1892/93).

Jimmy was marvellous player who undoubtedly would have won more honours had he not spent a significant part of his playing career confined to his medical studies and work. He was an expert at drawing an opponent and passing to his winger with perfect timing, a skill not universal at that time. While studying in Edinburgh and guesting for the local Edinburgh Institution club, he was twice selected for Scotland. After that he always wore his red Scottish socks in club matches.

In February 1892, now back in Swinton, Jimmy was uniquely selected for both England and Scotland on the same day. After choosing England he became the only man in history to have played for both countries. His last outing with Swinton was against Walkden in 1896 in what proved to be the Lions' final game under Rugby Union rules. Coincidentally he also set up a GP practice in Walkden, and remained an avid Swinton fan up to his death.

Born 1870 (Pendlebury); Died 1955 (aged 85).

Debut : v Durham City, 27 December 1890.
Last match : v Bristol, 16 April 1895.

Appearances 142, Tries 11, Goals 17.

Representative Honours:
Lancashire 3 caps (1892/93).

Clifton-man Herbie was a fine half-back who had the formidable task of coming into a team which had been dominated by Joe Mills and Walter Bumby. The fact that he was a success showed his quality, and in February and March of 1893 he earned three caps for Lancashire. These honours came against Durham, Glamorgan and Devon, at Sunderland, Swansea and Exeter respectively. Herbie, however, joined the Pendleton Britannia RU Club in 1896 when the Lions seceded to the Northern Union. His nephew Chris Brockbank played for the Lions' great 1920's team.

Tom Rothwell

Born 1868 (Swinton); Died n/k.

Debut : v Rochdale Hornets, 30 January 1886.
Last match : v Warrington, 17 March 1894.

Appearances 171, Tries 7, Goals 0.

Representative Honours:
Lancashire 16 caps (1 try) (1890/91 to 1892/93).

Tom was a local lad who joined the Lions from Clifton in 1886. He was a big aggressive forward who played consistently for his club and county over eight years before his retirement in 1894.

In the 1890/91 season Tom played in nine of Lancashire's 10 successive wins which saw them lift the national county championship under the captaincy of Jim Valentine. In all he gained a very impressive 16 county caps over three seasons.

Born 1860 (Pendlebury); Died 1905 (aged 45).

Debut : v Chorley, 2 April 1881.
Last match : v Cardiff, 6 April 1896.

Appearances 318, Tries 19, Goals 0.

Representative Honours:
Lancashire 9 caps (1885/86 to 1889/90).

Nat was another local man who joined the Lions from Pendlebury Blues, the same junior club that had supplied Walter Bumby. Nat was a formidable hard-as-nails forward who would take no nonsense on the field. He was known to warn opponents, "I'll punce thee off the field" in his broad Pendlebury accent. Nat had a long successful career with the Lions spanning some 15 years before his retirement in the 1895/96 season, and perhaps should have won more Lancashire caps. His number of appearances for Swinton under Rugby Union rules is bettered only by Jim Valentine and Walter Bumby.

Harold (GH) Murray

Born 1867 (Bolton); Died 1921 (aged 54).

Debut : v Sale, 3 November 1888.
Last match : v Blackley Rangers, 29 February 1896.

Appearances 186, Tries 29, Goals 0.

Representative Honours:
Lancashire 9 caps (1893/94 to 1895/96).

Originally from Bolton, Harold was a versatile player who started as a three-quarter and eventually moved to the forwards where he gained his nine Lancashire caps. Harold served on the club committee, and both he and his brother and fellow Swinton player, Jimmy, both acted as club secretary. Harold retired in 1896 just as the club resigned from the RFU.

Born 1874 (Swansea); Died 1955 (aged 81).

Debut : v Wigan, 14 November 1896.
Last match: v Broughton Rangers, 27 September 1902.

Appearances 144, Tries 48, Goals 12.

Representative Honours:
Lancashire 1 cap (1897/98); Rest of Northern Union 1 app (1897/98).

Bobby had played against the Lions for Swansea under Rugby Union rules, and Swinton induced him north very soon after they had defected to the Northern Union. He was small and slightly built, but a fast and a skillful handler of the ball, using perfect anticipation to intercept opponents' passes. Bobby won a cap for his adopted county in October 1897, when Lancashire defeated Yorkshire 11-10 at Watersheddings, Oldham. He was also a try scoring hero in the 1900 Challenge Cup Final victory against Salford at Fallowfield.

Bobby was surprisingly transferred to the Reds in 1903, and at the end of that campaign he appeared in a second Challenge Cup Final. However, on that occasion he was on the losing side as Salford went down to Halifax.

Billy Pearson

Born 1870 (Pendlebury); Died 4 November 1934 (aged 63).

Debut : v Huddersfield, 7 February 1891.
Last match : v Stockport, 18 November 1899.

1890/91 to 1895/96 : Appearances 197, Tries 70, Goals 23.
1896/97 to 1899/00 : Appearances 75, Tries 10, Goals 6.

Representative Honours:
Lancashire (RU) 3 caps (1 try) (1892/93 to 1895/96); Lancashire (NU)
1 cap (1898/99).

Billy was another local who joined the Lions from the Clifton junior club. He
was a clever and skilful half-back or centre who twice scored 20 or more tries
in a season. Billy was captain of the club for one season, but left for Leigh
after a dispute. Sons Jack (the full-back in the great 1920s team) and Stan
(one appearance), both played for the Lions. In October 1898, Billy won a
cap for Lancashire (Northern Union), but his side lost 5-4 to Cheshire at
Stockport. He had also previously gained three Lancashire caps under the
auspices of the Rugby Union. Along with Jim Valentine and forward Jack
Johnson, Billy therefore won representative honours under both codes.

Billy was the landlord of the Duke
of Wellington at Pendlebury
from 1912 to 1935, where he
was succeeded by his son, Jack.

Born 24 December 1877 (Swinton); Died 1959 (aged 82).

Debut : v Runcorn, 10 December 1898.
Last match : v St Helens, 25 January 1913.

Appearances 160, Tries 70, Goals 8.

Representative Honours:
Lancashire 2 caps (1 try) (1901/02).

Vernon was a speedy dodger of a winger who won running prizes on the track, as well as another member of the 1900 Challenge Cup winning team. He was a Swinton regular for six years and gained two Lancashire caps in February 1902, before being transferred to York in 1904. However, by 1908 Vernon had returned via Salford, but injury caused his retirement in 1910. He returned yet again as a player/trainer in 1912 and managed a couple more appearances.

Vernon was the son of the Lions' director RJ Hampson who owned a printworks at the top of Pendlebury Road, and Hampson Street still exists today in that vicinity.

Jim Valentine

150 GREATEST 1900

Born 29 July 1866 (Brindle Heath); **Died 25 July 1904** (aged 37 at Barmouth)

Debut : v Walton, 5 January 1884.
Last match : v St Helens, 16 March 1901.

1883/84 to 1895/96 : Appearances 356, Tries 262, Goals 145.
1896/97 to 1900/01 : Appearances 130, Tries 39, Goals 57.

Representative Honours: England 4 caps (1 goal) (1889/90 to 1895/96); Rest of England 2 apps (1 try) (1888/89 to 1891/92); The North 7 apps (2 tries, 2 goals) (1887/88 to 1895/96); Lancashire (RU) 57 caps (48 tries, 40 goals) (1884/85 to 1895/96); Lancashire (NU) 5 caps (2 tries, 2 goals) (1896/97 to 1898/99).

Jim was born at Brindle Heath in 1866, and was playing in that village's first team at the age of 14 before moving on to the more senior Pendleton club. As a 17 year old he was then persuaded to join Swinton by Lions Walter Dickenson and Charlie Horley. Without doubt "Val" would ultimately become the greatest and most famous Swinton player of all time, and indeed an all-time great of the Rugby Union era in general. His career spanned 18 seasons, a period which included the Lions' defection to the Northern Union. Val was equally at home as a winger or centre, and was a prolific try scorer in the days when tries were much harder to come by. He could score by using speed, strength, swerve or hand-off, and in just the five seasons between 1887 and 1892 he amassed an astonishing 212 tries in 184 club and representative matches. By the time Val took over the Lions' "A" Team in 1901 he had totalled 301 club tries, including an incredible 48 tries in the 1888/89 season – both of which are club records which still stand to this day. Jim was a fine captain who led by example, and he skippered both club and Lancashire for many years. His paltry four England caps owed more to class prejudice than his supreme talent as a player. Val was still a fine player in the Northern Union era, and now playing as a roving forward, he captained the club to their first major honour in 1900 when the Lions defeated Salford 16-8 in the Challenge Cup Final at Fallowfield. Val was granted a testimonial by both of rugby's governing bodies, which helped set him up as landlord of the Duchy Arms on Charles Street, Brindle Heath. In 1904 he was due to take up a position as a director of the newly formed Swinton Football Club Limited, when he was tragically struck by lightning and killed whilst on holiday at Barmouth. Jim was buried at St John's Church at Pendlebury on what would have been his 38th birthday.

A quite remarkable sportsman, and truly the "Lion of Swinton".

SWINTON LIONS 1866

Jack Lewis

Born 1874 (Prestwich); Died 1 December 1944 (aged 70).

Debut : v Huddersfield, 27 February 1892.
Last match : v Oldham, 26 December 1904.

1891/92 to 1895/96 : Appearances 121, Tries 37, Goals 1.
1896/97 to 1904/05 : Appearances 152, Tries 76, Goals 0.

Representative Honours:
Lancashire 5 caps (2 tries) (1895/96).

Jack came to Swinton from the junior club Rainsough. He was a small but exceptionally fast winger who had won prizes for sprinting on the running track. Jack was noted for his amazing runs down the touchline and was a great favourite at Chorley Road. He won all his Lancashire caps during the Lions' last season in the Rugby Union, and on one occasion he scored two tries in his county's victory over Northumberland at Newcastle. Arguably Northern Union football better suited his style, as many observers considered that he was a better player under the new code. Jack scored tries at a rate one every two games and was top try scorer in five separate seasons covering both codes. In the 1900/01 season he scored

tries in nine consecutive matches, which remains a club record only equalled by Derek Bate some 86 years later. Jack was also a try scorer in the 1900 Challenge Cup Final win against Salford, and he succeeded Jim Valentine as team captain.

He was eventually forced to retire due to persistent knee problems, and was granted a testimonial on Boxing Day 1905 when the Lions defeated a Lancashire XV.

Bob Valentine

Born 20 July 1877 (Brindle Heath); Died 16 January 1926 (aged 48).

Debut : v Victoria University, 26 February 1896.
Last match : v Ebbw Vale, 24 February 1908.

1895/96 : Appearances 3, Tries 0, Goals 0.
1896/97 to 1907/08 : Appearances 96, Tries 36, Goals 10.

Representative Honours:
Lancashire 5 caps (2 tries, 3 goals) (1900/01 to 1902/03)

Bob initially struggled to make the Swinton first team, possibly due to unfair comparisons with his famous brother, Jim. He made his debut towards the end of the Lions' membership of the Rugby Union, and soon developed a reputation as a classy centre. Bob scored a try in the 1900 Challenge Cup Final win over Salford, and he also scored a try on his debut for Lancashire against Yorkshire at Rochdale in the same year. He earned a fifth and final county cap in a win over Yorkshire at Salford's New Barnes ground in 1902, by which time he had also been installed as the Lions' skipper. Early in 1903, the club hired an engine and guard's van solely for the purpose of conveying Bob from his Sowerby Bridge workplace to Swinton's match at Brighouse! It came as quite a shock to the club and its supporters when in 1903 Bob joined Manchester United as a goalkeeper, but he only made ten first team appearances in over three seasons before sustaining a serious knee injury at Anfield from which he never fully recovered. In 1908 Bob attempted a return with the Lions, but he managed only one more appearance. He died in 1926 at the age of only 48 and is buried in the same plot as his famous brother.

Born 23 February 1871 (Llanelly)); Died 19 July 1924 (aged 53).

Debut : v Leigh, 23 October 1897.
Last match : v Rochdale Hornets, 13 October 1906.

Appearances 251, Tries 28, Goals 33.

Representative Honours:
Lancashire 9 caps (1 try) (1898/99 to 1902/03); Rest of Northern Union 2 apps (1 try) (1897/98 to 1899/00).

Jack was a huge dominating forward, very big and heavy even by the standards of the era in which he played. He began his Rugby Union career with Ammanford, but moved to Llanelly where he won two RU caps for Wales during the 1896 Home Nations Championship. After moving to the Llwynypia club in 1897 he won another cap, by which time he had gained a reputation as one of the finest forwards in Wales. The Lions decided to swoop for his services, and managed to persuade him to sign on the dotted line whilst he was washing having just completed a shift down the coal mine.

With his trade-mark scrum-cap, Jack was a fearless tackler and he was also known for his huge punts downfield. Jack played in the 1900 Challenge Cup Final victory over Salford, and in 1903 he gained his ninth and final cap for his adopted county, Lancashire.

In 1908, Jack assisted with the formation of the short-lived Mid-Rhondda Northern Union club, but returned to Swinton in 1914 to help out in a coaching capacity. In 1925, he became landlord at the Colliers Arms on Bolton Road in Pendlebury. His three sons, Jack junior, Bryn and Harold, each emerged as magnificent players for the club in their own right.

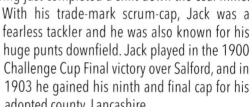

Walter Cheetham

Born c.1878; Died not known.

Debut : v Rochdale Hornets, 2 September 1901.
Last match : v Pontefract, 1 December 1906.

Appearances 161, Tries 7, Goals 0.

Representative Honours:
Lancashire 5 caps (1904/05 to 1905/06).

Walter was a local lad and signed for Swinton from the Pendlebury junior club, whose playing field was next door to Pendlebury Market. Walter was regarded as an effective tackler who was very smart at backing up breaks or kicks. In November 1904, he made his debut for Lancashire in a loss to Yorkshire at Oldham. He went on to win five caps in total, the last coming in a draw with Cumberland at Wigan in February 1906.

After five years with the Lions Walter was transferred to Wigan, but he's not to be confused with a notable player with exactly the same name who starred for Broughton Rangers and Wigan a decade later.

Born 1875 (Pendleton); Died 1928 (aged 53).

Debut : v Runcorn, 19 April 1894.
Last match : v Bradford, 29 April 1905.

1893/94 to 1895/96 : Appearances 62, Tries 3, Goals 0.
1896/97 to 1904/05 : Appearances 190, Tries 2, Goals 0.

Representative Honours:
Lancashire 1 cap (1895/96).

Bob was a hard-working pack member whose Swinton career covered both codes and 11 years. He was a real club man and was much respected by team mates, officials and supporters alike. It was about this time that the role of hooker was emerging as a specialised position, and Bob fell into the job almost by accident. He made over 250 appearances for Swinton, but was disappointed at being named 16th man for the 1900 Challenge Cup Final. However, the club commissioned an extra winner's medal for him. Bob's single Lancashire cap came against Durham at Fallowfield under Rugby Union rules.

After a distinguished career he retired from senior rugby in 1905. Bob then went on to assist the junior club, Radcliffe Rangers, whom he brought to Chorley Road in April 1906 for his own testimonial match.

Dan Davies

Born 1885 (Llanelly); Died April 1932 (aged 47).

Debut : v Morecambe, 11 November 1905.
Last match : v Oldham, 29 March 1913.

Appearances 201, Tries 14, Goals 0.

Representative Honours:
Other Nationalities 1 cap (1905/06); Lancashire 1 cap (1907/08).

Signed from Llanelly, Dan has the distinction of being the first Swinton player to earn international honours under the auspices of the Northern Union. As a Welshman, he was selected for the Other Nationalities team which drew 3-3 with England at Wigan on New Year's Day, 1906.

Dan was the brother of Lions' legend Dai Davies, although in contrast Dan was a tough-tackling forward. In the midst of his career at Swinton he joined brother Dai at Bolton Wanderers, but after failing to get into their first team he returned to the Lions. Dan played once for Lancashire in a loss to Cumberland at Wheater's Field, Broughton, in 1907.

Billy Simister

Born 1880 (Yorkshire); Died 1944 (aged 64).

Debut : v Leigh, 26 September 1903.
Last match : v Warrington, 24 September 1910.

Appearances 215, Tries 23, Goals 0.

Representative Honours:
Lancashire 1 cap (1907/08).

Although a Yorkshire man by birth, Billy came to the Lions from the short-lived Stockport club. He was a forward with wonderful energy who could keep running all day and never give up, qualities which endeared him to the Lions' supporters. Billy also had a touch of class and possessed good hands, skills which were not always common in a forward back then.

Billy was team captain towards the end of the Edwardian era, and indeed he led the Lions against the New Zealand "All Golds" in 1907 – the first-ever Northern Union tourists. He was still captain when Swinton welcomed Australian tourists for the first time 12 months later. Billy also won a single cap for Lancashire, this coming alongside Dan Davies in the loss to Cumberland in October 1907.

Joey Morgan

Born 20 March 1877 (Swansea); Died 1956 (aged 79).

Debut : v Morecambe, 12 December 1896.
Last match : v Salford 08 February 1908.

Appearances 199, Tries 25, Goals 13.

Representative Honours:
Lancashire 1 cap (1902/03).

Francis Augustine Morgan, or "Joey" as he was known, was a brilliant half-back. A Welshman, Morgan was the captain of Swansea and a former team mate of Bobby Messer whom he followed to Swinton. Both men represented major captures for the Lions as they adjusted to professionalism under the Northern Union. Joey was a very resourceful player and never at a loss for his next move, which made him a feared opponent. He would score many of his tries with a dash from the scrum, and on top of this his defence was fearless. He played in the 1900 Challenge Cup Final when the Lions defeated Salford, who ironically he joined in 1905.

Joey returned to Swinton in 1908, but by then he had lost his speed and in February he played his last game – again against Salford. His single cap for Lancashire came against Durham & Northumberland at Wheater's Field, Broughton, in December 1902.

Harry Barnett

Born 1878 (Altrincham); Died 1953 (aged 75).

Debut : v Huddersfield, 14 September 1901.
Last match : v Bradford Northern, 10 April 1911.

Appearances 273, Tries 47, Goals 2.

Representative Honours:
Lancashire 1 cap (1908/09).

Harry was signed in 1901 from the short-lived and beleaguered Altrincham club. His capture was a controversial affair which ultimately caused Swinton to be deducted two points by the Northern Union authorities. Barnett had won prizes for sprinting, and could play equally effectively as a speedy second-row forward or a winger. He had won county honours for Cheshire whilst at Altrincham, and he added a Lancashire cap when he played in the forwards against the first-ever touring Australians in March 1909, a game that was lost 14-9 at Leigh.

In both the 1907/08 and 1908/09 seasons Harry was the club's leading try scorer.

1909 150 GREATEST

Jack Preston

Born 1879 (Swinton); Died 1939 (aged 60).

Debut : v Bradford, 26 February 1898.
Last match : v Wigan, 1 January 1910.

Appearances 181, Tries 12, Goals 95.

Representative Honours:
Lancashire 2 caps (1901/02).

Another product of local junior football, Jack arrived at the Lions in the 1897/98 season from juniors Swinton Church. He was a tall rangy forward and yet another in this list who played in the 1900 Challenge Cup Final victory over Salford. Jack was also a more than useful goal-kicker who fell just short of kicking 100 for the club. Jack was transferred to Warrington where he remained from 1904 to 1907, but he then returned to Swinton for a further two seasons.

His brother Will Preston also played for the club during most of the same period. Jack won two Lancashire caps during the 1901/02 season, against Cheshire at Wheater's Field, Broughton, and against Cumberland at Barrow's Cavendish Park. On New Year's Day, 1910, Jack played his last match for the Lions, but went on to assist the Barton junior club.

Born n/k (Pendlebury); Died 1944.

Debut : v Runcorn, 14 November 1900.
Last match : v Bradford Northern, 10 April 1911.

Appearances 273, Tries 80, Goals 30.

Representative Honours:
Lancashire 1 cap (1902/03).

Pendlebury junior Billy was a speedy, cool and determined winger or centre, who scored on his Lions' debut in November 1900. He was a great crowd favourite and perhaps only needed a better physique to have reached the very top. Billy was three times the Lions' top try scorer in a season, and in December 1900 at Widnes he equalled the club record of scoring five tries in a match. His 22 points, courtesy of two tries and eight goals against Liverpool City in February 1907, was another club record that stood for over 50 years. In 1911, Billy retired from first-class rugby but joined the Barton club.

As a successful businessman he later returned to Swinton as a director, and shared in the glory years of the late 1920s.

Tommy Gartrell

Born 1881 (Cumberland); Died 1963 (aged 82).

Debut : v Widnes, 28 November 1903.
Last match : v Barrow, 4 October 1913.

Appearances 220, Tries 42, Goals 2.

Representative Honours:
Cumberland 1 cap (1906/07).

Tommy was a Cumbrian forward who came to the Lions from the Millom club, who were then full members of the Northern Union. He was strong and aggressive and quick enough to play on the wing when needed. Indeed Tommy finished the 1904/05 season as the club's joint top try scorer. He gained his one Cumberland county cap in October 1906 when they lost to Lancashire at Maryport.

Soon after that Tommy emigrated to South Africa where he worked as a miner and played Rugby Union. However, Tommy returned to England and to the Lions in 1908, for whom he twice played against touring Australian teams (in 1908/09 and 1911/12).

Born 1891 (Swinton); Died 1969 (aged 78).

Debut : v Widnes, 7 September 1912.
Last match : v Oldham, 25 December 1919.

Appearances 84, Tries 39, Goals 2.

Representative Honours:
Lancashire 2 caps (1913/14).

Frank was a prolific try-scoring winger who amassed tries at a rate of almost one every two games. He signed for the Lions from local junior side Wardley, at a time when the club was in dire financial straits and so did most of their recruiting in the Swinton area. He gained two Lancashire caps in late 1913, first against Cumberland at The Cliff, Broughton, and then against Yorkshire at Fartown, Huddersfield.

Frank was the club's top try scorer for three consecutive seasons between 1912/13 and 1914/15, and appeared briefly after the Great War before winding his career down at Seedley Rangers.

Jack Bailey

Born 1887 (Swinton); Died not known.

Debut : v Rochdale Hornets, 5 September 1908.
Last match : v Widnes, 21 January 1922.

Appearances 173 (plus war-time 1 appearance), Tries 28, Goals 0.

Representative Honours:
Lancashire 2 caps (2 tries) (1911/12 to 1912/13); Tour Trial 1 app (1919/20).

Jack was yet another local lad who joined the Lions from Swinton St Mary's. As well as being a speedy and fearless forward, he was also an accomplished boxer and wrestler. Jack played for the Lions against the 1911 Australians, and scored tries in both of his two appearances for Lancashire. His county debut came in a 13-12 win over Yorkshire at Halifax in January 1912.

During the Great War he served on the Western Front, and on 10 April 1916 he miraculously escaped death when he was shot clean through the chest by a machine-gun bullet. The bullet missed all of his vital organs and he somehow made a full recovery, to the extent that he was chosen to play in a Tour Trial match and narrowly missed selection for the 1920 Great Britain Ashes Tour. To this day, Jack's family still own his army tunic complete with bullet hole.

Born 12 May 1880 (Llanelly); Died 23 June 1944 (aged 64).

Debut : v Widnes, 3 April 1899.
Last match : v Batley, 8 March 1913.

Appearances 170, Tries 30, Goals 2.

Representative Honours:
Wales 1 cap (1910/11); Lancashire 3 caps (1 try) (1900/01);
Rest of Northern Union 1 app (1899/00).

Dai Davies was an 18 years old reserve international and leading light of Welsh rugby when the Lions snatched him from Llanelly in early 1899. Financial secretary Jack Scholes was in Wales trying to persuade another recent capture, a homesick Owen Badger, to return north when he saw an opportunity to snap up Davies. Hence Dai was persuaded to sign a hastily prepared £20 contract leaning against a shop window! He quickly formed a devastating half-back partnership with countryman Joey Morgan, with whom he would talk Welsh on the field in order to confuse the

opposition. Dai was a try scorer in the Lions' 1900 Challenge Cup Final win against Salford, but shocked the club when he accepted a significant financial offer from Bolton Wanderers to join them as a goalkeeper in 1902. He subsequently played for Bolton in the 1904 FA Cup Final against Manchester City, and remains the only man in history to have played in both codes' showpiece finals. Dubbed the "Prodigal Son", he returned to Swinton in 1909 and won an international cap for Wales when they lost to England at Coventry's Butts Ground in December 1910. Prior to that Dai had also won a cap playing soccer for Wales. He played on until the 1912/13 season before accepting an offer to play at Leigh. However, his connection with Swinton was not finished, because at the outset of the Great War, Dai volunteered for the 16th Lancashire Fusiliers. Dai and his brother Dan then became popular members of "E" Company, otherwise known as the "Swinton Pals". At their training base on the Morfa near Conway in 1915, the Davies brothers marked out football pitches and organised matches between the various platoons. Fortunately both brothers survived the war thanks to their evacuation from the trenches due to illness. When peacetime returned Dai assisted the junior Swinton Park club, and later became greenkeeper at the Pendleton Belmont Bowling Club which was near his home on Eccles Old Road.

Jack Daley

Born 1891 (Swinton); Died 14 September 1916 (aged 25, at Thiepval, France).

Debut : v Runcorn, 22 November 1913.
Last match : v St Helens, 13 March 1915.

Appearances 33, Tries 1, Goals 0.

Jack was from Watson Street just off Station Road, and he signed for the Lions for £5 from the Swinton St Mary's junior team in September 1913. His ability as a wrestler and occupation as a miner meant that he developed into an extremely tough forward. Jack was just establishing himself in the Lions' first team when war broke out in 1914.

He enlisted in February 1915 as a gunner in the Grenadier Guards, and played his last game for the Lions a few days later. Jack saw his first significant action at the Battle of the Somme in the summer of 1916. Sadly, it was an engagement that would claim his life, as he was reported Killed-in-Action on 14 September 1916. His body was never recovered and his name is listed on the Thiepval Memorial in northern France. Like George Crabtree on the next page, Jack is selected in this list as a representative of the known 40 Swinton players who served in the Great War.

Born 1893 (Pendleton); Died 20 April 1917 (aged 23 at Gorre, northern France).

Debut : v Wigan, 5 April 1913.
Last match : v Wigan, 13 December 1913.

Appearances 9, Tries 0, Goals 0.

George came from Pendleton and originally played rugby for his works team, Mandelberg and Co Ltd, who specialised in making waterproof garments. He came to the notice of the Lions in 1912 when he excelled in a work shop tournament organised by the club. George played a number of games at full-back before the Great War intervened, at which point he enlisted with the Lancashire Fusiliers.

Tragically George was Killed-in-Action in France on 20 April 1917, whilst assisting the 197th Trench Mortar Battery.

George has been listed here alongside the year that he died as a representative of all the Lions who fought in the Great War, and particularly those 14 men who lost their lives in the service of their country. Namely first-teamers Jack Daley, Jack Flynn, Tom Neen, Ernie Stephenson and Tom Williams; and reserve team players Charles Batty, Joe Cartwright, Ezra Gee, Bill Lever, Albert Sanderson, Herbert Shedlock, Harold White and William Wallwork.

Jack Flynn

Born 1884 (Cumberland); Died 4 May 1918 (aged 34 at Forceville, France).

Debut : v Wigan, 3 September 1904.
Last match : v Widnes, 18 October 1913.

Appearances 79, Tries 7, Goals 21.

Representative Honours:
Cumberland 6 caps (1904/05 to 1905/06).

John "Jack" Flynn was a 5′ 6″ Cumbrian who first made his mark with the amateurs Whitehaven Recreation, but it was from the Parton club that Swinton signed him for 15 shillings in 1904. He was quite a character and charmer, traits which earned him the nickname "Dandy". Jack was a very capable half-back or three-quarter, and he made six appearances for Cumberland before the Lions surprisingly sold him to Broughton Rangers in 1906. Whilst with Rangers he won an England cap and more county caps, before returning to Swinton in 1911.

After almost a year out of the game Jack intended to join Bradford Northern for season 1914/15, but owing to the outbreak of the Great War instead he returned to Cumberland and joined the Border Regiment as a Lance Corporal.

Sadly, Jack became one of Swinton's 13 fallen when he was Killed-in-Action on 4 May 1918. He is buried at Forceville cemetery in northern France on the Somme battlefield.

Born 1889 (Pendlebury); Died August 1959 (aged 70).

Debut : v Coventry, 9 December 1911.
Last match : v Rochdale Hornets, 27 August 1921.

Appearances 170, Tries 1, Goals 167.
War-Time 1915/16 to 1918/19 : Appearances 46, Tries 2, Goals 40.

Representative Honours:
Lancashire 2 caps (3 goals) (1919/20); Lancashire League 1 app (1915/16).

Matt was an extremely popular local lad from the Pendlebury junior club, who emerged as a very accomplished goal-kicking full-back or centre. On 13 September 1913, Swinton had the honour of opposing Broughton Rangers at the opening of the The Cliff, and Matt scored the new ground's first points. He was six times the club's top goal-scorer in a season, and during the 1914/15 season Matt was named team captain in the absence of the injured Jimmy Dawson. In April 1916, he was one of five Lions to represent the Lancashire League against the Yorkshire League at Halifax. During the Great War, Matt was in a reserved occupation as a mill foreman, but nonetheless

he volunteered for the Royal Field Artillery and became a gunner. He was wounded in the senseless slaughter at Passchendaele, but luckily he survived. After the war he returned to the Lions, and in the autumn of 1919 he won two official Lancashire caps. On his county debut he kicked three goals in a success over Yorkshire at Broughton, the ground where he had made his mark just before the war. In 1921 Matt was awarded £65 by the Lions in lieu of a benefit and rejoined Pendlebury. He later took up refereeing and lived out his life in the town.

Albert Jenkins

Born c.1897 (Machen); Died not known.

Debut : v St Helens Recreation, 6 November 1920.
Last match : v St Helens Recreation, 8 September1928.

Appearances 146, Tries 29, Goals 25.

Albert is arguably the most influential player in this list not to have achieved representative honours. A 5 foot 7 inches tall Welshman from Ebbw Vale RUFC, Albert (along with Hector Halsall) was greatly credited with kick-starting the club's great revival in the early 1920s.

Albert was an unorthodox attacking stand-off, and was one of the first players to use the scissors and reverse passes. He was a drop-goal expert and his career total of 21 was a club record at the time. In 1923, he played in the Lions' first post-war cup final in which the Lancashire Cup was lost to St Helens Recreation, but thereafter he had the misfortune to come up against Bryn Evans and Billo Rees for a regular berth at half-back. Albert became the club's coach in 1945, 25 years to the day after signing as a player, a position he held until the end of the 1950/51 season.

Jimmy Dawson

Born 30 September 1891 (Eccles); Died 5 November 1980 (aged 89 at Patricroft).

Debut : v Leigh, 14 October 1911.
Last match : v Rochdale Hornets, 1 November 1924.

Appearances 187, Tries 31, Goals 26.
War-time 1915/16 to 1918/19 : Appearances 63, Tries 13, Goals 6.

Representative Honours:
Lancashire 1 cap (1920/21); Lancashire League 1 app (1915/16).

Jimmy was born in Eccles and in 1910 he helped to re-form the junior club, Barton NUFC. As a boyhood Swinton supporter, he was thrilled when in August 1911 the Lions captured him for a £4 transfer fee and £20 signing-on fee. Jimmy's Swinton career would last some 14 years, primarily as a centre, although he could play anywhere in the back division. He was appointed captain in 1915 and continued in this role for six seasons. During the Great War, Jimmy continued his civilian work as a specialist motor-tyre maker which luckily was a reserved occupation. In October 1920, he was capped by Lancashire against Cumberland, playing full-back in a 16-12 win at St Helen's. Four years later the Rugby Football League granted Jimmy a benefit match against Hull KR which generated £400. In 1921, he captained

Swinton to a historic 9-0 victory over the touring Australians at Chorley Road. After his playing career finished Jimmy coached Swinton Juniors with such success that his services were requested by the great Lance Todd at The Willows. In 1938, Jimmy helped coach Salford to their only Challenge Cup victory at Wembley, having beaten the Lions in the semi-finals. Jimmy passed away at his Patricroft home in November 1980.

Henry Blewer

Born 24 January 1897 (Swinton); Died 1973 (aged 76).

Debut : v Leigh, 18 January 1919 (War-Time v St Helens, 9 September 1916).
Last match : v Leeds, 9 May 1931 (Championship Final).

Appearances 392, Tries 17, Goals 2.
War-Time 1916/17 to 1918/19: Appearances 51, Tries 4, Goals 0.

Representative Honours:
Lancashire 1 cap (1926/27).

Henry was a fitness fanatic who always stood erect and soldierly on the field, and he made his debut as a youngster during the Great War. He was a master ball-winning hooker, at a time when this was a very specialised position. In 1925, he was part of the Lions' team which defeated Wigan in the Lancashire Cup Final, and he followed this by scoring the only try of the 1926 Challenge Cup Final in which Oldham were defeated 9-3 at the Athletic Grounds, Rochdale. Henry was also central to the club's 1927 Championship success, and was a member of the great Five Cups team of 1927/28. Amazingly Henry only won one Lancashire cap, this coming in January 1927 when the touring New Zealanders were easily beaten 28-3 at Leigh. He missed the whole of the 1928/29 season because of a dispute with the club over his benefit, but happily Henry returned to the fold. In May 1931, he won his third Championship Final in his last ever appearance for the Lions, when Leeds were beaten at Wigan. His career was hampered to some extent due to the fact he was extremely hard of hearing, and thanks to this fact many amusing tales exist at poor Henry's expense.

Born 1898 (Parton, Cumberland); Died 18 December 1955 (aged 57).

Debut : v Wakefield Trinity, 3 February 1923.
Last match : v Salford, 3 October 1934.

Appearances 347, Tries 12, Goals 1.

Representative Honours:
Cumberland 21 caps (1923/24 to 1932/33).

Never has a Rugby League forward been more aptly named than Miller Strong, who was something of a man-mountain. A Cumbrian from the Broughton Moor club, he started off as he meant to go on by getting sent-off on his debut in 1923. He was also suspended for the last 11 matches of the 1929/30 season for "retaliating". Miller made his county debut for Cumberland in September 1923, and went on to amass a very impressive 21 county caps at prop-forward. He was also the cornerstone of the Lions' pack for over 10 years, and twice played in winning finals of each of the Championship, the Challenge Cup and the Lancashire Cup. A real character, Miller lived out his relatively short life in Pendlebury, and for a while he was the landlord of The Showboat pub on Hall Street.

Frank Evans

Born 3 April 1897 (Dafen, Llanelly); Died 30 November 1972 (aged 75 at Llanelly).

Debut : v Rochdale Hornets, 27 August 1921.
Last match : v Wigan, 22 October 1930.

Appearances 341, Tries 195, Goals 1.

Representative Honours: Great Britain 4 caps (3 tries) (1924); GB Tourist 10 apps (10 tries) (1924); Wales 7 caps (7 tries) (1921/22 to 1927/28); Other Nationalities 2 caps (1 try) (1924/25 to 1925/26); Glamorgan & Monmouth 1 cap (1 try) (1929/30); Tour Trial 1 app (1 try) (1927/28).

Frank, a Welsh Rugby Union international winger, was a major capture from Llanelly RUFC in the summer of 1921. Small in stature, he was a fast and elusive try scorer, amassing more than 20 in six out of seven seasons between 1923 and 1929. With a total of 195, he jointly holds the club record for tries in a career under Rugby League rules (and second overall only to Jim Valentine). He was the first Swinton player to be selected for an Ashes tour, and on 28 June 1924 he became the first Lion to gain a Test cap when Australia were beaten 5-3 at Sydney.

Amongst the many club tries he scored arguably the most important was the one which set the Lions on their way to an 11-0 Championship Final success over Featherstone Rovers in 1928, which secured the last of "All Four Cups". Evans also scored tries prolifically for Wales, including a hat-trick against New Zealand in December 1926 at Pontypridd, and two in a narrow loss to England in 1925. Upon retiring in 1930 Frank returned to his native South Wales.

Jack Evans (Junior)

Born 23 September 1897 (Llwynypia); Died 20 March 1940 (aged 42 at Pendlebury).

Debut : v Widnes, 19 February 1921.
Last match : v Huddersfield, 17 September 1932.

Appearances 276, Tries 99, Goals 27.

Representative Honours: Great Britain 3 caps (2 tries) (1926/27); GB Tourist 3 apps (1 try) (1928); England 5 caps (1924/25 to 1927/28); Lancashire 11 caps (4 tries) (1922/23 to 1927/28); Tour Trial 1 app (1927/28).

Evan "Jack" Evans was born in South Wales, but came to Swinton at the age of 5 months when his father, Jack senior, signed for the Lions. He was also elder brother to Bryn and Harold. After excelling with the Swinton Park junior side, Jack was snapped up the Lions in early 1921. He soon developed into a very clever player and tactician, and many experts of the day credit him with being the real mastermind of the great Swinton side of the 1920s. Jack captained Swinton to victory in the 1926 Challenge Cup Final, and kicked the dropped-goal which won the 1928 final against Warrington, 5-3. Jack twice played in Lancashire Cup Final victories over Wigan, and was key to the Lions' first Championship success in 1927. He missed Swinton's 1928 Championship victory on account of his selection for the Ashes Tour, which had set sail ahead of the final. Sadly, appendicitis ruled him out of much of the 1928 tour, and he therefore didn't get chance to add to the three Great Britain caps he gained against the touring New Zealand team in the winter

of 1926/27. Prior to that he had won the first of five England caps in a win over Wales in January 1925. During the Great War, Jack had been gassed and held prisoner for eight months, and these were ultimately major factors in the ill-health which dogged him after his retirement from playing. After a stint succeeding his father at the Colliers Arms, Jack became landlord of the Royal Oak in Pendlebury in 1932, where he died eight years later at the age of just 42.

Bert Morris

Born 30 August 1896 (Coventry); Died 1956 (aged 60).

Debut : v Huddersfield, 17 November 1923.
Last match : v Leeds, 9 May 1931 (Championship Final).

Appearances 301, Tries 16, Goals 377.

Bert was signed from Coventry RUFC in the autumn of 1923, and soon became an unsung hero of the Lions' great 1920s team. He was a brilliant all round prop-forward, with good ball handling ability as well as being a skilled scrummager. Added to this he was a very dependable goal-kicker, who notched a then club record 91 goals in 1925/26 and 95 a year later. In the 1925/26 season, Bert twice kicked three goals in winning cup finals – firstly in the 15-11 success against Wigan in the Lancashire Cup, then again when Oldham were beaten 9-3 in the Challenge Cup Final.

In all Bert would win three Championships, two Challenge Cups, two Lancashire Cups and four Lancashire Leagues in an illustrious career with the Lions, which perplexingly did not bring about any representative honours.

Chris Brockbank

Born 1901 (Swinton); Died 1963 (aged 62).

Debut : v Leigh, 18 January 1919 (War-Time v Broughton Rangers, 29 March 1918).
Last match : v Salford, 1 January 1931.

Appearances 272, Tries 136, Goals 28. (War-Time Apps 11, Tries 3, Goals 0).

Representative Honours:
England 1 cap (1926/27); Lancashire 2 caps (1927/28); Tour Trial 1 app (1 try) (1927/28).

Chris made his debut at a tender age during the Great War after signing from Clifton via the St Peter's School club, and when peace-time came he was initially loaned out to Salford. After returning to the Lions he established himself as a brilliant free-scoring winger in the great Swinton team of the 1920s. He had a habit of scoring on big occasions, such as in the Championship Final of 1925 which was lost to Hull KR; the 1925 Lancashire Cup Final victory over Wigan; the 1927 Challenge Cup Final defeat to Oldham; and perhaps most famously, in the 1928 Challenge Cup Final victory over Warrington. He was twice the Lions' top scorer, and his 29 efforts in season 1924/25 was at the time a club record under RL rules. In April 1927, he won an England cap, ironically in opposition to his fellow Swinton winger Frank Evans, as the Welsh were beaten 11-8 at The Cliff, Broughton. During his Lions' career he ran a tobacconist's on Cemetery Road, Swinton, but in 1931 he signed briefly for Bradford Northern. He then later coached at Huddersfield before becoming secretary-manager at Warrington after World War Two. In 1954, Chris was an instrumental figure in the formation of Blackpool Borough, for whom he also served as secretary. He was a nephew of Herbie Brockbank, who had starred for the Lions just prior to the formation of the Northern Union.

Hector Halsall

Born 1900 (Wigan); Died September 1966 (aged 66).

Debut : v St Helens Recreation, 6 November 1920.
Last match : v Widnes, 22 February 1930.

Appearances 369, Tries 55, Goals 17.

Representative Honours: Great Britain 1 cap (1929/30); Lancashire 2 caps (1926/27 to 1929/30); Northern RL 1 app (1929/30).

Hector Halsall is one of the most famous names in the club's history, as it is he that will be forever remembered as the captain of the immortal Swinton team which carried off "All Five Cups" in 1928. Yet he came to the Lions from Wigan almost by accident in 1920, after Swinton had initially enquired about a different player. Hector soon established himself as a great defensive centre with a noted body swerve when in attack. More than this he had great leadership and sportsmanship qualities, and he was appointed club skipper at the start of the 1922/23 season at the age of only 22. He then led the Lions to all of their major triumphs of the 1920s, except for the 1926 Challenge Cup Final that he missed through injury. He scored a try in the 1928 Championship Final against Featherstone Rovers, this being the game which marked the pinnacle of all the Lions' achievements. Hector twice played for Lancashire, with a county debut against New Zealand in early 1927. On 4 January 1930, he was drafted into the Great Britain team that faced Australia in the deciding Ashes Test at Station Road, the Lions' new ground that had opened 10 months earlier under his captaincy. His playing career ended soon afterwards, but he was landlord of the Buckley Arms, Swinton, between 1929 and 1933. Hector also had coaching spells at Leigh and more latterly Barrow, whom he led to the 1938 Challenge Cup Final.

COPYRIGHT)

H. HALSALL (CAPTAIN)   LANCS: LEAGUE   R.L. CHALLENGE   R.L. CHAMPIONSHIP

CUPS

SWINTON R.F.C. 1927-28

Frank Buckingham

Born 4 January 1905 (Birmingham); Died December 1958 (aged 53).

Debut : v Barrow, 18 February 1928.
Last match : v Widnes, 7 November 1936.

Appearances 172, Tries 69, Goals 0.

Frank was born in Birmingham but moved to New Zealand as a child, and he was playing for Waikato RUFC when he came to the Lions' attention in early 1928. He subsequently became recognised as Swinton's first-ever overseas signing. Frank was a strong and speedy winger who gave the club excellent service for almost nine years. On 2 March 1929, he gained ever-lasting fame by scoring Swinton's first ever try at Station Road (in a 9-3 win over Wigan). In season 1930/31, he was the club's top try scorer as Swinton won the Championship by defeating Leeds in the final. Frank won another Championship Final in 1935 when Warrington were beaten at Wigan, and it had been his two tries in the semi-final that had seen off arch rivals Salford.

He became a publican after his playing career ended, taking over the Golden Lion in Eccles. On the night of 8 May 1941, the pub was flattened by a German bomb, but Frank and his family emerged unscathed from the cellar. He was later landlord of the Crown and Volunteer pub in Eccles.

Fred Butters

Born 3 July 1904 (Pendlebury); Died 16 August 1988 (aged 84).

Debut : v St Helens, 16 April 1927.
Last match : v Barrow, 11 May 1940.

Appearances 351, Tries 70, Goals 0.

Representative Honours: Great Britain 2 caps (1929/30); GB Tourist 1 app (1 try) (1932); England 1 cap (1932/33); Lancashire 15 caps (3 tries) (1928/29 to 1936/37); Northern RL 1 app (1 try) (1929/30); Tour Trials 2 apps (1931/32).

Fred was a native of Pendlebury and worked for Gerrard's, but he was also without doubt one of the club's greatest ever loose-forwards. Fred was a formidable long-striding attacker and resolute defensive player, always noticeable by the trademark skull-cap which he wore for good reason. He established himself in the Swinton team in season 1928/29 when he won the first of his impressive 15 Lancashire caps. Fred scored a try in the 1931 Championship Final, and was an instrumental figure in the club's 1935 Championship success (despite missing the final through injury), a period in which Swinton had a very powerful forward line. Fred was selected for the Ashes Tour of Australasia in 1932, but agonisingly broke his ankle in his first outing against a provincial team. Fred had, however, already made his test debut in a win against Australia at Leeds in November 1929, a result which set up the Third Test at Swinton as an Ashes decider. With the deciding Test locked at 0-0 and approaching the dying seconds, Fred produced a miraculous tackle to prevent the Aussie stand-off Joe "Chimpy" Busch from scoring in the corner. With Great Britain then going on to win a hastily arranged Fourth Test, Butters had literally saved the Ashes for his country. The collision with Busch and the corner flag had almost torn Fred's ear off, and he remained out of the game for several months afterwards.

Born 25 November 1899 (Swinton); Died 10 July 1975 (aged 75).

Debut : v Batley, 17 January 1920.
Last match : v St Helens Recreation, 29 February 1936.

Appearances 467, Tries 102, Goals 0.

Representative Honours: Great Britain 10 caps (1926/27 to 1933/34); GB Tourist 11 apps (1 try) 1928 and 9 apps (2 tries) 1932; England 4 caps (1 try) (1930/31 to 1933/34); Lancashire 21 caps (1 try) (1923/24 to 1932/33); Tour Trials 3 apps (1 try) (1927/28 to 1931/32).

Bryn was the middle brother of Jack and Harold, and the son of Jack senior, all of them Swinton stars in their own right. He emerged through the Swinton Park amateur club, who were based at the Farmers Arms. Bryn was a clever and defensively sound scrum-half who played a pivotal role in the club's most successful era, usually alongside Billo Rees whom he also often partnered for Great Britain. His list of honours is remarkable. He assisted the Lions to four Championships in 1927, 1928, 1931 and 1935 (the latter two as captain), as well as two Challenge Cups, two Lancashire Cups and four Lancashire Leagues. Bryn was also a try scorer when Swinton first won the Lancashire Cup in 1925, and he scored twice when the Lions defeated St Helens Recreation in 1927 to secure their first ever Championship. He also had an impressive list of representative honours, with 14 international caps

and 21 Lancashire county caps. Bryn was twice selected for Ashes Tours, first in 1928 and then in 1932 when he had the honour of being named vice-captain to Jim Sullivan. He retired partway through the 1935/36 season by which time he had made a then record 467 club appearances. In 1936, Bryn became club coach, but he was less successful in that role. Bryn was a true gentleman, and one of the most popular and successful players in the entire history of the club.

Joe Wright

Born 28 June 1908 (Carlisle); Died 1967 (aged 58).

Debut : v Halifax, 3 November 1928.
Last match : v Workington Town, 17 November 1945.

Appearances 419, Tries 14, Goals 7.

Representative Honours: Great Britain 1 cap (1932); GB Tourist 15 apps (3 tries) (1932); England 3 caps (1931/32 to 1933/34); Cumberland 19 caps (2 tries) (1930/31 to 1938/39); Tour Trials 2 apps (1931/32).

Joe was a tough Cumbrian prop-forward who came to Swinton from Carlisle RUFC. He played throughout the 1930s when the Lions had one of the most feared packs in the game. Joe twice won the Championship with the Lions (in 1931 and 1935), and he was a member of Swinton's successful 1940 Lancashire Cup team. He also played in four losing major finals for the Lions. Joe made his county debut in a victory over Yorkshire at York in October 1931, and remained a regular for Cumberland for nine seasons. He was selected for England when they defeated Wales at Salford in 1932, and this timely good form ensured selection for the 1932 Ashes Tour of Australasia. It was on that tour that Joe won his only Great Britain cap in a win over New Zealand at Carlaw Park, Auckland.

The latter end of his career was disrupted by World War Two, but he did briefly continue playing when peacetime resumed. Joe's last appearance came ironically in Swinton's first ever league match against Cumbrian opposition – when appropriately Joe scored the winning try in a 3-2 victory at Workington Town in November 1945, some 17 years after his debut.

Born 14 April 1899 (Glanamman); Died 1968 (aged 68).

Debut : v St Helens, 3 December 1921.
Last match : v St Helens Recreation, 21 October 1933.

Appearances 360, Tries 38, Goals 2.

Representative Honours: Great Britain 11 caps (2 tries) (1926/27 to 1929/30); GB Tourist 13 apps (3 tries) (1928); Wales 6 caps (1925/26 to 1929/30); Other Nationalities 2 caps (1928/29 to 1930/31); Glamorgan & Monmouth 2 caps (1928/29); Tour Trial 1 app (1927/28).

The 22 years old William or "Billo" Rees, was a cult hero at his local Rugby Union club, Amman United, which represented the villages of Garnant and Glanamman. Billo's talents had been recognised by the much bigger Swansea club, and he was also a Welsh international trialist when the Lions swooped to whisk him north in November 1921. Almost tiny in physical stature, he was lightning quick in both thought and movement, as well as being a master of the short grubber-kick. Initially Billo covered for the injured Bryn Evans, a man with whom he would later form a brilliant half-back partnership at both club and international level. He gained the first of his seven Wales caps when England won at Pontypridd in April 1926, then in October of the same year he was capped by Great Britain when the touring New Zealanders were beaten at Wigan. Billo was selected for the 1928 Ashes Tour and starred in all six Tests against Australia and New Zealand. The Aussies took Billo to their hearts and many regarded him as the finest British player on that tour. He missed Swinton's 1928 Championship Final success due to the Ashes tour, but he did play in the Lions' 1927 and 1931 Championship Final victories. He also played in four Challenge Cup Finals for Swinton (two of them won), and both Lancashire Cup Final victories over Wigan in 1925 and 1927. He finally retired in 1933, aged 34, after 12 years of astonishing success. Billo initially took up the position of steward of the Swinton Social Club, but in November 1934 he left for Swansea to take over a public house.

Born 26 October 1907 (Pendlebury); Died November 1994 (aged 87).

Debut : v St Helens Recreation, 6 December 1930.
Last match : v Keighley, 18 September 1937.

Appearances 229, Tries 112, Goals 0.

Representative Honours:
England 1 cap (1935/36); Lancashire 2 caps (1932/33 to 1933/34); Northern RL 1 app (1933/34).

Although signed from Leigh, Jack Kenny was originally from Pendlebury and he had emerged through the junior ranks with Chloride Recreation. Jack was a speedy winger who scored 20 tries in a season three times, and five times topped the Lions' tries in a season charts. He played in the 1931 Championship Final success over Leeds, but was on the losing team a year later in the Challenge Cup Final against the same opposition.

Jack twice won caps for Lancashire, and was a try scorer when he played for a representative Northern RL XIII which beat the touring Australians at York in November 1933. He gained a single cap for England, when his side was surprisingly beaten by Wales at Hull KR in February 1936. Jack's son Peter also starred for the Lions in the late 1960s and early 1970s.

Born 21 February 1903 (Warrington); Died March 1970 (aged 67).

Debut : v Widnes, 27 September 1924.
Last match : v Warrington, 11 May 1935 (Championship Final).

Appearances 396, Tries 83, Goals 6.

Representative Honours:
Lancashire 5 caps (1 try, 2 goals) (1927/38 to 1934/35).

Fred was considered the most exciting young prospect in the Manchester area when the Lions signed him from Irlam & Cadishead Juniors in the summer of 1924. He was a fast second-row or loose-forward who played in 13 major cup finals and won 12 major honours for Swinton between 1924 and 1935. Fred scored a crucial try in the 1927 Championship Final victory against St Helens Recreation at Warrington, and another to help his club defeat the 1926 touring New Zealanders. He was a prolific try scorer for a forward, and four times he reached double figures in a season. Fred won five Lancashire caps, the first coming against Yorkshire at Warrington in October 1927 when he scored a try.

His final match was arguably his proudest moment, as he produced a man-of-the-match display to help defeat Warrington in the 1935 Championship Final. Fred's home town of Warrington had played a part in many of his most memorable moments, and after his playing career ended he became a director at Wilderspool, where he often insisted on wearing his Swinton blazer complete with rampant lion badge.

Born 1 April 1904 (Manchester); Died 15 October 1972 (aged 68).

Debut : v Barrow, 29 August 1931.
Last match : v Leigh, 19 October 1946.

Appearances 355, Tries 25, Goals 6.

Representative Honours: Great Britain 8 caps (1933/34 to 1937/38); GB Tourist 8 apps (1936) England 10 caps (1 try) (1934/35 to 1939/40); Lancashire 13 caps 1 try (1933/34 to 1938/39); Lancashire League 1 app (1939/40); Northern RL 3 apps (19933/34 to 1938/39); 1936 Tourists 1 app (1939/40); Tour Trial 1 app (1935/36).

Tommy was not only arguably Swinton's finest ever hooker, but he was also the sport's best number nine throughout the 1930s. He was a late developer in Rugby League terms having previously had a taste of professional soccer with Crewe Alexandra. However, despite his soccer background, Tommy was signed from Seedley Juniors amateur RL club in 1931 and made his debut at the opening of Barrow's Craven Park. In his first two seasons with the Lions he was a loser in three major cup finals, but he did play in the 1935 Championship Final victory over Warrington and the 1940 Lancashire Cup Final success over Widnes. A winner of eight Great Britain caps, Tommy had a fine record against the Australians. Twice he helped win the Ashes, firstly as a Tourist in 1936, and again in England during the 1937/38 season. He also played in two victories for Swinton over touring Australian teams. Tommy was still playing for England at the age of 35, and he didn't hang up his Lions' boots until the age of 42, by which time he had played in the same reserve team line-up as his son, Charlie.

Born 23 November 1901 (Aspatria); Died 1981 (aged 79).

Debut : v Hunslet, 8 December 1928.
Last match : v Keighley, 23 January 1937.

Appearances 337, Tries 9, Goals 127.

Representative Honours:
Cumberland 9 caps (1 goal) (1929/30 to 1935/36).

Bobby was a Cumbrian who was signed from the short-lived Carlisle City RLFC in 1928. He succeeded Jack Pearson at full-back and played against Wigan at the opening of Station Road in March 1929. Later that year he gained the first of his nine county caps for Cumberland, when he played alongside Martin Hodgson and Miller Strong in a loss to Lancashire at Whitehaven. Although small in stature he was an excellent last line of defence, not to mention a useful stand-in goal-kicker for Martin Hodgson. Bobby twice won Championship Finals with Swinton, in 1931 and 1935, against Leeds and Warrington respectively. He retired in 1937 having also played in three losing major cup finals for the Lions.

Gomer Hughes

Born 13 May 1910 (Neath); Died 14 November 1974 (aged 64 at Salford).

Debut : v Halifax, 25 August 1934.
Last match : v Barrow, 10 May 1947.

Appearances 293, Tries 16, Goals 0.

Representative Honours:
Wales 3 caps (1934/35 to 1940/41); Wales War-Time 1 app (1943/44).

Gomer was a tough-as-iron no-nonsense prop-forward. He was signed from Penarth RUFC in 1934 having played in all three Triple Crown matches for Wales earlier that year. Disgracefully, however, the Welsh Rugby Union withheld his caps until after his death. Gomer had a reputation for being able to drink extraordinary amounts of beer, and he would often be seen in the Bull's Head ahead of matches "calming his nerves". In his first season the Lions won the Championship with a 14-3 victory over Warrington at Wigan, and he produced outstanding performances when Widnes were defeated in the two-legged Lancashire Cup Final of 1940. Gomer also won three caps for Wales under Rugby League rules, losing in Bordeaux to France on his debut on New Year's Day, 1935. However, he was a winner when the Welsh famously beat England 17-9 at Llanelly in November 1938.

Like many others of his era, Gomer's career was hampered by the war. He eventually retired in 1947, but remained in the Swinton area.

Harold Evans

Born 10 March 1907 (Swinton); Died 1981 (aged 74).

Debut : v Leigh, 28 March 1927.
Last match : v Bramley, 18 February 1939.

Appearances 399, Tries 94, Goals 16.

Representative Honours:
Lancashire 1 cap (1933/34); Northern RL France Tour 1 app (1 try) (1936/37).

As the younger brother of the Lions' more famous Jack and Bryn, Harold was always known as "Chick". He made his debut in 1927 at the age of 20, but it wasn't until the 1928/29 season that he began to earn a regular place. Harold played mainly at centre, but he could also slot in effectively at stand-off. His absence through suspension was thought to be a contributory factor behind the Lions' last-minute 10-8 loss to Salford in the 1931 Lancashire Cup Final at The Cliff. However, Harold gained adequate compensation through playing his part in the 1931 and 1935 Championship Final successes alongside his brother, Bryn.

He won a single Lancashire cap against Yorkshire at Oldham in September 1933, and was also selected for promotional Rugby League Tour of France in 1936. Upon retirement in 1939, and following 12 years of loyal service, Harold was awarded a joint-testimonial alongside Fred Butters.

1939 150 GREATEST

Martin Hodgson

Born 26 March 1909 (Egremont); Died 23 July 1991 (aged 82 at Swinton).

Debut : v St Helens, 16 April 1927.
Last match : Oldham, 25 December 1940.

Appearances 473, Tries 39, Goals 870.

Representative Honours: Great Britain 16 caps (8 goals) (1929/30 to 1937/38); GB Tourist 13 apps (2 tries, 13 goals) (1932) and 14 apps (3 tries, 58 goals) (1936); England 9 caps (14 goals) (1927/28 to 1936/37); Cumberland 29 caps (4 tries, 17 goals) (1927/28 to 1938/39); Lancashire League 1 app (1 try, 2 goals) (1939/40); Northern RL 1 app (1933/34); 1936 Tourists 1 app (2 goals) (1939/40); Tour Trial 1 app (1 try) (1935/36).

It is difficult to argue against Martin being regarded as the greatest ever player of the club's Rugby League era. A Cumbrian from the Egremont Rugby Union club, Martin was a second-row forward of such talent that he deservedly holds his place in the RFL's illustrious Hall of Fame. In his first full season with the Lions, 1927/28, he collected an unprecedented six winners' medals. Swinton of course had swept the board, but Cumberland also lifted the County Championship. Martin would eventually gather a colossal 29 county caps over a period of 12 seasons. He is also the Lions' most-capped Great Britain player with 16 to his credit. Hodgson's Test debut came during the successful Ashes campaign of 1929/30, whilst he was twice selected for tours of Australasia (in 1932 and 1936). The latter tour confirmed his status as one of the greatest second-row forwards that the game had ever known. A massive man in height and stature, he was also remarkably quick, as well as being a deadly cover-tackler. His power extended to kicking, and for 12 successive seasons he was the Lions' top goalscorer. His goals helped win the 1931 and 1935 Championship Finals, and he also kicked four in the lost 1932 Challenge Cup Final. Martin's 108 efforts in the 1931/32 season was the first time any player had kicked a century of goals for the club, whilst his mighty boot at Rochdale Hornets in April 1940 from 77.75 yards remains an all-time world record. That same year Martin was the League's top goal-kicker, whilst he also captained the Lions to the Lancashire Cup. Martin finished his Swinton career having been involved in the winning of 11 major club honours, with another seven as a runner-up. Martin guested for Huddersfield during the war having accepted a pram for his new-born twins as a signing-on fee, and he later became landlord of the Black Horse in Pendlebury. Martin was a true gentleman and he lived out his life in Swinton, being a frequent visitor to Station Road until his death in 1991.

Born 1878 (Barnsley); Died 25 September 1958 (aged 80).
Secretary : 12 July 1906 to May 1948.

Debut : v Dewsbury, 20 April 1907.
Last match : Dewsbury, 20 April 1907.

Appearances 1, Tries 0, Goals 0.

Samuel Alfred Jones is included in this list by virtue of his remarkable contribution to the club during his 42 years as secretary. A native of a village near Barnsley, he moved to Salford as a youngster. Sam married Maud Harvey in December 1901 at St Luke's, Weaste, and they went on to have three children. As a young man he became the player-secretary of Manchester League club, Egerton (later renamed Swinton Hornets), who in

1905 were invited to share the Lions' Chorley Road ground. Sam was offered a trial by Rochdale Hornets, but following the resignation of Swinton secretary Charlie Platt the vacant role was offered, and he took up duty on 12 July 1906. Sam actually played one match for the Lions, this being against Dewsbury on 20 April 1907, when he filled in at winger when the team was a man short. Sam became a hugely popular figure around the club. He was responsible for the day to day administration of the club through the glory years of the 1920s and 1930s, but he also played a critical role in keeping the club alive during two world wars. He also acted as team manager in 1945 immediately after the war. This arrangement lasted for 11 matches until a full-time coach, Albert Jenkins, was appointed. Sam finally resigned as secretary in 1948, after which his son, Vic, succeeded him as secretary. Vic himself would then hold the post until 1976 as part of a remarkable family dynasty.

Born 6 August 1910 (Skewen); Died 1 February 1995
(aged 84 at Salford).

Debut : v Halifax, 25 August 1934.
Last match : v York, 2 May 1942.

Appearances 165, Tries 45, Goals 0.

Arthur was a Welshman signed from Neath RUFC, and who had won a couple of international caps in 1930 and 1933. He came to Lions for a reported fee of £350 in 1934. Arthur was a fine centre, but also quick enough to play on the wing as he did later in his Swinton career. In his first season at Station Road (1934/35), he helped the Lions to win the Championship, and indeed played in the final against Warrington at Wigan. Arthur also played in the Lions' 5-3 victory over Australia in 1937, and was part of the team which won the 1940 Lancashire League and Cup double. He was well regarded and would deputise as club captain whenever Martin Hodgson was unavailable. His last appearance for the club came in a cup tie in 1942, shortly after which Station Road was requisitioned for the remainder of the war by the Home Guard and Ministry of Works.

Arthur remained in the Swinton area, and in the 1980s he could still be seen at Station Road exercising his duties as match-day commissionaire.

Born 26 April 1913 (Wigan); Died 22 March 1943 (aged 29 at Enfidha, Tunisia).

Debut : v Keighley, 18 April 1933.
Last match : v Bradford Northern, 25 May 1940.

Appearances 109, Tries 20, Goals 0.

Representative Honours:
Northern RL France Tour 1 app (3 tries) (1936/37).

Tommy joined the Lions in the summer of 1932 at the age of 19 from Wigan Old Boys RUFC. He therefore followed his friend Dick Green who had made the same switch a few months earlier. Tommy was a small but tigerish scrum-half, who was initially lined up to replace the ageing Bryn Evans. Tommy remained a loyal club man for the rest of the 1930s, despite facing severe opposition for the number seven jersey. His only representative honour came by way of selection for a Northern RL XIII tour of France in 1936/37.

After playing in the losing Championship Final against Bradford Northern in May 1940, Tommy enlisted with the Durham Light Infantry. He was subsequently posted to North Africa, where in March 1943 he was Killed-In-Action fighting Rommel's German forces. He was aged just 29, and is included in this list as a tribute to his sacrifice.

Dick Green

Born 2 April 1913 (Wigan); Died 15 November 1944
(aged 31 at Faenza, Italy).

Debut : v Dewsbury, 2 April 1932.
Last match : v Bradford Northern, 26 April 1939.

Appearances 155, Tries 29, Goals 0.

Like his friend Tommy Holland, Dick joined the Lions from Wigan Old Boys
RUFC. He was an excellent stand-off or centre who gained a regular place
during season 1934/35, which he finished as the club's joint top try scorer.
That particular campaign culminated in a try scoring performance against
Warrington in the Championship Final which was won 14-3. Dick also played
in the Lions' victory over the 1937 Australians, but following the outbreak of
war he joined Huddersfield as a guest player for three seasons.

Dick enlisted with the Lancashire
Fusiliers and attained the rank of
corporal. By September 1944, he
was in the thick of the fighting in
Italy where he was wounded. He
spent two months convalescing
before re-joining his unit on 15
November. Sadly, just a few days
later, he was Killed-in-Action at
Faenza near Bologna. Although
from Ince near Wigan, he is
remembered on the Swinton
Cenotaph alongside his pal,
Tommy Holland.

Randall Lewis

Born 1913 (Port Talbot); Died Sept 2009 (aged 96).

Debut : v Barrow, 9 January 1937.
Last match : v St Helens, 26 April 1947.

Appearances 206, Tries 74, Goals 0.

Randall represented a major capture for the Lions when he was signed from Aberavon RUFC for a reputed record club fee of £1,000 in January 1937. He was a policeman by trade and had just taken part in international trial matches for Wales. Randall was a strong-running centre who became a particular favourite of the younger Swinton fans. He was an ever present and leading try scorer during the 1939/40 season when the Lions won a Lancashire League and Cup double, and he also gained a Challenge Cup winners medal in 1944/45 whilst guesting for Huddersfield.

In January 1946, Randall scored a club record equalling five tries in a match against Keighley. In 2003, at the age of 90, he was a special guest of the club at the Lions' Moor Lane ground.

Ralph Morgan

Born 15 January 1920 (Machen); Died May 2009 (aged 89 at Swinton).

Debut : v Warrington, 11 January 1947.
Last match : v Barrow, 4 October1952.

Appearances 151, Tries 8, Goals 327.

Representative Honours:
Wales 3 caps (2 goals) (1948/49 to 1949/50).

Douglas "Ralph" Morgan was a 6 foot 2 policeman, and a Welsh international trialist from Newport RUFC. He was also an accomplished baseball player, and indeed he won a cap for his country at that sport in 1938. Ralph almost signed for Leeds and would have done so had a police re-location request been successful. Instead it was Swinton who landed his signature after the Lions arranged a job for him at Gerrard's, where he would ultimately spend the rest of his working life outside of rugby. Ralph was a stylish full-back and excellent place-kicker, although he did manage to burst the ball on his debut! For five seasons starting in 1946/47 he was the club's top goalscorer. In November 1948, he captained Swinton to a 21-0 defeat by the powerful

Australian tourists, and in the following season he led the Lions to a top three finish. Ralph won three caps for Wales between April 1949 and March 1950, his debut coming in a heavy defeat to the French at Marseille. He was eventually edged out of the Lions' team by the emerging Albert Blan, and subsequently he went to Leeds and later Belle Vue Rangers. Despite these transfers Ralph continued to live on Moss Lane in Swinton, where he died in 2009 at almost 90 years of age.

Born 1919 (Caernarfon); Died 1997 (aged 78 at Aberconwy).

Debut : v Leeds, 12 April 1947.
Last match : v Barrow 25 August 1948.

Appearances 41, Tries 8, Goals 2.

Representative Honours:
Wales 2 caps (1 try) (1947/48).

Bob was a Welsh prop-forward who came to the Lions from Aberavon RUFC towards the end of the 1946/47 season. He made a quick impression, and in November 1947 played for Wales in a 29-21 defeat to France at Bordeaux. Bob retained his place a fortnight later when England beat Wales at Swansea.

His proudest moment in a Swinton jersey was when the Lions defeated New Zealand, 8-6, in September 1947. At the start of the 1948/49 season Bob was snapped up by St Helens.

Jack Stoddart

Born 22 July 1914 (Grasslot, Maryport); Died 5 June 1983 (aged 68).

Debut : v St Helens, 1 October 1932.
Last match : v Halifax, 28 April 1951.

Appearances 368, Tries 18, Goals 0.

Representative Honours:
Cumberland 6 caps (1 try) (1937/48 to 1947/48).

Jack was a Cumbrian from the village of Grasslot, and he signed for the Lions at the age of 18 in 1932 from his local amateur club, Brookland Rovers of Maryport. The Lions helped him find work as a miner at Pendlebury's Wheatsheaf Colliery, and initially he lodged over the road at the Butcher's Arms. Jack started out as a prop or second-row forward and went on to give the club remarkable service. He started to edge his way into the first team during the Lions' Championship season of 1934/35, and by the end of the decade he was a regular. However, on a personal level, other than the 1940 Lancashire War League, major honours eluded him. Jack played in both of the Lions' agonising semi-final defeats of 1938 (against Salford in the Challenge Cup, and Leeds in the Championship), then in 1940 he didn't feature in the Lancashire Cup Final success over Widnes, but did play in the Championship Final defeat to Bradford Northern. Jack made his debut for Cumberland in a side which included Martin Hodgson and Joe Wright in November 1937, and ended with six county caps spread equally either side of the war - the last arriving in 1948. During the war, Jack had served with the Irish Guards, whilst his younger brother, Fletcher, also played for the Lions around the war years. Jack captained Swinton to their 8-6 victory over the 1947 New Zealanders, and a year later he was granted a testimonial. In 1950, and in the twilight of his career, Jack was a surprise strong contender for the 1950 Great Britain Ashes Tour to Australasia. However, he ruled himself out amidst the illness of his eldest daughter, who subsequently tragically died. Jack retired at the end of the 1950/51 season, 19 years after his Swinton debut.

Charlie Armitt

Born 10 January 1926 (Manchester); Died 17 April 2004 (aged 78).

Debut : v Keighley, 18 October 1947.
Last match : v Whitehaven, 11 April 1953.

Appearances 144, Tries 31, Goals 3.

Representative Honours:
England 1 cap (1949/50); Lancashire 1 cap (1948/49).

Charlie was the son of the Lions' legendary hooker, Tommy Armitt. But unlike his dad he was a mobile second-row forward - skilful enough to play at loose-forward and quick enough to occasionally play on the wing. Charlie was the Lions' top try scorer in season 1948/49, a campaign he completed by earning a Lancashire cap against Yorkshire at Halifax.

In September 1949, Charlie's meteoric rise was completed when he was selected for England to play against Other Nationalities at Workington. Charlie twice played in losses for Swinton against Australia (in 1948 and 1952), and in 1953 he was transferred to Huddersfield.

Frank Osmond

Born 31 January 1920 (Newport); Died January 1973 (aged 53).

Debut : v Hunslet, 25 January 1947.
Last match : v Wakefield Trinity, 6 October 1956.

Appearances 305, Tries 12, Goals 0.

Representative Honours:
Great Britain 1 unofficial app (1950/51); Great Britain Tourist 10 apps (4 tries) (1950); Wales 14 caps (1947/48 to 1951/52).

Frank is a real contender alongside Tommy Armitt, Henry Blewer, Trevor Roberts, Derek Clarke and Dick Evans for the title of the Lions' greatest ever hooker. Osmond was an old-fashioned master ball-winner in the scrum, a skill which sadly no longer exists. Swinton signed him from Newport RUFC on the advice of the recently captured Ralph Morgan. Frank was a regular for Wales over six seasons, during which time he won an impressive 14 caps. He went on the 1950 Great Britain Ashes Tour as first choice hooker, but in the event Wigan's Joe Egan prevented him from winning a full test cap. Frank did play for Great Britain against a combined Australasian team at Leeds in May 1951, but the game wasn't accorded Test status. In 1956, Frank was allowed to join Keighley on a free transfer, but part of the deal was that he could return with his new club later in the season to claim a Testimonial. Frank subsequently received some £282 from his Benefit, whereupon he returned to Newport to become a grocer.

Born n/k (Swansea); Died n/k.

Debut : v Liverpool Stanley, 31 December 1949.
Last match : v Wigan, 5 March 1955.

Appearances 112, Tries 4, Goals 0.

Representative Honours:
Wales 6 caps (1951/52 to 1953/54); International Select 1 app (1953/54).

Owen had previously played for Swansea RUFC before switching codes to join the Welsh (RL) League side, Ystradgynlais. He was then signed by the Lions in contravention of a Rugby League directive asking clubs not to raid the fledgling Welsh competition to prevent it from collapsing. Owen scored a rare try on his debut and soon earned a reputation as an uncompromising prop-forward. He gained the first four of his six Welsh caps during season 1951/52, but was a loser on each occasion against England, Other Nationalities, New Zealand and France respectively.

Owen finally enjoyed success when the Welsh beat the French at Leeds in October 1952. In January 1954, he was also selected for an International Select XIII which faced France at Lyon to help the hosts celebrate the 20th Anniversary of French Rugby League. In 1955, Owen retired and returned to his home town of Swansea.

Joe Knowles

Born 16 November 1916 (Leigh); Died 20 July 1982 (aged 66).

Debut : v Leigh, 1 May 1937.
Last match : v Widnes, 1 March 1952.

Appearances 184, Tries 21, Goals 1.

Representative Honours:
Lancashire 1 cap (1 try) (1950/51).

Joe was a strong running second-row forward whose loyal Swinton career spanned 15 years either side of World War Two. He celebrated his 21st birthday in 1937 by being carried off the field injured during a match against Batley, but that same year he was also in the Swinton team which beat the touring Australians, 5-3. Eleven years later Joe played on a losing Swinton team against the Australians, but by this time his career was embarking on something of a renaissance. In October 1950, at the age of 34, he was awarded a Lancashire cap and scored a try although his team went down to Yorkshire at Fartown.

Upon his retirement in April 1952, he was granted a testimonial with the Lions playing a Lancashire Select team to mark the occasion. Joe then briefly held the position of President of the Swinton Supporters' Association.

Peter Norburn

Born 31 December 1930 (Wigan).

Debut : v Workington Town, 26 August 1950.
Last match : v St Helens, 30 March 1964.

Appearances 440, Tries 166, Goals 0.

Representative Honours:
England 1 cap (4 tries) 1953/54; Lancashire 4 caps (1 try) (1953/54 to 1961/62); Northern RL 1 app (1957/58); Tour trial 1 app (1 try) (1953/54).

Peter had already achieved county and international honours at amateur level whilst with the Wigan based Worsley Boys Club, when he signed for Swinton as a 19 year old in the summer of 1950. He started out as a winger, and between seasons 1950/51 and 1954/55 was the club's top try scorer in all but one campaign. From season 1955/56 onwards Peter was successively re-invented by coach Cliff Evans as a rampaging second-rower, to the extent that in 1957/58 he again topped the club's try scoring charts. In November 1953, he made his England debut and produced a brilliant display to score four tries in a 30-22 victory over Other Nationalities at Wigan. Peter then scored another try in an official Tour Trial game at Station Road, so he must have been bitterly disappointed to be omitted from selection for the 1954 Ashes Tour. Earlier that same campaign he had won the first two of his four Lancashire caps. In 1956, Peter looked set to play for Great Britain against the touring Australians, but agonisingly he again missed out through injury having been selected for the Third Test. Peter did, however, play against the Australians three times for Swinton, in 1952, 1959 and 1963 – the latter ending in an epic 2-2 draw. He was a member of the Swinton side which won the Lancashire League in 1961, and was a regular at second-row during the Lions' epic back-to-back Championship successes of 1962/63 and 1963/64. Peter, however, was on the losing side in three Lancashire Cup Finals against St Helens between 1960 and

1962. Throughout his Swinton career he had personal disputes with the Board, but despite this he remained loyal to the club for 14 seasons. By the time he departed for a sojourn with Salford in 1964, only eight players in the history of the club had achieved more appearances for the Lions. Peter's striking looks also earned him non-speaking parts in television programmes such as Coronation Street and Z Cars, which no doubt supplemented his day job as a window cleaner. Today he still lives in Swinton with his wife, Marjorie, who he married in 1953.

Albert Cartwright

Born 1932 (Warrington); Died December 2006 (aged 74).

Debut : v Widnes, 27 December 1954.
Last match : v Wigan, 9 March 1966.

Appearances 213, Tries 19, Goals 0.

Albert hailed from the Warrington area and came to the Lions from the amateur side, Rylands Recreation. He was a supremely talented scrum-half who for many years formed a marvellous partnership with George Parkinson. Albert was a master tactician around the scrum and initiated many of the dazzling moves devised by coach Cliff Evans as the Lions emerged as a major force. He was eventually ousted from a regular spot in the team by the up and coming Graham Williams in the run in to the 1963 Championship, but Albert remained an important squad member during Swinton's follow-up title of 1964. He also played in the 1961 and 1962 Lancashire Cup Finals, both of which were lost to St Helens. Albert didn't win any representative honours, this being the result of enormous competition in his particular position.

Like his half-back partner, George Parkinson, the modest but cheeky Albert was tremendously popular amongst the Station Road faithful and he was given a well-earned testimonial in 1966. By trade he was a motor mechanic.

Born 31 August 1926 (Maesteg); Died March 1984 (aged 57).

Debut : v Dewsbury, 17 September 1949.
Last match : v Widnes, 27 April 1960.

Appearances 218, Tries 15, Goals 0.

Representative Honours:
Wales 1 unofficial app (1954/55).

Rees was a Welshman who was signed in the summer of 1949 from Devonport Services RUFC, where he had played since being demobilised from the Royal Navy. He had previously played for Maesteg and only missed out on a full Welsh RU cap due to appendicitis. He was a tactically proficient scrum-half who formed fine partnerships with first Cyril Moran and then George Parkinson. Rees played for the Lions in their loss to the 1952 touring Australians, and he also played for Wales against France at Nantes in May 1955. Sadly, this match was not awarded full international status owing to the French fielding what was described as a "B" Team. With Albert Cartwright fast emerging, the Lions felt able to let Rees go to Wigan at the start of the 1956/57 season. He then went on to win the coveted Lance Todd Trophy for Wigan after their victory over Workington Town in the 1958 Challenge Cup Final. Rees returned to Swinton in autumn 1959, ironically to cover for Cartwright who had suffered a badly broken arm, before retiring at the end of that season. In the early 1970s he would return yet again as "A" team coach, and following the sacking of Dave Mortimer in November 1972 he was appointed first team coach. However, he too was eventually dismissed following a disappointing 18 months in charge.

Gordon Haynes

Born 21 December 1928 (Warrington); Died 2015 (aged 86).

Debut : v Belle Vue Rangers, 13 April 1953.
Last match : v Liverpool City, 11 April 1959.

Appearances 128, Tries 19, Goals 0.

Representative Honours:
Great Britain 1 unofficial app (1955/56); Northern RL 1 app (1955/56).

Gordon was a cultured loose-forward who came to Swinton towards the end of the 1952/53 season from the Warrington amateur club, Orford Tannery. He was initially a key component of Cliff Evans' emerging team, but had departed for Oldham before the Lions hit the highlights. Gordon was selected for a RLXIII which beat New Zealand 24-11 at Odsal in December 1955, and he became the first Swinton player in almost 19 years to play for Great Britain when he was selected against France on the same ground in April 1956. However, this was just before France was accorded full Test status, and therefore a Test cap was not awarded.

Born 29 May 1932 (Warrington); Died 30 September 2016 (aged 84).

Debut : v Barrow, 29 September 1956.
Last match : v Workington Town, 24 August 1964.

Appearances 239, Tries 12, Goals 0.

Representative Honours:
Lancashire 4 caps (1 try) (1960/61 to 1961/62).

Alfred "Trevor" Roberts was a fine tough-tackling hooker and a Lions' stalwart from the late 1950s to the early 1960s. He was the successor to Frank Osmond, and spent eight years with the Lions before having to retire following a severe shoulder injury. By this time his regular place in the team had come under threat from Derek Clarke. Trevor was a wire-drawer by trade and a native of Warrington, who came to the Lions from the amateur club, Rylands Recreation. In May 1961, he earned the first of his four county caps and scored a try as Lancashire defeated Cumberland 32-18 at The Willows. Four months later he also played for his county in a 15-13 victory over the touring New Zealanders in his home town, Warrington.

Trevor was the subject of an infamous situation in January 1961 when he arrived late for a game at Featherstone Rovers owing to fog. The short-handed Lions played with 12 men in the first half and then Trevor joined them for the second half! He was a key component of the Lions' 1963 Championship success, but was understudy to Clarke by the time this feat was repeated in 1964. Trevor also played in all three Lancashire Cup Final defeats to St Helens in 1960, 1961 and 1962.

George Parkinson

Born 2 January 1935 (Wigan).

Debut : v Bramley, 26 December 1952.
Last match : v Oldham, 22 March 1966.

Appearances 457, Tries 114, Goals 3.

Representative Honours:
Lancashire 4 caps (2 tries) (1958/59 to 1964/65); English Services 1 app (1955/56); Tour Trial 1 app (1957/58).

The Lions snatched George from under the noses of his local club, Wigan, in 1952. He was signed from the Whelley Boys club and made his full Swinton debut at the Barley Mow, Bramley, on Boxing Day of that same year. George became regarded as the toughest stand-off of his era, but this reputation as a hard man undermines the skill and speed which he also possessed in abundance. He was a critical cog in Cliff Evans' great side which went on to win back to back Championships in 1963 and 1964. George also won the 1961 Lancashire League with the Lions, but four times he lost out to St Helens in Lancashire Cup Finals (1960, 1961, 1962 and 1964). George also missed out narrowly on the 1958 Ashes Tour of Australasia despite playing well in a trial game at Station Road. In terms of representative honours his four Lancashire caps also do not do justice to his talents, but the likes of Alex Murphy and Lewis Jones often blocked his path. He did, however, win four Lancashire caps, and indeed he scored a try on his county debut against Yorkshire at Hull City AFC, with his last Lancashire appearance coming in the same city six years later. Only five players have made more appearances for the Lions, and just seven have scored more tries. George's longevity and cheeky never-say-die spirit over 14 years being other reasons why he was regarded as a cult hero by many Lions' fans. But with injuries starting to get the better of him, he finished his career in a low-key manner at Rochdale Hornets. In later life George ran a pub in his home town, and he still lives in Wigan with his wife to this day.

Born 2 October 1937 (Atherton).

Debut : v Blackpool Borough, 10 March 1956.
Last match : v Oldham, 23 April 1963.

Appearances 201, Tries 33, Goal 19.

Representative Honours:
Lancashire 1 cap (1959/60).

Ken, a grocer, came to the Lions via Tyldesley RUFC and Leigh junior rugby league in late 1955. He was regarded as a highly promising prop or second-row forward. Ken was also usually a reliable stand-in goal-kicker, although it was his simple late miss that caused the Lions to lose 25-24 in November 1959 to the touring Australians. A couple of weeks earlier Ken had gained a county cap for Lancashire in a loss to Yorkshire at Leigh. He was a regular scorer of tries for a prop-forward, with season 1959/60 representing his best haul of 12. Ken won the Lancashire League with the Lions in 1960/61, and was a regular in the side which won

the 1962/63 Championship. He also appeared in three losing Lancashire Cup finals for Swinton between 1960 and 1962. Ken was a regular first teamer for seven seasons, but lost his place to Harold Bate in the run-in to the Lions' 1963 Championship success. He subsequently went to Halifax for a fee of £5,500, where he would gain domestic and international honours, including a place on the 1966 Ashes Tour. Ken's son, Ken junior, also later played for the Lions.

Cliff Evans

Born 14 July 1913 (Resolven); Died July 1982 (aged 69 in Wiltshire).

Debut as coach: v Salford (Red Rose Cup), 7 August 1954; v Batley, 14 August 1954 (League).
Last match : v Warrington, 16 December 1967.

Matches 572, Won 335, Drawn 27, Lost 210.

Clifford Handel Evans earns his place in this list as the Lions' most celebrated post-war coach. Although he had finished his playing career at Leeds, it was as a member of the legendary Lance Todd's successful Salford side of the 1930s that Evans would have learnt much about coaching. During the war he held a position as a PT and parachute instructor, and earned a commission in January 1944. In 1943, Cliff actually played as a guest for Swinton, in a game played under Rugby Union rules against a Blackpool RAF unit in aid of the Red Cross Prisoner of War Fund. After the war he took up employment in California, USA, and it was from there that he successfully applied for the vacant Swinton coaching post in May 1954. Cliff also landed a job as a PE teacher at St Ambrose Barlow school in Swinton. His coaching techniques were said to be years ahead of his time, and he would work methodically on the training ground to perfect attacking moves that would perplex the opposition. Even so it took a few years of patient team building before Cliff's side began to emerge as a real force. After finishing sixth in 1959, he guided the Lions to their first major post-war silverware when in 1961 they won the Lancashire League. Then in 1962/63 Evans instilled such belief and team spirit that they negotiated the final 18 games of the season undefeated to come from nowhere to lift the Rugby League Championship. In 1963/64 the title was retained, giving the Lions six in total. However, Cliff had less luck in knockout football with Swinton, with Wembley somehow eluding him as well as presiding over six cup finals which were all lost. After almost 13 years in the hot seat at Station Road Cliff sought new challenges, and he went on to enjoy great success with both St Helens and Salford.

Ron Morgan

Born 21 January 1936 (Bradford).

Debut : v Liverpool City, 7 October 1961.
Last match : v Halifax, 27 May 1964.

Appearances 90, Tries 18, Goals 0.

Representative Honours:
Great Britain 2 caps (1962/63 to 1963/64), Wales 1 unofficial app (1962/63); Yorkshire 1 cap (1 try) (1963/64).

Yorkshire born Ron was a major capture from Ebbw Vale RUFC in the close season of 1961. He would remain at the Lions for only three seasons before departing for Leeds for £4,500, but during that time he made an indelible mark on the club's history. He certainly got off to a fine start, scoring a hat-trick on his debut against Liverpool City. Ron was a tough prop or second-row forward who was often in the thick of the battle during the Lions' successive Championship campaigns of 1962/63 and 1963/64. He played in the 1962 Lancashire Cup Final defeat to St Helens, a game in which he was sent-off for fighting. Ron gained two caps for Great Britain, with his Test debut coming in a 42-4 victory over France in April 1963 at Wigan.

His second cap came in the infamous 50-12 reverse to Australia at Station Road six months later. Ron also made one appearance for Wales against France at Toulouse, and another for Yorkshire when he scored a try in a heavy loss to Lancashire at St Helen's.

John Speed

Born 1939 (Wigan); Died 1991 (aged 52).

Debut : v Wakefield Trinity, 11 April 1960.
Last match : v St Helens, 2 January 1967.

Appearances 224, Tries 79, Goals 0.

John, a cousin of Albert Blan, was an appropriately named fast and strong winger who was otherwise employed as a colliery electrician. He came to the Lions from Wigan junior outfit Triangle Valve partway through the 1959/60 season at the age of 20. John initially formed a three-quarter partnership with Peter Smethurst, but it was his devastating combination with Bob Fleet in the Lions' Championship teams of 1962/63 and 1963/64 for which he is better remembered. John played in all four of the losing Lancashire Cup Finals against St Helens in the early 1960s, but he did help win the 1960/61 Lancashire League for the Lions. Four times he contributed 16 tries or more in a season, and in 1961/62 he was the club's top scorer with 19.

In an era of intense competition for the wing positions, representative honours eluded him, but he will always be remembered for his role in the Lions' successes of the early 1960s. In 1967, and after scoring 79 tries in seven years, John was transferred to Blackpool Borough.

Albert Blan

Born 13 January 1930 (Wigan); Died 27 September 2015 (aged 85).

Debut : v Liverpool Stanley, 9 April 1949.
Last match : v Halifax, 27 May 1964.

Appearances 447, Tries 75, Goals 744.

Representative Honours: England 1 cap 1952/53; Lancashire 5 caps (3 tries, 12 goals) (1952/53 to 1961/62).

Window cleaner Albert joined Swinton at the age of 18 in July 1948 from the Wigan amateur club, Whelley Juniors. He made a spectacular debut against Liverpool Stanley a few months later by kicking nine goals, which is still a club record for a debutant. By season 1951/52 he had ousted Ralph Morgan at full-back, and in the same season he was appointed captain by coach Griff Jenkins. In October 1952, Albert captained the Lions and kicked a goal in a loss to the touring Australians. During the same season, he made his debut for Lancashire and kicked another goal in a defeat at The Boulevard against Yorkshire. Between that appearance and season 1961/62 he won a total of five Lancashire caps, scoring three tries and 12 goals. In April 1953, Albert was selected for England and played in a 15-13 win against France in Paris, but although he was also named as Great Britain reserve for that season's Ashes series a Test cap would unjustly elude him. With an emerging reputation of master tactician and excellent tactical kicker, new coach Cliff Evans saw Albert as key to his plans, and although not the quickest he certainly had a very astute, quick and mischievous rugby brain. Albert was awarded a testimonial in season 1958/59, but his best years were yet to come. By now he had switched first to stand-off, then by season 1959/60 to loose-forward. Albert scored a hat-trick of tries in a narrow loss to the 1959 touring Australians, and captained the Lions in their 2-2 draw against the 1963 Kangaroos. By then Albert had led the Lions to their first post-war silverware, the 1960/61 Lancashire League. However, despite kicking goals in all three finals, Albert had the misfortune of skippering the Lions to all three of their Lancashire Cup Final defeats to St Helens between 1960 and 1962. But ultimately in the twilight of his career Albert would not be denied, and in 1962/63 he led the Lions on a remarkable 18 match unbeaten run which saw Swinton end the season as Champions. Remarkably the Lions retained the trophy a year later, and in doing so Albert

elevated himself to equal the double-Championships that had been won by former captains Hector Halsall and Bryn Evans. He then retired from playing to become assistant to Cliff Evans, before becoming first team coach in his own right in 1968. In November 1969, Albert succeeded as a coach where he had missed out as a player, by lifting the Lancashire Cup after Swinton defeated Leigh 11-2 in the final at Wigan. The legendary Albert Blan currently stands seventh in terms of club appearances, and third in terms of career goals.

Johnny Stopford

Born 23 August 1936 (Wigan); Died 21 August 1998 (aged 61).

Debut : v Batley, 11 October 1958.
Last match : v St Helens, 7 April 1969.

Appearances 298, Tries 195, Goals 1.

Representative Honours:
Great Britain 12 caps (7 tries) (1960/61 to 1965/66); Great Britain Tourist 15 apps (16 tries, 1 goal) (1966); Lancashire 5 caps (1 try) (1963/64 to 1965/66).

Wigan born John came to the Lions from Highfield Juniors, and soon developed into a speedy winger with a devastating swerve and sidestep. Forming a brilliant partnership with centre Alan Buckley, he was the club's top try scorer on five occasions between seasons 1959/60 and 1964/65. His haul of 42 tries in the Lions' Championship winning season of 1963/64 not only created a club record under Rugby League rules, but also made him the top try scorer in the whole league. John's career return of 195 tries also makes him the club's all-time joint top scorer alongside Frank Evans (under RL rules). Amongst his try scoring feats were five against Bramley in December 1962 (which at the time equalled the club tries in a match record), plus two hat-tricks in direct opposition to the St Helens great, Tom Van Vollenhoven. John's absence through injury for all four of the Lions' Lancashire Cup Final defeats to St Helens between 1960 and 1964, was arguably a critical factor in those losses. John became the first Swinton player to win a post-war Great Britain cap when he played against France and scored a try in January 1961. He went on to win 12 Test caps in total, and was chosen for the 1966 Ashes Tour of Australasia. His try against Australia in GB's infamous 50-12 defeat in November 1963, is the only time that a Swinton player has scored a try for Great Britain in a Test match played on the Swinton ground. John showed great courage to come back from two serious shoulder operations, but following a testimonial in 1969 he was allowed to join Blackpool Borough. He returned to the Lions as coach in season 1976/77, but sadly his appointment was short-lived as Swinton continued with an alarming fall in fortunes.

Barry Simpson

Born 4 October 1942 (Oldham); Died 24 December 2011 (aged 69).

Debut : v Huddersfield, 6 October 1962.
Last match : v Oldham, 8 August 1971.

Appearances 189, Tries 7, Goals 0.

Representative Honours:
Lancashire 3 caps (1 try) (1964/65 to 1965/66).

Although born in Oldham, Barry was brought up locally and came to the Lions via the Swinton based amateur club, Folly Lane. His father was George Simpson, landlord of the Red Lion and an ex-Broughton Rangers player. Barry edged into the first team squad during the successive Championship campaigns of 1962/63 and 1963/64, but it wasn't until the 1964/65 season that he established himself as a regular. He played in the 1964 Lancashire Cup Final loss to St Helens, but sadly missed the 1969 victory over Leigh in the same competition through injury.

Barry was a hard-working grafter who was effective at both prop-forward and second-row forward. He played three times for Lancashire but all were on losing occasions, including against New Zealand at St Helen's in October 1965 when he scored a try. Barry also played for the Lions against the Kiwis that same month, this time in a 14-7 victory. In addition, he was an unused substitute for Great Britain Under 24s against France in November 1966. After almost nine years of excellent service Barry was transferred to Leigh in 1971.

Born 1 August 1944 (Swinton).

Debut : v Leigh, 21 March 1964.
Last match : v Batley, 6 March 1977.

Appearances 203, Tries 32, Goals 0.

Representative Honours: Great Britain 12 caps (1 try) (1965/66 to 1967/68); Great Britain Tourist 17 apps (4 tries) (1966); England 1 cap (1969/70); Lancashire 6 caps (3 tries) (1965/66 to 1969/70); Great Britain U24s 1 app (1965/66); 1966 Tourists XIII 1 app (1 try) (1966/67).

As an ex-pupil of Moorside Secondary School and player at Folly Lane, Dave was very much a local product. His young talent was such that he was trusted to fill the gap left by Albert Blan at loose-forward, and in his first full season he was just 80 minutes from Wembley when the Lions lost to Wigan in the 1965 Challenge Cup semi-final. Dave was terrifically fast in the loose, and his prompting of the Swinton attack from his pivot position soon brought him to the attention of the representative selectors. In October 1965, he was chosen for Lancashire to play the touring New Zealanders, then found himself in the full Great Britain team for the Third Test which was drawn 9-9 against the Kiwis a month later. From thereon he became a regular in the Great Britain line-up and won 12 consecutive caps. This sequence included all five Tests on the Ashes Tour of 1966, when he was one of four Swinton men to make the trip. He had an outstanding match for the Lions in the 1969 Lancashire Cup Final victory over Leigh, and he also played for his club against the 1965 Kiwis and 1967 Kangaroos. In January 1970, Dave was controversially sold to Wigan for a club record £10,000, where he earned a place on the 1970 Ashes Tour and played in a Challenge Cup Final. He returned to the Lions in February 1976 in an unsuccessful effort to stem the Lions' slide towards the second division, and retired towards the end of season 1976/77.

Graham Williams

Born 28 July 1944 (Swinton); Died 1 July 1994 (aged 49 at Sydney).

Debut : v Leigh, 1 September 1962.
Last match : v Whitehaven, 29 November 1968.

Appearances 179, Tries 62, Goals 9.

Representative Honours: Lancashire 6 caps (1 try) (1963/64 to 1968/69); Rest of League 1 app (1 try) (1966/67).

Graham was Swinton born and bred and came through the ranks at Folly Lane. He took over the scrum-half position from Albert Cartwright and played a crucial role in the Lions' unbeaten 18 match run to the 1963 Championship. Although only 5 foot 6 tall, he was tremendously fast and nippy, and his dynamic runs from behind the scrum added a whole new dimension to the Lions' attack. Graham contributed ten tries during the 1963/64 season as Swinton retained the Championship in style, whilst in 1966/67 he was the club's top try scorer with 19. Graham was arguably the best scrum-half never to have received an international cap, although he did pick up six Lancashire caps. His county debut came at the age of 19 when he scored a try in Lancashire's 13-11 win over Australia at Wigan in September 1963. A few weeks later he played in the Lions' 2-2 draw with Australia, but then in 1968 he announced his intention to emigrate down-under. Graham was signed by North Sydney, but tragedy struck soon

afterwards when his wife drowned in a parachuting accident. He later played for Manly and coached at the Queensland club, Burleigh.

In a further tragic twist, Graham was killed in a motorcycle accident at Sydney shortly before his 50th birthday.

Billy Davies

Born 14 March 1948 (Leigh).

Debut : Rochdale Hornets, 3 October 1964.
Last match : v Hull, 1 January 1972.

Appearances 204, Tries 69, Goals 0.

Representative Honours: Great Britain 1 cap (1968/69); England 1 cap (1968/69); Lancashire 2 caps (1969/70 to 1970/71).

"Daz" Davies was so named due to a curious fashion at school to call each other after soap powders. At the age of just 16 he became the Lions' youngest ever debutant when he took to the field against Rochdale Hornets in October 1964. Although Billy became recognised as a skilful, fast and elusive stand-off, he could also play at centre and occasionally on the wing. He might also have become the youngest player ever to grace Wembley, but sadly Billy was on the losing side when the Lions met Wigan in the Challenge Cup semi-final of April 1965. In October 1965, Billy scored a try in the Lions' 14-7 win over New Zealand, and six years later he scored another try as the touring Kiwis were beaten again at Station Road. In December 1966, he was on the losing side for Swinton against Castleford in the BBC2 Floodlit Trophy Final. However, Billy did win domestic honours with the Lions, as in November 1969 he and fellow half-back Peter Kenny were crucial to Swinton's 11-2 Lancashire Cup Final success against Leigh. Billy's ability to glide effortlessly through opposition defences earned him county and international honours, and in November 1968 he won both England and Great Britain caps. Firstly, he played for England in a shock defeat to Wales at Salford, then three weeks later he featured in a 34-10 victory for Great Britain against France at St Helen's. Hence he became the last Swinton player ever to have won a Great Britain cap. Early in 1972, Billy was the subject of a shock joint £8,000 transfer to Wigan along with forward Terry Cramant. Amazingly he was still only 23, but injuries would sadly curtail his career.

Bob Fleet

1969 150 GREATEST

Born 16 February 1943 (Torquay).

Debut : v Rochdale Hornets, 28 January 1961.
Last match : v Doncaster, 26 September 1976.

Appearances 376, Tries 90, Goals 0.

Bob had already played the union code at county level for Devon, when in 1960 he signed for the Lions at just 17 years of age from Torquay RUFC. Bob used his height and long-striding style to help him adapt quickly to Rugby League, primarily playing at centre inside of John Speed. He was a stylish player and an integral member of the great Swinton back-line which helped carry off the 1962/63 and 1963/64 Championships. He also played in three Lancashire Cup Finals for the Lions. These were the 1961 and 1964 lost matches against St Helens, but also the 1969 victory over Leigh when he was the proud captain. Bob also played three times for Swinton against touring sides from down under, winning against the 1965 New Zealanders, drawing against the 1963 Australians, and losing narrowly to the Australians in 1967. Prior to the 1970/71 season Bob was transferred to Warrington, but he returned as a player and assistant coach to Austin Rhodes in March 1974.

He helped guide the Lions to promotion, then took over as first team coach in November 1975. But sadly the newly promoted Lions were in the midst of a nightmare campaign which ended in immediate relegation. On 5 September 1976, Bob picked himself for a trip to Blackpool Borough, but by the end of October he'd resigned as coach. He stayed on at the club and became a Director and county representative, thereby uniquely filling a notable set of positions in service of the club. Indeed "supporter" can be added to that list, because gentleman Bob remains an avid match-going fan of the Lions to this day.

SWINTON LIONS 1866

Derek Clarke

Born 20 April 1941 (Widnes); Died 9 February 2015 (aged 73).

Debut : v Huddersfield, 20 January 1962.
Last match : v St Helens, 19 September 1970.

Appearances 228, Tries 20, Goals 0.

Derek was a process worker and a native of Widnes. He came to Swinton from the Widnes St Marie's club at the age of 20 in August 1961. Derek was a tenacious tackler and hugely combative hooker, always recognisable by his trademark headband. During the Lions' 18 match unbeaten march to the 1963 Championship, Derek shared hooking duties with Trevor Roberts, but he had become first choice by the time the title was retained in 1963/64. Derek played in the Lions' epic 2-2 draw with Australia in November 1963, whilst he also appeared on the losing side in three major finals for Swinton. These were the 1963/64 Western Division Championship Final against St Helens, the 1964 Lancashire Cup Final also against St Helens, and the

1966/67 BBC Floodlit Trophy Final against Castleford. However, Derek got his hands on more silverware when he starred in the Lions' 1969 Lancashire Cup Final victory over Leigh at Wigan.

Derek's last appearance came in September 1970, as by the end of that month he was controversially transferred to Salford for £7,000. He subsequently played for Leigh, but retired at the end of the 1973/74 season due to a neck injury.

Peter Kenny

Born 14 January 1948 (Swinton).

Debut : v Workington Town, 23 August 1967.
Last match : v Leigh, 5 November 1972.

Appearances 164, Tries 54, Goals 39.

Representative Honours:
Lancashire 1 cap (1 try) (1971/72).

Former Ambrose Barlow pupil Peter is the son of the former Swinton and England winger, Jack Kenny. He was a fast and elusive scrum-half with a knack for following up breaks made by his forwards. Peter was something of a drop-goal expert as well, and his finest hour came in the 1969 Lancashire Cup Final when the Lions defeated Leigh 11-2 at Wigan. Not only did Peter outplay his opposite number Alex Murphy that day, but he also contributed eight points from four successful drop-goal attempts. In October 1971, Peter contributed a try as Swinton defeated New Zealand 26-15, this coming just nine days after he had made his county debut for Lancashire and scored a try in a loss to Yorkshire at Leigh.

Peter would finish the 1971/72 season as the club's top try scorer alongside Don Preston with 18. One of his last games for the Lions was the 1972 Lancashire Cup Final defeat to Salford, when again he scored a drop-goal. Peter now resides in the United States.

Born 4 July 1939 (Whitehaven).

Debut : v Workington Town, 7 September 1968.
Last match : v Salford, 21 October 1972 (Lancashire Cup Final).

Appearances 94, Tries 5, Goals 59.

Representative Honours:
Cumberland 2 caps (1 try, 4 goals) (1968/69).

Swinton signed the former Great Britain captain Bill Holliday for a then club record fee of £6,000 from Hull KR in 1968. Although a fraction past his best, Bill was still a formidable prop or second-row forward, and he played a leading role in the Lions' 1969 Lancashire Cup Final victory over Leigh. Bill's final game for Lions was also a Lancashire Cup Final, but this time it was lost against Salford in 1972. Whilst with the Lions, Bill added two Cumbrian caps to his collection during season 1968/69. Firstly he kicked two goals in a loss to Yorkshire in his home town of Whitehaven, then he kicked two more goals and scored a try in another defeat, this time to Lancashire at St Helen's.

Following a dispute he left for Rochdale Hornets, but he later returned as joint-coach and led the Lions to a promotion and Second Division Premiership double in season 1986/87 alongside Mike Peers. In his team at Old Trafford that day were his sons, Les and Mike. Bill is still a resident of Swinton today.

Born 15 October 1936 (Wigan).

Debut ; v Belle Vue Rangers, 20 November 1954.
Last match : v Oldham, 21 April 1973.

Appearances 601, Tries 55, Goals 970.

Representative Honours: Great Britain 14 caps (21 goals) (1962/63 to 1965/66); Great Britain Tourist 12 apps (53 goals) (1966); England 1 cap (1962/63); Lancashire 12 caps (27 goals) (1958/59 to 1966/67); Northern RL 1 app (1958/59); English Services 1 app (1955/56).

Ken is the son of the former Rochdale Hornets player and Great Britain tourist, Walter Gowers. He signed as a scrum-half from the Rochdale amateurs Kirkholt Juniors in 1954, but would eventually make his name as a brilliant all-round full-back. Ken was like a rock in defence, but he could also dodge and skip past opponents when in attack. He also possessed brilliant hands, either in terms of receiving or giving a pass, or in catching an awkward high ball. Ken was also an excellent goal-kicker, and his 970 club goals is a record unlikely ever to be beaten. The 12 goals that he scored in a game against Liverpool City in 1959 was also a club record which has only recently been surpassed. Five times Ken played and scored for Swinton against touring Australian or New Zealand teams, but more importantly he was critical to the Lions' successes of the 1960s. Ken won four major honours with Swinton - the 1963 and 1964 Championships, the 1961 Lancashire League, and the 1969 Lancashire Cup. In addition, he received eight runners-up medals. Ken is also the most decorated Swinton player of the post-war era in terms of representative honours. He won the first

of his 14 Great Britain caps in a match against France at Perpignan in December 1962, this coming just a few months after he had been unjustly left out of the 1962 Ashes Tour. He did tour in 1966, but this came as scant consolation despite being chosen as vice-captain. Ken's first class Swinton career eventually spanned a record 19 seasons, and by the time he retired in 1973 he had chalked up a club record 601 appearances (leaving even Jim Valentine trailing by more than a hundred). He was granted a testimonial match against Salford which was kicked-off by Bobby Charlton - recognition from one great sportsman towards another. After retirement Ken concentrated on his business as a builder and property repairer.

Alan Buckley

Born 23 October 1941 (Ardwick); Died 12 March 2008 (aged 66 at Walkden).

Debut : v Barrow, 9 January 1960.
Last match : v Barrow, 24 March 1974.

Appearances 466, Tries 192, Goals 3.

Representative Honours: Great Britain 7 caps (1 try) (1963/64 to 1965/66); Great Britain Tourist 13 apps (4 tries) (1966); England 1 cap (1968/69); Lancashire 10 caps (2 tries, 1 goal) (1962/63 to 1970/71); 1966 Tourists XIII 1 app (1966/67).

Alan was from Manchester and admitted to preferring soccer to rugby, but it was at the latter named sport that he excelled. He came to the Lions' attention playing for Broughton Park RUFC around his 18th birthday, and made his first team debut shortly afterwards. A draughtsman by trade, Alan quickly developed into a devastating centre with blistering pace as well as being hard as nails in the tackle. He formed a brilliant partnership with his winger John Stopford, for whom he set up numerous tries. Alan's own final tally of 192 tries was just three behind the (RL) club record of Stopford and Frank Evans, and indeed had he not missed the whole of the 1961/62 season with a bad shoulder injury then that record would surely have been smashed. He won the Lancashire League in his first full campaign of 1960/61, but lost out in the Lancashire Cup Final to St Helens in the same season. Alan also figured in the lost Lancashire Cup Finals of 1962 and 1964, but in 1969 he set up the game's only try for Mick Philbin when Swinton defeated Leigh to finally lift the trophy. Before that he had been central to the Lions' back-to-back title triumphs of 1963 and 1964. In 1963/64 he scored 25 tries, including a club record equalling five against Salford in a 47-0 victory. Alan also scored a try for the Lions to help defeat the Kiwi tourists of 1965, whilst he twice faced Australia in Swinton colours. Alan's first representative honours came in September 1962, when aged just 20 he was selected for Lancashire against Cumberland at Widnes. He won a further nine county caps over the next nine years, including one for a 13-11 victory over Australia in September 1963. This performance brought Alan into the Great Britain set-up, and he earned his first cap in the Third Test against the Aussies at Leeds a couple of months later. Alan was selected for the 1966 Ashes Tour and played in both Sydney Tests against the Kangaroos and the First Test against the Kiwis. He was awarded a testimonial in 1970, and in 1972 played in another Lancashire Cup Final, although this one was lost against Salford. Alan finally retired at the end of the 1973/74 season, after a soul-destroying campaign in which the club failed to achieve top flight football after the league had split into two divisions 12 months previously. Alan went on to run a sports shop on Swinton Precinct, and later went into the licensed trade. Many fans will remember him as the landlord of the Cricketer's Arms, which sits by the site of the Lions' old Chorley Road ground.

Born 26 January 1945 (St Helen's).

Debut : v Dewsbury, 9 January 1971.
Last match : v Widnes, 27 February 1977.

Appearances 195, Tries 2, Goals 4.

Representative Honours:
Wales 3 caps (1974/75 to 1975/76); Lancashire 6 caps
(1973/74 to 1975/76).

Dick was a brilliant ball winning hooker and hard worker in the loose, who came to the Lions from Barrow in late 1970 for £5,000. He made history in October 1971 by becoming the first player to kick a one-point drop-goal in Britain when Swinton defeated New Zealand, 26-15. Even when the Lions found themselves languishing in the second division Dick continued to excel, and eventually it came as no surprise when he was sold to Salford in March

1977. Dick was an extremely popular player amongst fans, and he was Swinton's most honoured player in terms of representative appearances during the 1970s. He was selected for Lancashire twice in September 1973, and went on to win six county caps whilst with Swinton.

Dick qualified for Wales through his father, and made his international debut against England at Salford in February 1975. He then became part of the 1975 Welsh World Cup squad, playing in narrow defeats to France at Toulouse and New Zealand at Auckland.

Bob Fleay

Born 15 January 1949 (Neath).

Debut : v Hunslet, 23 October 1970.
Last match : v Bramley, 10 October 1976.

Appearances 211, Tries 88, Goals 0.

Representative Honours:
Other Nationalities (county level) 1 cap (1974/75).

Flame-haired Bob Fleay was a Welsh international trialist winger from Aberavon RUFC. He was signed after notching two tries as AN Other in a victory over Hunslet in October 1970. Bob went on to play in the Lions' victory over the 1971 New Zealanders, and scored Swinton's only try during their 1972 Lancashire Cup Final defeat to Salford. Bob was the club's leading try scorer in both the 1972/73 and 1973/74 seasons, grabbing 46 in the process. In September 1974, he gained his only representative honour, which came by way of an appearance for Other Nationalities (alongside club mate Brian Butler) against Yorkshire in the county championship. Bob assisted Swinton to promotion in 1975, but left the club early in the 1976/77 season following an apparent disagreement with his coach, Bob Fleet. At the same time Bob relinquished his position as manager of the recently constructed Swinton Sports Centre. Having played in every single game between 25 August 1972 and 22 August 1976 to create an all-time club record of 149 consecutive appearances, this was a sad end to his Swinton career. Bob, however, had remained a firm crowd favourite throughout a difficult period for the club. He re-emerged briefly with the newly formed Cardiff City RLFC in 1981.

Born 21 May 1941 (St Helen's).

Debut : v Whitehaven, 15 March 1969.
Last match : v St Helens, 28 August 1977.

Appearances 180, Tries 18, Goals 0.

Kevin was from St Helen's and came to the Lions early in 1969 from the top amateur club, Pilkington Recreation. He was a hard-working and hard tackling second-row forward who always gave his all, and consequently became a firm favourite on the Station Road terraces. Kevin helped the Lions to promotion to the First Division in 1974/75, and played with great endeavour in the difficult season which followed.

In all Kevin gave eight years of honest service to the Lions, but sadly in August 1977 he was forced into retirement after sustaining a badly broken arm. He then went into coaching with his old club, Pilkington Recs.

Les Bolton

Born 14 February 1949 (Wigan).

Debut : Featherstone Rovers, 9 April 1972.
Last match : v Keighley, 23 October 1983.

Appearances 175, Tries 25, Goals 1.

Les started his career at Swinton as a stand-off, but was also versatile enough to slot in at centre or scrum-half. He started to win a regular place in the team towards the end of the 1974/75 promotion season, and was a popular player throughout the Lions' turbulent years of the mid to late 1970s with his "no-nonsense" style. He was named Player of the Year in season 1977/78, but was transferred to Wigan partway through the following campaign. He returned to the Lions in the summer of 1981, this time re-invented as a mobile loose-forward. However, Les had lost none of the fire in his belly and he was no stranger to early baths, all of which seemed to simply endear him even more to the Swinton faithful. Les even managed to break his own arm whilst stiff-arming a Huyton player in September 1982. The following season, nearly 12 years since his original Swinton debut, he made way for the emerging talent of Les Holliday.

Les later went back to the amateur game and was successful in coaching the Wigan St Cuthbert's team.

Kevin O'Loughlin

Born 25 May 1947 (Wigan); Died 7 November 2016 (aged 69).

Debut : v St Helens, 28 August 1977.
Last match : v Cardiff City, 4 December 1983.

Appearances 168, Tries 29, Goals 3.

Kevin was the brother of Keiron and the uncle of Sean, both of whom found fame with Wigan in different eras. He had already earned Great Britain Under 24 and Lancashire representative honours whilst at Wigan, when the Lions secured his signature in August 1977. Tough-tackling Kevin came as a hard-working loose forward, but thanks to his pedigree he also had a touch of class about him. Kevin could also play full-back, centre or wing, and Swinton fans greatly appreciated his contribution during the tough times of the late 1970s.

Kevin's most celebrated moment in a Swinton shirt came when he touched down in the last minute at The Willows in November 1981, which sealed a legendary 6-0 victory over Salford in the quarter-finals of the John Player Trophy. After six years of service, he fell out of favour in the autumn of 1983, when new coach Jim Crellin began to mould his own young team.

Born 3 December 1956.

Debut : v York, 23 January 1977.
Last match : v Blackpool Borough, 21 August 1983.

Appearances 108, Tries 13, Goals 228.

John was a former Liverpool FC trialist who came to Lions from the amateur game in Wigan, primarily as a full-back. However, John could also play centre and would often do so until the sale of Graeme Johns to Salford together with the retirement of David Watkins, enabled him to stake a regular claim at number one. He was a reliable full-back at the time of the Lions' revival under Frank Myler and Peter Smethurst, and in season 1980/81 he gained the distinction of playing and scoring in every match. This feat covered 31 games (or 41 including the end of the previous season and the start of the next). It was the first time this feat had ever been achieved by a Swinton player, and indeed across the whole game only a handful of players have managed it. Eventually John lost his place to the more youthful Paul Mellor, and was transferred to Halifax.

Born 1955 (Cardiff).

Debut : v Huddersfield, 2 March 1980.
Last match : v Halifax, 1 January 1988.

Appearances 180, **Tries** 62, **Goals** 49 (including a club record 39 drop-goals).

Representative Honours: Wales 4 caps (1 try, 3 goals) (1980/81 to 1984/85).

Danny was an enigma. A mixture of extraordinary natural talent coupled with a recurring ability to live on the edge and court controversy. However, it was arguably thanks to his unpredictable personality that he would remain with the Lions during his best years, when perhaps under other circumstances he would have joined a top first division club. Danny, a native of Cardiff's notorious Tiger Bay area, came to the Lions in early 1980 as an "AN Other" from Bute Town RUFC, having previously played for both Newport and Cardiff. He had also earlier dipped his toe in the Rugby League water as a trialist with both Widnes and Barrow. Danny reputedly had the best pair of hands in South Wales and few at Station Road would ultimately dispute it. He soon broke into the Wales national team, and earned the first of four caps against France at Narbonne in January 1981. His last cap came against the English in 1984 at Ebbw Vale, when he scored a try and won the man-of-the-match award despite playing with a heavily strapped thigh in a losing team. Danny was a confident and extravagantly talented stand-off or occasional centre who could, and did, win matches on his own with dazzling pace, a mesmerising sidestep, or some amazing sleight of hand. The downside was that his team mates usually didn't know what he was going to do next, or whether in fact he would turned up on match day in the right mood to perform. Arguably his best seasons were 1983/84 when he was both the club's Player of the Year and top try scorer, and 1984/85 when he assisted Swinton to the Second Division Championship. Indeed the Lions' 1983 John Player Trophy run was arguably a microcosm of his career. In the first round against Hunslet, Danny equalled the sport's drop-goals in a match record with five in a 17-16 victory. In the second round at Keighley, he started a brawl which soon involved every player on the pitch apart from himself, and in the quarter-finals he terrorised high-flying Leeds with two tries and a drop-goal, only for the Lions to lose unluckily in the

last minute. Injuries during Swinton's first division campaign of 1985/86 were a blow to himself and his ultimately relegated team, and he would also miss the end of the Lions' successful 1986/87 promotion and Premiership winning season through injury. Danny's last game for Swinton was at Halifax on New Year's Day 1988, after which he left quietly for Springfield Borough in an exchange that brought Tommy Frodsham to Station Road. Danny, the father of Manchester United legend Ryan Giggs, is still held in affection and awe by those Swinton fans that were fortunate to see him at his best.

Paul Mellor

Born 31 July 1963 (Salford).

Debut : v Batley, 22 February 1981.
Last match : v Ryedale York, 6 January 1991.

Appearances 91, Tries 10, Goals 94.

Representative Honours:
Great Britain Colts 1 cap (1 try, 4 goals) (1981/82).

Paul was a 17 years old full-back who followed his older brother, Johnny, to Station Road in early 1981 from local amateurs Langworthy Juniors. With bags of natural talent and youthful energy, both he and his brother soon emerged as crowd favourites. Paul was a fine goal-kicker and landed 86 in season 1981/82. Nine of those came against Salford in a 45-3 thrashing at Station Road in May, and another capped the Lions' epic 6-0 success over Salford at The Willows six months earlier in a John Player Trophy quarter-final. Paul gained a Great Britain Colts cap against France at Limoux in 1982, when he scored a try and kicked four goals to win the man-of-the-match award. He remains the only Swinton player to have won honours at international Colts level. Sadly, however, injuries would ultimately ruin Paul's career. In 1983, he suffered a badly broken jaw, then on his comeback in April 1986 he broke a leg at Halifax. Again he tried to re-launch his career in 1990 as the Lions headed towards a successful promotion campaign, but a shattered cheek-bone brought matters to an end at the age of just 27, and just a few days short of the tenth anniversary of his debut.

Born 2 March 1961 (Leigh).

Debut : v Dewsbury, 14 March 1982.
Last match : v Barrow, 5 February 1989.

Appearances 148, Tries 75, Goals 3.

Martin was a quick and clever scrum-half who came to Lions in early 1982 from the junior club, Leigh East. As an amateur he had already won county and international honours, and it wasn't long before he established himself as the Lions' first choice number seven. He had an eye for a speedy burst through a gap and became a prolific scorer of tries, including four when in April 1984 Swinton defeated Keighley 66-1 to record their best win for 78 years. Martin was the club's top try scorer in season 1982/83, a feat he held jointly with Ken Jones in 1984/85 when Swinton lifted the Second Division championship. Indeed Martin scored a hat-trick against Rochdale Hornets on the night that the title was confirmed, and he then had the added bonus of being named Player of the Year.

His 1985/86 campaign was affected by injuries, but he did captain Swinton "A" (the Crusaders) to a remarkable win over Leeds in the Alliance Challenge Cup Final at Headingley. Martin won promotion with Swinton for a second time in 1986/87, and was a try scorer for the Lions when Hunslet were defeated 27-10 in the inaugural Second Division Premiership Final at Old Trafford that same season.

Steve Snape

Born 17 September 1963 (Urmston).

Debut : v Halifax, 5 February 1984.
Last match : v London Crusaders, 11 October 1992.

Appearances 216, Tries 49, Goals 3.

Steve was a Clifton lad who emerged through the amateur ranks of Folly Lane. He was the first signing made by coach Jim Crellin following his appointment in November 1983. Steve could play at centre or stand-off, and would often chip in with important tries. Added to a sound defence, he was a coach's dream player. Three times Steve helped the Lions to promotion (in 1984/85, 1986/87 and 1990/91), and although they were relegated in each subsequent season, Steve never looked out of place in the top division. He was a member of the Lions' team which won the 1987 Second Division Premiership Final at Old Trafford, but was on the losing side in the same event against Sheffield Eagles two years later. As a local lad he was upset by the loss of Station Road, and only made two appearances after the Bury FC relocation before calling time on his career.

Steve remains a keen supporter of the Lions, and in 2016 he generously donated his coveted medals to the club.

Born 8 December 1957 (Wigan).

Debut : v Hull, 2 January 1977.
Last match : v Warrington, 6 December 1987.

Appearances 198, Tries 26, Goals 5.

Alan was signed as a loose-forward or second-rower in late 1976 during the short coaching reign of Johnny Stopford. He had come through the ranks at Wigan St Cuthbert's, but had also done well for the Wigan Colts team. Alan couldn't really be described as a flamboyant player, but he was always steady, reliable and trusted. A switch to hooker in the early 1980s gained him a regular spot in the first team, but he later reverted to the second-row and was appointed skipper by coach Jim Crellin.

It was under the captaincy of Alan that the Lions lifted the Second Division Championship in 1985. He was never a prolific scorer of tries, but his two most memorable efforts came courtesy of lucky rebounds off the goal posts. On Boxing Day 1984, he plunged over during the Lions' epic 18-5 win over Salford at Station Road after Danny Wilson's grubber-kick rebounded into his arms off the foot of a post. Then in 1987, he scored off a rebounding Les Holliday drop-kick during the Lions' Second Division Premiership win over Hunslet at Old Trafford. Alan was the recipient of a deserved Testimonial in 1987, after which he joined Rochdale Hornets.

John Allen

Born 5 June 1964 (Widnes).

Debut : v Huyton, 11 March 1984.
Last match : v Wigan, 29 September 1992.

Appearances 152, Tries 12, Goals 0.

John signed for the Lions from the Widnes amateur club, Simms Cross. He joined Swinton in early 1984 as a 19 years old second-rower, but he could also operate at loose-forward. John soon established himself as a real crowd favourite with his never-say-die spirit and honest endeavour. He was regarded as something of a tackling machine and was always in the thick of the action. John helped the Lions to the Second Division Championship in 1985, and he was also an integral member of the team which won the double of promotion and Second Division Premiership in 1987. He was also in the team which lost the 1989 Second Division Premiership Final to Sheffield Eagles, as well as being a regular member of the side which won promotion to the top division in 1990/91.

John retired shortly after the tragic loss of Station Road with a serious knee injury, feeling bitterly let down by the old Board with regards to an unpaid medical bill.

Les Holliday

Born 8 August 1962 (Whitehaven).

Debut : v Doncaster, 14 December 1982.
Last match : v Rochdale Hornets, 27 July 1997.

Appearances 182, Tries 39, Goals 28.

Representative Honours:
Cumbria 1 cap (1 try) (1986/87).

Les is the son of the former Great Britain captain Bill Holliday and although a Cumbrian by birth, he was brought up in Swinton following his father's transfer from Hull KR to the Lions. Les joined Swinton from Folly Lane ARLFC around his 20th birthday, and his talent and maturity soon catapulted him into the first team. As a gifted ball-playing loose-forward, he had awareness and time on the ball only typified by great players, with an ability to pick the right pass and offload in dangerous areas of the field. Les helped inspire the Lions to promotion to the top flight in 1984/85, and his personal injuries may well have been the deciding factor in the Lions' relegation a year later by a narrow margin. In autumn 1986, he had the honour of being selected for Cumbria, and scored his team's only try during a loss to the all-conquering Australian tourists. As an inspirational skipper he led the Lions to promotion again in 1987, and was the proud recipient of the inaugural Second Division Premiership Trophy at Old Trafford that same year (a team which contained his brother, Mike, and was jointly coached by his father). Following much speculation Les joined high-flying Halifax for a fee of £65,000 in the autumn of 1987, for whom he played in a couple of losing major cup finals. Les later moved to Widnes with whom he

enjoyed club success and gained Great Britain selection honours. He also enjoyed a stint at Dewsbury before returning to Swinton for a second spell in 1995. In 1996, Les captained Swinton to promotion to the middle tier, before playing his last game in 1997 almost 15 years since his original debut. Les later coached the Lions, both in a head coach and assistant coach capacity. Arguably Les Holliday is the finest player to pull on a Swinton jersey since the heady days of the 1960s. He is still greatly respected by his peers and the Swinton faithful, and currently holds the post of club ambassador.

Paul Topping

150 GREATEST 1988

Born 18 September 1965 (Wigan).

Debut : v St Helens, 30 August 1985.
Last match : v Oldham, 22 April 1990.

Appearances 138, Tries 28, Goals 270.

Paul was a fine young full-back or occasional centre, whom the Lions signed from Wigan St Patrick's following their promotion to the top flight in 1985. He soon settled into Swinton's first team, taking the huge step up in class in his stride. Coach Jim Crellin described him as one of the best defensive full-backs in the game, and he also had good pace which he often used to good effect when joining the attacking line. Paul is the club's seventh highest goal-scorer of all time, and four times he topped the Lions' seasonal goal-kicking charts. He helped the Lions to promotion in 1986/87, but fractured his cheek-

bone in three places during the Second Division Premiership Final success over Hunslet at Old Trafford. Ahead of the 1990/91 season he was involved in a controversial player exchange which saw him and another crowd favourite Mark Sheals join Leigh, with Chris Johnson, John Kerr and Tim Street coming in the opposite direction.

Paul later played at Super League level with the ill-fated Oldham Bears, and is currently a deputy headmaster on Merseyside.

Derek Bate

Born 17 August 1962 (Leigh).

Debut : v Batley, 28 August 1983.
Last match : v Sheffield Eagles, 10 December 1989.

Appearances 185, Tries 119, Goals 0.

Derek was a winger with exceptional pace and balance who came to Station Road in 1983 from the amateur club, Leigh Miners' Welfare. He was a scorer on his debut just as the value of a try had been increased to four points. He was the Second Division's top try scorer in the Lions' promotion season of 1986/87 with 31, and when he grabbed 32 in season 1988/89 only two men across the entire RFL had scored more. Such was the Lions' confidence in his ability that they would often kick early in the tackle count and rely on Derek's

speed to outrun defences and score spectacular tries. His tries helped the Lions to the 1984/85 Second Division Championship, and he was the club's joint-top scorer with Tony Hewitt during the top division campaign of 1985/86. Derek scored in an all-time club record equalling nine successive matches during 1986/87, and at the climax of that great campaign he was a try scorer again at Old Trafford when Hunslet were defeated in the Second Division Premiership Final. However, he was on the losing side to Sheffield Eagles a couple of years later at the same occasion and venue. Derek had a number of successful centre partners during his Lions' career, including the likes of Alan Ratcliffe and Tex Evans, but he particularly profited from playing alongside Steve Snape. In late 1989, he was transferred to Oldham in a deal which brought Terry Flanagan in the opposite direction.

Only seven players in the entire history of the club have scored more tries than Derek's 119.

Born 20 September 1967 (St Helen's).

Debut : v Widnes, 13 December 1987.
Last match : v Hull KR, 6 January 1992.

Appearances 129, Tries 69, Goals 0.

Scott had just reached the age of 20 when he was signed from the St Helen's amateur club, Thatto Heath, shortly after the Lions' commenced their ill-fated Division One campaign in 1987. He had already won county and international honours as an amateur. Scott was a speedy winger whose arrival gave the Lions a big threat down either flank along with Derek Bate. He scored a try in Swinton's loss to Sheffield Eagles during the 1989 Second Division Premiership Final at Old Trafford, then in season 1989/90 he was the Lions' top scorer on 22 tries. He was top try scorer again the following campaign, when under coach Jim Crellin the Lions achieved promotion to the First Division. Scott was involved in a controversial player exchange deal with Oldham in early 1992 after the club hit severe financial problems. Swinton received three players, including Tony Barrow junior, in return.

Born 17 December 1965 (Oldham).

Debut : v Chorley Borough, 3 September 1989.
Last match : v Carlisle, 19 May 1996.

Appearances 79, Tries 12, Goals 0.

Tony was signed from Oldham at the start of the 1989/90 season for a fee of around £8,000. He was a fine tackling second-rower who always led by example, and he was club skipper when the Lions surprisingly won promotion to the top division in 1991. He regained the captaincy following the departure of player-coach Chris O'Sullivan at Christmas 1991, and has the distinction of being the last player to skipper a Swinton team at Station Road. That infamous match against Salford on 20 April 1992, was Tony's last outing before being sold to Castleford for a fee of £30,000.

He returned briefly to Swinton at the advent of summer rugby, and captained the newly named "Swinton Lions" in their first-ever Super League era match. But within a couple of months Tony had moved on to Rochdale Hornets in a swap for Steve Gibson.

Ian Pickavance

Born 20 September 1968 (St Helen's).

Debut : v Workington Town, 12 February 1989.
Last match : v Keighley, 2 July 2000.

Appearances 121, Tries 27, Goals 0.

EThe Lions picked Ian up from the St Helens Colts team early in 1989. He was introduced into the Swinton first team as a winger, but progressed to the centre and second-row positions as his career matured. Ian seemed to have the ability to run with more weight than he actually possessed, and this gangly all-action style led coach Jim Crellin to comment that trying to tackle him "was like trying to bring down a demented giant spider". Ian was the Lions' top try scorer in season 1991/92, the club's last at Station Road. Indeed he also goes down in history as the last ever player to score a try at Station Road, coming as it did on that infamous day on 20 April 1992 when the Lion lost 26-18 to Salford. Despite constant speculation that he would be sold to balance the books, he remained with the Lions for the inaugural season at Gigg Lane.

Finally, however, he joined his home-town club St Helens, and went on to score a try at Wembley when Saints won the Challenge Cup in 1996. He returned briefly to the Lions in season 2000.

Alex Melling

Born 12 August 1964 (Oldham).

Debut : v Workington Town, 25 September 1983.
Last match : v Hunslet, 28 November 1993.

Appearances 198, Tries 24, Goals 0.

Alex "Little Beaver" Melling came to the Lions from Oldham St Anne's towards the end of coach Tom Grainey's reign. A keen cricketer, he was well known in the dressing room for his pranks and sense of humour, coupled with a determined and professional approach. He could arguably be described as the last of Swinton's conventional hookers, but perhaps a slight lack of pace was his Achilles heel. Alex was injured towards the end of the 1985 Second Division Championship winning season, and Gary Ainsworth filled the number nine position towards the end of the successful 1987 campaign. He therefore had to wait until the Second Division Premiership Final of 1989

before appearing on a major stage. Unfortunately, of course, the Lions lost to Sheffield Eagles on that occasion at Old Trafford. Alex played a pivotal role in Swinton's promotion to the top division in 1990/91, by which time his short pass routine to Shane Tupaea, which produced lots of tries, had been perfected. As well as Ainsworth, Alex also faced tough competition from the likes of Steve Garner and Joe Graziano, and at one point he was loaned out to Leigh. But always he stayed loyal to the Lions and he was in the line-up against Rochdale Hornets when Swinton opened their stay at Gigg Lane in 1992. Alex was rewarded with a benefit in season 1993/94, which included a testimonial match against Salford in which he opened the scoring.

Born 27 June 1970 (Prescot).

Debut : v Rochdale Hornets, 30 August 1992.
Last match : v Rochdale Hornets, 1 August 1999.

Appearances 203, Tries 120, Goals 0.

Simon "Sticks" Ashcroft performed admirably well with the league's perennial easy-beats Highfield during season 1991/92, and this was enough to persuade the Lions to give the slim speedster a chance following their controversial move to Gigg Lane. He made his debut against Rochdale Hornets in the first match at Bury, and ended both of the first two seasons at Gigg Lane as the Lions' leading try scorer. Simon had pace to burn, and was unquestionably one of the most feared wingers outside the top division. In all he was Swinton's leading try scorer in a season on four occasions, and he eventually finished with a career total of 120.

In the post-war era only Alan Buckley and Johnny Stopford have scored more tries for the Lions than "Sticks", whilst only six men in total have outscored him. Simon was also amongst the most approachable and friendly of the Gigg Lane crop of players, and his popularity transcended the controversial club politics of that era.

Mark Welsby

Born 17 September 1971 (Wigan).

Debut : v Rochdale Hornets, 30 August 1992.
Last match : v Rochdale Hornets, 6 February 2000.

Appearances 195, Tries 62, Goals 1.

Mark was one of the Lions' first signings following the loss of Station Road in 1992. Although he emerged as one of the finest full-backs outside of the top division, he was originally signed as a potential half-back, and indeed he made his Swinton debut at stand-off against Rochdale Hornets in the first-ever game at Gigg Lane.

A Wiganer, the Lions picked him up from his hometown club where he had been on the cusp of the first team. Over the next seven years Mark developed into a stylish and defensively excellent full-back, heralding the terrace chant of "You'll never beat Mark Welsby", a song since stolen by other clubs for various players.

He retired due to a serious hernia problem at the beginning of the 2000 season, despite still being only 28 years old. Mark was unquestionably one of the Lions' success stories of the Gigg Lane era.

Mark Riley

150 GREATEST 1996

Born 16 June 1967 (New Zealand).

Debut : v York, 31 March 1996.
Last match : v Wakefield Trinity, 20 July 1997.

Appearances 45, Tries 30, Goals 0.

Mark "Flicker" Riley was a diminutive Kiwi who first made his name with the Otahuhu Leopards in the Auckland League. Having taken his career to England, he had a successful career with London Broncos before Swinton made him a major signing in early 1996 at the advent of summer rugby. Mark's services were acquired thanks largely to the significant, but ultimately controversial, investment of Bury FC owner, Hugh Eaves. His time with the Lions was relatively short, but during his stay he made quite an impact, and many supporters rate him as one of the best half-backs Swinton have had in the past 50 years.

On 11 August 1996, Mark broke the all-time Swinton tries in a match record when he scored six against Prescot Panthers at Gigg Lane. He was the Lions' Player of the Year in 1996, but retired at the end of the 1997 campaign.

Born 19 December 1970 (Hemel Hempstead).

Debut : v Huddersfield, 4 September 1994.
Last match : v Oldham, 23 May 1999.

Appearances 138, Tries 44 Goals 37.

Representative Honours:
Wales 2 caps (1995).

Gavin was born in England, but brought up in Australia with a Welsh father! He arrived at Gigg Lane via Canberra Raiders in 1994. Thanks to his parentage he picked up a couple of Welsh international caps on a tour of the USA in 1995. Gavin was a very versatile player, and was equally effective at centre, winger or second-row. He was a regular try scorer, and he grabbed two against Leeds in the Challenge Cup when the Lions' went down

agonisingly in the last moments of what was the last game of the winter era. Gavin had the curious distinction of being red-carded twice within the space of a few days (against Batley and Dewsbury) only to be found not guilty on each occasion. He was a consistent and whole-hearted player, and he carried off the club's Player of the Year awards in the successive campaigns of 1997 and 1998.

Not long after the failure of the Lions' bid for Super League status in 1998, he left for Rochdale Hornets. Gavin currently holds a teaching position back in his home country.

Ian Skeech

Born 4 February 1967 (Warrington); Died 28 September 1998 (aged 31).

Debut : v Hunslet, 22 November 1987.
Last match : v Hull KR, 25 August 1996.

Appearances 106, Tries 20, Goals 0.

Ian started his rugby career as a junior with Newton-le-Willows RUFC, and later played amateur Rugby League with Parkside Golborne. After impressing in "A" Team trials, Ian signed for the Lions in November 1987, on the recommendation of coach Frankie Barrow when the club was in the First Division. Ian preferred loose-forward, but it was as a second-rower that he found his niche. Although not always first choice on the team sheet, Ian's inclusion in this book is thanks to his honest endeavour, longevity, and club loyalty. Ian himself described his favourite game as being the epic battle in the mud and rain against Warrington in late 1991, which the Lions won, 10-8. His Swinton career transcended the despair of losing Station Road, but on a personal level nothing could compare with his diagnosis for leukaemia in 1997.

Sadly, that dreadful disease claimed his life at the age of just 31 in September 1998. Swinton fans continue to perform an annual charity walk in his memory.

Born 3 June 1982 (Wigan).

Debut : v Featherstone Rovers, 8 August 1999.
Last match : v York City Knights, 3 May 2015.

Appearances 114, Tries 52, Goals 221.

Representative Honours:
Northern Ford Premiership U21s v Super League U21s 1 app (2001).

Wigan-born Mick emerged through the Lions' Academy system, and made his senior debut as a teenager in the 1999 season when the club was still based at Gigg Lane. The son of an ex-Wigan and Blackpool Borough player of the same name, he emerged as a talented centre and reliable goal-kicker over the next three seasons, before being tempted away by Rochdale Hornets in 2003. Mick subsequently played for Whitehaven, Widnes, Oldham and Leigh, and would have added Halifax to that list in 2012 had it not been for injury. In 2013, Mick returned to the Lions where his career began, and remained until his retirement in 2015. But when Mick scored two tries for Swinton in a victory at Barrow in August 1999, it was the start of a Rugby League odyssey. Not only would he represent Scotland in the 2008 World Cup in Australia and win the Northern Rail Cup Final with Leigh in 2011 amongst many other highlights, he would also write his name into the record books as the sixth highest points scorer in the history of the sport. Year after

year he consistently plundered tries and goals, breaking numerous individual club records along the way. Mick is eleventh on Swinton's all-time goal-kicking list, and eighth on the club's all-time points scoring list - both remarkable facts considering he spent 10 seasons with other clubs! Furthermore, only four other Swinton players, namely Jim Valentine, Albert Blan, Ken Gowers and Ken Jones, have scored at least 50 tries and 100 goals in their Lions' career. Mick was undoubtedly a modern era phenomenon.

Sean Casey

Born 9 December 1971 (St Helen's).

Debut : v Wakefield Trinity, 9 February 1997.
Last match v Keighley, 2 July 2000.

Appearances 103, Tries 38, Goals 14.

Representative Honours:
West of Pennines v East of Pennines 1 app (1999).

Sean joined his local club St Helens at the age of 18 in 1990. But facing tough competition for a first team place he joined Whitehaven in 1995, from whom he joined the Lions in 1997. Sean was a talented ball-playing loose-forward with an eye for a try, and he came to Gigg Lane as part of the Hugh Eaves investment which Swinton hoped would catapult them to Super League. That didn't happen of course, but he did skipper the Lions to fifth place in the second tier in 1998 which culminated in a controversial play-off defeat at Featherstone Rovers. Sean spent just over three seasons at the club during which time he gave solid leadership and service.

He left the Lions in 2000 owing to injury, but later turned to playing Rugby Union for the Liverpool-St Helens club.

Tony Barrow

Born 19 October 1971 (St Helen's); died 16 March 2017 (aged 45).

Debut : v Halifax, 16 February 1992.
Last match : v Leeds, 11 February 2001.

Appearances 243, Tries 25, Goals 0.

Representative Honours:
West of Pennines v East of Pennines 1 app (1999).

When Tony retired in 2001, following the Lions' brutal annihilation at the hands of Leeds in the Challenge Cup, gone was the last link with the Lions' Station Road playing days. It may also come as a surprise to learn that no player in the last 40 years has made more appearances for the Lions. The former Thatto Heath amateur was signed from Oldham early in 1992 as part of the player exchange that took Scott Ranson to Watersheddings. Tony arrived when his father, Tony senior, was the Swinton coach, and therefore perhaps he always felt an added pressure to prove himself. But this he did successfully with consistent and honest displays over a period of some nine years, eight of which were at Gigg Lane.

Tragically, Tony recently succumbed to a serious illness that he had battled bravely for some considerable time. Despite his illness, Tony had been a welcome visitor to Heywood Road during the 2016 season.

Lee Hansen

Born 23 July 1968.

Debut : v Chorley Lynx, 3 December 2000.
Last match : v London Skolars, 8 June 2003.

Appearances 66, Tries 2, Goals 0.

Liuaki "Lee" Hansen was a Tongan international prop-forward who played in the 2005 Rugby League World Cup, and he joined Swinton from Widnes ahead of the 2001 season. He had also previously played for both Leigh and Wigan. Lee's association with the Lions was relatively short, but at a time of significant off-field problems Lee's honesty and efforts were a shining light, and he soon became a cult hero. In mid-2002 the Lions were forced out of Gigg Lane, and found temporary solace at Moor Lane, Salford. Chairman Malcolm White and Chief Executive Tony Barrow had left the club by then, which was saved and taken forward by Dave Jones, assisted by the newly formed Supporters' Trust which had been the brainchild of Steve Wild.

During all this upheaval Lee continued to lead from the front, often in the face of great adversity on the scoreboard, and he never took a backward step. Early in 2003 he left the club and later played for Rochdale Hornets.

Born 27 September 1978.

Debut : v Chorley Lynx, 3 December 2000.
Last match : v Hunslet, 9 May 2004.

Appearances 79, Tries 11, Goals 0.

With a martial-arts black-belt Rob had a tackling technique second to none, and he put this to great effect from his position at hooker. Signed from Warrington, and always recognisable by his head-band, Rob was another who stuck with the club through uncertain times in a Swinton career spanning four years either side of the departure from Gigg Lane. His unrelenting efforts earned an appreciative terrace chant in his honour, and the highlight of his Lions' career was the unexpected run to a Challenge Cup quarter-final in 2003. He tackled Featherstone Rovers into the Moor Lane mud in the last 16, and then helped keep Wigan at bay for 25 minutes in the quarter-final at the JJB Stadium which ultimately was comfortably lost.

Jason Roach

Born 2 May 1971 (St Helen's)

Debut : v Bramley, 20 August 1995.
Last match : v Chorley, 27 August 2004.

Appearances 139, Tries 94, Goals 3.

Representative Honours:
Scotland 4 caps (2003 to 2004).

Jason was a big barn-storming winger who enjoyed three separate spells with the Lions over a period spanning nine years. He first joined Swinton from St Helens in 1995, and early in 1996 scored twice against Leeds in the Challenge Cup when Swinton were minutes away from causing a sensational upset. In August 1996, he equalled the all-time club tries in a match record when he scored five against Prescot Panthers, but it was just his luck that Mark Riley went and grabbed six on the same day! Jason left Swinton to play Super League at Castleford and Warrington between 1997 and 1999, but returned to the Lions for the 2000 season. After leaving the Lions for a third time at the end of 2004, he saw his career out with Barrow and Blackpool Panthers.

Jason's haul of 94 Swinton tries is a total surpassed only by Simon Ashcroft and Wayne English in the post-Station Road era. Through family links he also qualified for Scotland for whom he won eight caps, four of which came whilst a Swinton player.

Born 5 March 1963.

Debut : v Rochdale Hornets, 13 February 2005.
Last match : v Oldham, 16 September 2007.

Appearances 69, Tries 34, Goals 220.

Lee began his career with Salford but joined the Lions from Oldham in time for the start of the 2005 campaign, and by the end of that first season he had entered the club's record books. Lee could play just as effectively in the forwards or the backs, being able to combine skill and guile at stand-off, or size, strength and ball-handling skills at loose-forward. His 2005 haul of 20 tries, 114 goals and two drop-goals, for a total of 310 points, exceeded the legendary Albert Blan's points in a season record. Albert's record of 283 points had stood since 1961, and even taking into account the rise in value of a try from three to four points, Lee had still smashed the record. That 2005 campaign saw the Lions flatter to deceive and they ultimately heart-breakingly lost by a point in a play-off match at Workington Town, despite

Lee's final four goals of the campaign. In 2006, again the Lions entered the promotion play-offs, winning sensational games against Barrow, Featherstone Rovers and Celtic Crusaders to reach the final against Sheffield Eagles at Warrington. In that never-to-be-forgotten semi-final at Bridgend, Lee was arguably man-of-the-match with two tries and a sure-footed conversion that took the game into extra-time. At the end of the 2007 season he joined Leigh Centurions.

Chris Hough

Born 30 August 1981 (Oldham).

Debut : v Salford, 19 January 2003.
Last match : v Oldham, 16 September 2007.

Appearances 57, Tries 12, Goals 121.

Representative Honours:
National League 2 v New Zealand "A" 1 app (2003).

Chris started his career with Waterhead ARLFC, before joining Rochdale Hornets for whom he made his debut at the age of only 16. He joined the Lions in 2003 as a typical talkative and cheeky, but creative, scrum-half. Chris inspired the Lions to a sensational 32-10 victory over higher-division Featherstone Rovers in the last 16 of the Challenge Cup, but after just one season he joined Doncaster before moving to Blackpool Panthers. However, he returned to Lions in 2006, and it was at the climax of that season that he went down in Swinton and Rugby League folklore. This came about in the promotion play-off semi-final at the Brewery Field, Bridgend, when Swinton defeated the much-fancied Celtic Crusaders 27-26 with the British game's first-ever golden-point drop-goal. Level at full-time and still level after extra-time, it was a Chris Hough drop-kick which heralded a delirious pitch invasion and sent the Lions through to the final against Sheffield Eagles at Warrington. He re-joined Rochdale Hornets at the start of the 2008 season, but left when he wasn't retained in the player-coaching role that he'd fulfilled towards the end of the 2012 campaign. Chris was always approachable and a great fans' favourite at Sedgley Park, and even after leaving for Rochdale he would often be seen watching Swinton games with his family.

Martin Moana

Born 13 August 1973 (Huntly, New Zealand).

Debut : v Widnes, 12 February 2006.
Last match : v Oldham, 12 September 2009.

Appearances 112, Tries 45, Goals 0.

Martin was a skilful, ball-playing, but tough, stand-off or loose-forward, who served the Lions well in the twilight of his career. Perhaps in many respects Martin could be described as a journeyman professional, and he'd certainly had more than his fair share of clubs by the time he arrived at the Lions in 2006 at the age of 32. Martin, a New Zealander, was born at Huntly and first made his name with Waikato in the New Zealand domestic league. He then came under the wing of the Auckland Warriors, and he was in their team when they played their inaugural NRL match in 1995. Martin also gained selection for the NZ Maori team at the 2000 World Cup, as well as the NZ World Nines team in 1995. However, by 1996 he had moved to England and joined Halifax, who were then members of Super League. He spent five years with Halifax, scoring a highly impressive 119 tries in 186 appearances. From there he had spells with Doncaster, Wakefield Trinity, Halifax (again), Salford, and Doncaster (again), before signing for Paul Kidd's Swinton team in 2006. Martin made an immediate impact with the Lions and soon became a great favourite at Sedgley Park. He played a starring role in Swinton's epic victories over Featherstone Rovers and Celtic Crusaders, which took the Lions to the

2006 National League 2 play-off final. Sadly that game ended in defeat against Sheffield Eagles. In all Martin gave four years of great service to the Lions in what were generally difficult times, but never did his efforts or talents go unnoticed. After retiring in 2009 he spent some time as the club's Commercial Manager.

Marlon Billy

Born 22 November 1973 (Huddersfield).

Debut : v Moldgreen, 31 January 1999.
Last match : v Oldham, 12 September 2009.

Appearances 170, Tries 88, Goals 0.

Marlon was a prolific try scoring winger who was signed by coach Les Holliday from Keighley in 1999. For a while he enjoyed the same Gigg Lane dressing rooms as his brother, Chris, who at the time played for Bury FC. After two years with the Lions, Marlon joined Rochdale Hornets and later Doncaster, but he returned to Swinton in 2005 and remained for five seasons. Perhaps the highlight of that period was the Lions' run to the National League 2 play-off final against Sheffield Eagles at Warrington in 2006, which along the way saw great wins over Barrow, Featherstone Rovers and Celtic Crusaders. Marlon had the physique of a 100 metre runner, and his power and athleticism delivered 88 tries for the Lions – which included the distinction of club leading try scorer in both 2005 and 2008.

Marlon enjoyed a great rapport with the Swinton fans, and it was a popular move when he was appointed assistant coach under Ian Watson. But after Watson left to take up a position at Salford in 2014, Marlon went to Halifax to become number two to the former Lion, Richard Marshall.

Wayne English

Born 8 March 1980 (Rochdale).

Debut : v Waterhead, 1 February 2000.
Last match : v Dewsbury, 5 July 2009.

Appearances 226, Tries 97, Goals 0.

Representative Honours:
National League 2 v New Zealand "A" 1 app (2003).

Wayne signed professional forms in July 1998 after impressing for John Prince's Swinton Academy team. The then 17 years old full-back had come through the ranks at Kirkholt WMC, in remarkably similar circumstances to Swinton legend, Ken Gowers, some 44 years earlier. Wayne then had to endure a serious cruciate knee ligament injury, which meant that his debut didn't arrive until some 18 months later. He was handed his debut by coach Mike Gregory, and took full advantage of the retirement of Mark Welsby to cement his place at full-back. Although not large in stature, Wayne had the heart of a lion. Defensively sound, and with lightning quick feet, he trained hard and made the most of his abilities. His Swinton career traversed three home grounds, Gigg Lane, Moor Lane and Park Lane, but always Wayne's was the first name down on the team sheet. He was much respected amongst the non-Super League fraternity, and in both 2004 and 2005 he was chosen in the National League 2 "All Stars" team at full-back. Wayne played a pivotal

role in the Lions' remarkable run to the National League 2 Grand Final in 2006, but unfortunately Swinton lost to Sheffield Eagles at Warrington. Having been granted a well-earned testimonial in 2008, Wayne was surprisingly allowed to join his home-town club Rochdale Hornets at the end of the 2009 campaign. Many supporters thought this was a grave error of judgment on the part of the Lions, and indeed Wayne went on to give equally remarkable service to Hornets, culminating in promotion to the Championship in his last game before retirement at the climax of 2016.

Dana Wilson

Born 22 May 1983 (Auckland, New Zealand); Died 4 September 2011 (aged 28 at Burtonwood).

Debut : v Doncaster, 7 February 2010.
Last match : v Rochdale Hornets, 2 September 2011.

Appearances 44, Tries 12, Goals 0.

Pareu Pera Takatatia Wilson, or "Dana", was a much-loved south sea islander who joined the Lions from Halifax in 2010, and went on to play a major role in Swinton winning the 2011 Championship One title. His father was Samoan and his mother a Cook Islander, but Dana first saw representative honours with New Zealand schoolboys before winning full caps for the Cook Islands. He was a prop-forward of considerable power and purpose, and during that successful 2011 campaign he was usually used as a devastating weapon off the bench. Dana plundered 12 tries during his Swinton career at a rate of nearly one every three games, and was a great crowd favourite during the club's brief time at The Willows.

Tragically, only two days after celebrating the Lions' title triumph of 2011, Dana was killed in a car crash in the early hours of 4 September. In a small but heartfelt tribute, Swinton supporters subsequently named their lion mascot in Dana's honour.

Born 9 June 1981 (Leigh).

Debut : v Workington Town, 17 February 2010.
Last match : v Gateshead Thunder, 14 April 2012.

Appearances 47, Tries 15, Goals 0.

Lee was signed from Leigh early in 2010, and was made captain for season 2011 when the Lions played out of The Willows under coach Steve McCormack. At the end of that campaign he had the honour of being presented with the Championship One trophy, the Lions' first silverware in 24 years. In May of that year Lee produced a tremendous individual performance as the Lions won at Dewsbury in the Challenge Cup, which until the win over Huddersfield in April 2017 was the only time in the club's history that they have beaten a team from a higher division away from home in a competitive match.

Shortly after the club's relocation to Leigh Sports Village in 2012, he reluctantly retired at the age of 31 to take care of his business interests. Lee had previously played for Oldham, and was a real work-horse of a second-rower or prop-forward.

Kevin Penny

Born 3 October 1987 (Warrington).

Debut : v Hunslet, 19 February 2012.
Last match : v Whitehaven, 7 September 2014.

Appearances 54, Tries 31, Goals 2.

Kevin made his debut for Warrington in 2007 at the age of 19 and made an immediate impact. In that first season he scored a hat-trick in nine minutes against Salford, and finished the year by being chosen for the Super League Dream Team. However, a loss of form saw his career punctuated with loan moves to Widnes, Harlequins RL and Wakefield Trinity, before coach Steve McCormack unveiled him as a surprise signing for the Lions ahead of their bow in the Championship in 2012. Kevin made a tremendous impact with Swinton, and his tries at a rate of one in every two games were instrumental in consolidating the Lions' status during 2012 and 2013. Such was his return to form that Warrington signed him back for the 2014 campaign. However, part of that season was subsequently spent back on loan with the Lions where he ended up as leading try scorer.

Kevin was a winger with pace to burn, and he scored some spectacular tries often out of nothing. He was also a great team player, and although the

likelihood was always that he would one day return to Super League, he gave everything to the Lions' cause. As such he was a great favourite amongst fans, team mates and coaching staff alike.

Born 27 October 1976 (Manchester).

Debut : v Folly Lane, 1 February 1998.
Last match : v Barrow, 22 June 2014.

Appearances 239, Tries 39, Goals 180.

Representative Honours:
Wales 9 caps (1999 to 2011); West of Pennines v East of Pennines 1 app (1999).

Local-lad Ian made his Station Road "debut" as a ball-boy whilst enjoying his junior Rugby League with Eccles. He turned professional with Salford in 1994, although it was with Workington Town that he made his Super League debut whilst being on loan there in 1996. After struggling to gain regular first team football at The Willows, he signed for Swinton for a reported fee of £15,000 in 1997. Ian made his Lions' debut in the memorable local derby against Folly Lane ARLFC at Gigg Lane in the 1998 Challenge Cup, and quickly established himself as a goal-kicking scrum-half. There quickly developed an assuredness about his on-field demeanour that was vital to the Lions' play, and he would influence and direct his team around the field like a general. In 2001 he joined Widnes, then a year later returned to Super League with Salford. Once again, however, Salford allowed him to leave, and following stints with Rochdale Hornets and Oldham he returned to the Lions in 2005. Ian's journey then took him to Halifax and Leigh between 2006 and 2009, before he returned to the Lions for a third time in 2010. He greatly influenced Swinton's Championship One title success of 2011, and then helped maintain the Lions' stay in the middle tier for the next two seasons.

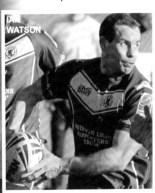

In January 2014, he was appointed Swinton's player-coach, but in July of that year he accepted a position at Salford, where he later became head coach. Ian also enjoys the great accolade of having won a record number of caps for Wales, for whom he qualifies through family connections. He won nine Welsh caps as a Lion, but in total he made 30 appearances for the Principality and scored seven tries, one of which was in a World Cup semi-final against Australia at Huddersfield in 2000.

Mike Morrison

Born 9 September 1987 (Wigan).

Debut : v Halifax, 4 February 2011.
Last match : v London Broncos, 12 June 2016.

Appearances 114, Tries 7, Goals 0.

Self-employed joiner Mike previously played for Widnes, but came to the Lions from Leigh at the start of the 2011 season. He then immediately played a prominent role in the club winning the Championship One title. In 2012, Mike helped the Lions consolidate in the middle tier, before deciding to try his luck in Australia along with fellow Lion, Dale Cunniffe. But in early 2014 he rejoined Swinton, and again became the mainstay of the Lions' pack. However, Mike was unable to prevent the Lions from suffering relegation, but under new coach John Duffy, he helped the Lions to promotion for a second time in 2015. This was a dramatic campaign which culminated with thrilling play-off victories over York and Keighley, both of which were won with drop-goals. Following the departure of skipper Ritchie Hawkyard, Mike was appointed captain for season 2016, but sadly he was forced into premature retirement due to repeated concussions.

Mike was a player who never took a backward step, and led by example. Friendly and approachable off the field, Swinton fans took him to their hearts and dubbed him "Iron Mike" for his on-field passion and leadership. At the end of season presentation night in September 2016, the club's Man of Steel award was renamed in Mike's honour.

Born 21 January 1986 (Huddersfield).

Debut : v Oldham, 1 February 2008.
Last match : v Keighley, 4 October 2015 (League 1 Play-off Final).

Appearances 168, Tries 49, Goals 53

"Titch", a plasterer by trade, hails from Slaithwaite near Huddersfield, but emerged through the Academy system at Bradford Bulls. He played three Super League games for the Bulls during 2007 at the age of 21. To gain more regular match experience, Ritchie joined Paul Kidd's Swinton at the start of 2008, and soon became an essential name on the Lions' team sheet. Although modest in physical stature, hence his nickname, Ritchie was as brave as a lion. He was signed essentially as a stand-off, but it was as a full-back where he mainly made his name for Swinton following the departure of Wayne English. Darren Hawkyard, his older brother, later also joined the Lions from the Huddersfield amateur game. Ritchie was always willing to drive the ball out from defence, using his speed, swerve and bravery to evade opponents, relieve his defence, and gain valuable yards. He was excellent under the high ball, and could join the attacking line to great effect and grab more than his fair share of tries. He was also a useful stand-in goal-kicker. Ritchie played a major part in helping the Lions lift the Championship One title in 2011, but most significantly he was captain of the Swinton team which won the League One promotion play-off final against

Keighley at Widnes in October 2015. But with promotion secured, the club and Ritchie were unable to agree terms for 2016, and he consequently left for Keighley alongside his brother, Darren.

Stuart Littler

Born 19 February 1979 (Wigan).

Debut : v Hemel Stags, 1 March 2015.
Last match : v Whitehaven, 18 September 2016.

Appearances 55, Tries 25, Goals 0.

Representative Honours:
Ireland 2 caps (2016)

Although born at Wigan, Stuart is a life-long resident of Leigh and that's the town he regards as home. In 2008, at the age of 19, he was signed by Salford, and soon became a mainstay in a Reds career that lasted some 12 years. During his time at Salford, he chalked up an impressive 329 appearances, primarily at centre and second-row, and scored 112 tries. He also gained international recognition for Ireland through family connections, and wore the green shirt at the 2008 World Cup down-under. In 2011, he made an emotional move to Leigh, where he chalked up just shy of another hundred appearances, and scored tries at a rate marginally under once every three games. In 2014, he dallied briefly with Rochdale Hornets, but then welcomed the opportunity to join John Duffy's revamped Swinton Lions at the start of the 2015 season. That campaign ended with sensational play-off victories over York and Keighley which secured promotion to the Championship, during which Stuart played a key leadership role for the young Lions team. On a personal level in 2015, he also contributed 21 tries in 30 appearances and formed a fine centre-wing partnership with Shaun Robinson. Shrugging aside rumours of retirement, Stuart then made the step up to the Championship and notched four more tries in 21 appearances, as the Lions successfully consolidated their higher status. Following the last game of the 2016 season at Whitehaven, Stuart finally confirmed his retirement and in doing so brought to an end a remarkable professional career which had spanned some 19 seasons and in excess of 500 appearances. Stuart then joined the Lions' coaching staff for season 2017, in the safe knowledge that he could now enjoy more time with wife Tiffany and his young family.

Every player – Heritage Number and Career Statistics

The following section reveals full career details of every single player known to have played for Swinton since the club's formation in 1866. Essentially this incorporates two lists of Heritage Numbers, the first covering the pre-Rugby Union and Rugby Union eras (seasons 1868/69 to 1895/96 inclusive), and the second covering the club's Northern Union/Rugby League era (season 1896/97 to 2016 inclusive). All players are accredited with a unique Heritage Number based on the chronological order of his debut.

Qualification for a Heritage Number is one appearance in one competitive first-team match, including substitute appearances. (Players who only ever appeared for the reserve team are therefore not included). Individual player information includes the dates of his debut and last appearance, as well as his usual field position and full career records (i.e. appearances, tries and goals). Substitute appearances are included amongst the overall total, and no distinction is made between placed goals and dropped-goals.

For the period 1896 to date, that is, from the time that the Lions defected to the Northern Union (Rugby League), our records are complete. We know the first name of every single player, plus the identity of all the "AN Others". The compilation of this information represents an extraordinary achievement on the part of Les Smith and John Edwards, who for many years have painstakingly researched the club's statistical history. We are not aware of any other club that can match this level of detail.

Unlike other Rugby League clubs, we also have remarkably complete records from the Lions' Rugby Union Days from 1871 to 1896.

Indeed except for just four matches, for which we hold partial information, we have complete records for every game played from the start of the 1877/78 season. For the six seasons between 1871/72 and 1876/77 we hold partial information.

But in addition to this, we know the line-ups from what are thought to be Swinton's first ever two matches, both played in 1869, at a time which even pre-dates the Rugby Football Union (which was not founded until 1871).

The Heritage Numbers begin with those pioneer matches in 1869 (numbers 1 to 13), and continue into the club's Rugby Union era. Numbers 39 to 100 have not been utilised due to the gaps in those very early records, whilst numbers 14 to 38 are subject to alteration for the same reason. During the 1871-1877 period only known appearances, tries and goals are stated, therefore these figures are subject to confirmation and are marked with an asterisk. However, the list then continues from number 101 at the start of season 1877/78, from when we have virtually complete records.

The careers of 19 players straddled both the Rugby Union and Northern Union eras, and those players are given Heritage Numbers in both lists. The most notable of these being Jim Valentine who has number 170 in the Rugby Union list and Number 1 in the Rugby League list.

To arrive at the overall correct records for these 19 players then the two sets of figures need adding together. For example, Valentine made 356 appearances under Rugby Union rules and 130 under Northern Union rules, for a total of 486.

HERITAGE NUMBERS

Another unique feature, again thanks to the efforts of Les Smith and John Edwards, is the identification of those men that played for Swinton during the unofficial Great War seasons of 1915/16 to 1918/19. Where a player appeared in both peace-time official games and war-time unofficial games, his appearances, tries and goals are given separately under each category. If a player didn't make any official appearances in addition to war-time appearances, then he is not given a Heritage Number, but rather a "W" signifying "war-time only".

In order to provide an accurate representation of the careers of those players who enjoyed more than one playing spell with the club, each period is shown separately. For example, Number 695 Les Holliday made 134 appearances in his first spell with Swinton, and 51 in his second spell, for a total of 185.

Players that have achieved representative honou[rs] are indicated in bold capitals, and relevant deta[ils] are provided in the end column (including tri[es] and goals scored). Note that these figures are [a] record of representative honours won whilst ea[ch] man was a Swinton player only. If, for example, [a] player won Great Britain caps whilst with anoth[er] club, then this isn't reflected in the figures state[d]. Details of representative honours are, howeve[r] fully complete. Again this represents a[n] impressive feat of research, especially in tracin[g] those Lancashire caps won during the Rugb[y] Union era. Keys to both field positions an[d] representative honours are also given.

Finally, for ease of searching and cros[s] referencing, a full alphabetical list is also provide[d]. In this list Rugby Union Heritage Numbers ar[e] given in the left-hand column, and Rugby Leagu[e] Heritage Numbers are given in the right-han[d] column.

The victorious Swinton team following their epic giant-killing victory over Super League club, Huddersfield, in April 2017. The most recent men to earn a heritage number:

HN	Player	Position	Debut	Last
1238	Josh Woods	SO	23/04/2017	Current
1239	Caine Barnes	SR	23/04/2017	Current
1240	Liam Carberry	HK	23/04/2017	Current

	Season 1868/69	Position	Debut	Last	Apps	Tries	Goals	Honours as a Lion	150
	WALTER LONGSHAW	F	02/01/1869	15/11/1879	49*	7*	1*	LRU1	1877
	John Dorning	HB	02/01/1869	27/10/1877	11*	2*	4*		1869
	James Bowers (jnr)	n/k	02/01/1869	pre-1877/78	1*	0*	0*		
	Thomas (AT) Morris	n/k	02/01/1869	pre-1877/78	1*	0*	0*		
	John Owen	HB	02/01/1869	20/01/1883	76*	15*	3*		1868
	Richard Lee	n/k	02/01/1869	pre-1877/78	1*	0*	0*		
	William Shovelton	n/k	02/01/1869	pre-1877/78	1*	0*	0*		
	Season 1869/70	Position	Debut	Last	Apps	Tries	Goals	Honours as a Lion	150
	Edward (EL) Farr	FB	18/12/1869	13/04/1878	27*	3*	1*		1872
	Ted Barker	F	18/12/1869	29/10/1881	71*	3*	0*		1870
	Brooks	n/k	18/12/1869	pre-1877/78	1*	0*	0*		
	William Evans	F	18/12/1869	27/12/1880	45*	3*	0*		
	J Ormrod	n/k	18/12/1869	pre-1877/78	3*	1*	0*		
	W Radcliffe	n/k	18/12/1869	pre-1877/78	1*	0*	0*		
	Seasons 1871/72 to 1876/77	Position	Debut	Last	Apps	Tries	Goals	Honours as a Lion	150
	Harry Longshaw	F	1871/72	pre-1877/78	1*	0*	1*		1871
	John Denwood	n/k	1871/72	pre-1877/78	1*	1*	0*		
	Radcliffe Dorning	n/k	1871/72	pre-1877/78	1*	1*	0*		1867
	Nathan Howarth	n/k	1871/72	pre-1877/78	1*	1*	0*		
	Richard Ashton	F	pre-1876/77	22/12/1877	3*	0*	0*		
	James Barlow	F	pre-1876/77	01/11/1879	40*	4*	0*		
	Tom Clegg	n/k	pre-1876/77	pre-1877/78	8*	1*	2*		
	Arthur (AH) Dorning	F	pre-1876/77	02/02/1878	9*	0*	0*		
	H Dorning	n/k	pre-1876/77	pre-1877/78	1*	0*	0*		
	Henry (HP) Farr	TQ	pre-1876/77	15/03/1879	39*	7*	3*		
	HERBERT (HF) FARR	TQ	pre-1876/77	15/03/1879	38*	16*	6*	LRU2(2t)	1878
	TOM (TS) FARR	TQ	pre-1876/77	10/11/1883	107*	58*	11*	LRU5(4t)	1883
	Mills	F	pre-1876/77	pre-1877/78	2*	1*	0*		
	Tom Morrison	F	pre-1876/77	02/10/1880	46*	2*	0*		
	Murgatroyd	n/k	pre-1876/77	pre-1877/78	1*	0*	0*		
	L Nicholson	TQ	pre-1876/77	pre-1877/78	1*	0*	0*		
	Bob Ogden	F	pre-1876/77	21/04/1883	117*	6*	1*		1875
	Stancliffe	n/k	pre-1876/77	pre-1877/78	2*	0*	0*		
	George Townsend	F	pre-1876/77	03/11/1877	11*	0*	0*		1873
	HENRY YATES	F	pre-1876/77	19/02/1881	38*	3*	3*	LRU2	1874
	JOE MILLS	HB	18/03/1877	21/03/1891	267	85	26	NRU2, LRU29(4g, 7t)	1876
	James Banks	HB	pre-1877/78	08/11/1879	5*	2*	0*		
	Arthur Knowles	TQ	pre-1877/78	17/04/1880	2*	2*	0*		
	E Morley	F	pre-1877/78	02/10/1880	11*	1*	0*		
	John Yates	F	pre-1877/78	01/03/1879	7*	0*	1*		
N	Season 1877/78	Position	Debut	Last	Apps	Tries	Goals	Honours as a Lion	150
1	F Pearson	F	20/10/1877*	06/11/1880	33*	0*	0*		
2	J Ainsworth	F	27/10/1877*	27/10/1877	1*	0*	0*		
3	Richard Blears	F	27/10/1877*	27/10/1877	1*	0*	0*		
4	James Crossley	F	27/10/1877*	15/02/1879	11*	1*	0*		
5	Jim Jeanes	F	27/10/1877*	01/03/1884	3*	0*	0*		
6	Walter Pearson	F	27/10/1877*	30/10/1880	33*	2*	0*		
7	William Simister	F	27/10/1877*	29/10/1881	12*	1*	0*		
8	Charles Jones	TQ	16/11/1877*	02/10/1880	13*	2*	0*		
9	John Brierley	F	08/12/1877	02/03/1878	3	1	0		
0	L Kay	F	05/01/1878	22/02/1879	12	1	0		
1	L Scheele	F	02/03/1878	29/10/1878	2	0	0		
2	William Emery	HB	16/03/1878	13/04/1878	4	1	0		
N	Season 1878/79	Position	Debut	Last	Apps	Tries	Goals	Honours as a Lion	150
3	William Yates	F	19/10/1878	19/10/1878	1	0	0		
4	H Wood	TQ	26/10/1878	23/11/1878	6	0	0		
5	James Wright	HB	26/10/1878	09/11/1878	4	0	0		
6	ALBERT HOPE	F	26/10/1878	01/03/1890	112	16	0	LRU3	1879
7	W Chadwick	HB	29/10/1878	15/03/1879	4	0	0		
8	J Fletcher	F	29/10/1878	29/10/1878	1	0	0		
9	C J Glossop	F	29/10/1878	29/10/1878	1	0	0		
0	F Wild	F	29/10/1878	27/12/1880	3	0	0		
1	Charles Sawyer	TQ	23/11/1878	11/10/1879	2	1	0		
2	J Sawyer	TQ	23/11/1878	11/10/1879	2	0	0		
3	Wignall	TQ	30/11/1878	30/11/1878	1	0	0		
4	James Marsh	FB	22/02/1879	01/11/1879	3	0	0		
N	Season 1879/80	Position	Debut	Last	Apps	Tries	Goals	Honours as a Lion	150
5	TED BESWICK	TQ	11/10/1879	20/11/1886	105	49	15	ERU2, NRU1, NERU1, LRU5(4t)	1882
6	Cowper	F	11/10/1879	11/10/1879	1	0	0		
7	Johnson	F	11/10/1879	11/10/1879	1	0	0		
8	BOB SEDDON	F	11/10/1879	18/04/1887	121	10	0	LRU3(2t)	1886
9	James Haworth	TQ	18/10/1879	15/11/1879	3	0	0		
0	Tom Hunter	F	18/10/1879	06/03/1880	6	2	0		
1	Neil Marr	F	18/10/1879	06/03/1880	6	4	0		
2	CHARLIE HORLEY	F	01/11/1879	08/04/1893	261	28	4	ERU1, NRU3(1t), LRU20(2t), NERU1	1885
3	Edward Seddon	F	01/11/1879	12/02/1881	18	1	0		
/a	three players unidentified	F	15/11/1879	n/a	3	0	0		
4	James Sutton	HB	20/12/1879	20/12/1879	1	0	0		
5	Fred Blackburn	F	20/12/1879	20/12/1879	1	0	0		
6	Billy Howarth	F	20/12/1879	26/02/1887	141	7	0		

HN	Name	Position	Debut	Last	Apps	Tries	Goals	Honours as a Lion	
137	Noah Jackson	F	10/01/1880	27/12/1880	20	0	0		
138	Tom Kneen	TQ	31/01/1880	31/01/1880	1	0	0		
139	Harry Hope	F	13/03/1880	01/11/1890	163	12	0		
140	Robert Hope	F	13/03/1880	02/10/1880	4	0	0		
141	J Ogden	TQ	20/03/1880	20/03/1880	1	0	0		
142	Smith	TQ	20/03/1880	20/03/1880	1	0	0		
HN	**Season 1880/81**	**Position**	**Debut**	**Last**	**Apps**	**Tries**	**Goals**	**Honours as a Lion**	
143	E James	TQ	02/10/1880	02/10/1880	1	0	0		
144	**BILLY COOKE**	**FB**	**09/10/1880**	**15/11/1890**	**123**	**0**	**116**	LRU1	
145	**WALTER BUMBY**	**HB**	**09/10/1880**	**30/03/1896**	**333**	**87**	**2**	T1888(23)(5t), NRU1, LRU23(1t)	
146	W Mason	HB	06/11/1880	06/11/1880	1	0	0		
147	**JOHN (JT) SEDDON**	**F**	**06/11/1880**	**23/03/1885**	**82**	**4**	**0**	LRU4(2t)	
148	Jim Cheetham	F	18/12/1880	08/04/1882	28	4	0		
149	Hugh Williamson	TQ	27/12/1880	27/12/1880	1	0	0		
150	G Meach	F	12/02/1881	02/04/1881	2	0	0		
151	James Kenyon	TQ	19/03/1881	20/11/1886	49	8	1		
152	Edward Kay	F	19/03/1881	14/11/1885	29	3	0		
153	Charles Simister	F	19/03/1881	25/03/1882	2	0	0		
154	**NATHAN HOTCHKISS**	**F**	**02/04/1881**	**06/04/1896**	**318**	**19**	**0**	LRU9	
155	L Howarth	F	02/04/1881	02/04/1881	1	0	0		
HN	**Season 1881/82**	**Position**	**Debut**	**Last**	**Apps**	**Tries**	**Goals**	**Honours as a Lion**	
156	**TOM BANKS**	**TQ/F**	**24/09/1881**	**14/03/1892**	**146**	**25**	**2**	T1888(7)(1t), LRU6(1t)	
157	J Bowring	F	24/09/1881	01/10/1881	2	1	0		
158	**WALTER DICKENSON**	**F**	**24/09/1881**	**14/11/1885**	**75**	**1**	**0**	LRU2	
159	H Worthington	TQ	24/09/1881	15/10/1881	4	0	0		
160	**JOE BAGSHAW**	**F**	**15/10/1881**	**23/04/1887**	**116**	**5**	**0**	LRU4	
161	C Ashton	TQ	22/10/1881	29/10/1881	2	0	1		
162	Sam Pollitt	F	29/10/1881	21/09/1889	170	13	0		
163	A Venables	F	31/12/1881	07/01/1882	2	0	0		
164	Archie Sutherland	HB	21/01/1882	08/04/1882	5	2	0		
HN	**Season 1882/83**	**Position**	**Debut**	**Last**	**Apps**	**Tries**	**Goals**	**Honours as a Lion**	
165	W Ellarby	F	11/11/1882	11/11/1882	1	0	0		
166	A C Smith	TQ	07/12/1882	21/04/1883	6	2	1		
HN	**Season 1883/84**	**Position**	**Debut**	**Last**	**Apps**	**Tries**	**Goals**	**Honours as a Lion**	
167	Harry Distin	F	20/10/1883	27/10/1883	2	0	0		
168	J Jones	F	20/10/1883	27/10/1883	2	0	0		
169	Roger Wilcock	F	15/12/1883	15/12/1883	1	0	0		
170/1	**JIM VALENTINE**	**TQ**	**05/01/1884**	**16/3/01**	**356**	**262**	**145**	ERU4(1g), NRU7(2g, 2t), LRU58(39g, 48t), ROERU2(1t)	
171	Charles Hopewell	TQ	12/01/1884	19/01/1884	2	1	0		
172	Squire Lindley	F	26/01/1884	16/04/1887	71	1	0		
HN	**Season 1884/85**	**Position**	**Debut**	**Last**	**Apps**	**Tries**	**Goals**	**Honours as a Lion**	
173	Jack Roberts	TQ	27/09/1884	27/09/1884	1	0	0		
174	William Smethills	F	04/10/1884	05/04/1886	7	0	0		
175	Fred Shaw	TQ	11/10/1884	17/10/1885	24	3	0		
176	William Marsh	F	15/11/1884	12/04/1890	104	3	4		
177	Walter Sherlock	TQ	29/11/1884	23/03/1885	10	0	0		
178	George Parr	TQ	31/01/1885	05/12/1885	2	1	0		
179	**TOM COULTHWAITE**	**F**	**21/02/1885**	**16/03/1889**	**82**	**15**	**0**	LRU1	
180	Fred Allen	F	21/03/1885	03/09/1892	12	0	0		
181	John Kenyon	F	25/04/1885	22/09/1888	25	1	0		
182	Tom Valentine	F	25/04/1885	25/04/1885	1	0	0		
HN	**Season 1885/86**	**Position**	**Debut**	**Last**	**Apps**	**Tries**	**Goals**	**Honours as a Lion**	
183	**JIMMY (JH) MURRAY**	**TQ**	**31/10/1885**	**31/03/1888**	**50**	**21**	**1**	LRU1(1t)	
184	J Crossley	F	14/11/1885	27/04/1886	4	0	0		
185	J Fielding	F	14/11/1885	14/11/1885	1	0	0		
186	Jack Scholes	F	21/11/1885	04/12/1886	10	0	0		
187	**SAM ROBERTS**	**FB**	**26/12/1885**	**13/02/1892**	**93**	**13**	**23**	ERU2, NRU1, LRU7(7g)	18
188	**JIMMY MARSH**	**TQ**	**26/12/1885**	**18/04/1896**	**103**	**21**	**10**	ERU1, SRU2, NRU2, LRU14(6t)	18
189	**TOM ROTHWELL**	**F**	**30/01/1886**	**17/03/1894**	**171**	**7**	**0**	LRU16(1t)	18
190	Walton	HB	05/04/1886	05/04/1886	1	0	0		
191	Arthur Harrison	F	05/04/1886	05/04/1886	1	0	0		
192	William Kinnish	F	05/04/1886	05/04/1886	1	0	0		
193	James (JH) Harris	F	27/04/1886	07/03/1887	4	0	0		
194	**TOM KENYON**	**F**	**27/04/1886**	**07/09/1889**	**84**	**2**	**1**	LRU1	
HN	**Season 1886/87**	**Position**	**Debut**	**Last**	**Apps**	**Tries**	**Goals**	**Honours as a Lion**	1
195	James Lord	TQ	20/11/1886	20/11/1886	1	0	0		
196	Cornelius Atkinson	HB	20/11/1886	19/02/1887	4	0	0		
197	Herbert Cooke	TQ	04/12/1886	06/12/1890	9	1	0		
198	**JOE BIRCH**	**F**	**04/12/1886**	**21/09/1889**	**52**	**3**	**0**	LRU1	
199	H Hughes	FB	28/12/1886	28/12/1886	1	0	0		
200	Munro	F	03/01/1887	03/01/1887	1	0	0		
n/a	*eight players unidentified*	*misc*	03/01/1887	*n/a*	8	0	0		
201	Jack Hurst	FB	22/01/1887	28/03/1887	10	0	0		
202	Tom Morris	TQ	29/01/1887	29/01/1887	1	0	0		
203	Jacob Sharples	TQ	29.01.1887	21/03/1891	14	0	0		
204	Charlie Buxton	TQ	19/02/1887	01/11/1890	30	8	1		
205	**TOM CLAYTON**	**F**	**05/03/1887**	**19/04/1890**	**93**	**10**	**0**	LRU1	
206	Tom Hardman	F	05/03/1887	11/04/1887	4	0	0		
207	A Smith	HB	07/03/1887	12/03/1887	2	0	0		
208	James Hope	FB	12/03/1887	16/04/1887	3	0	0		
209	John Buxton	TQ	12/03/1887	02/11/1889	8	0	0		

	Name	Position	Debut	Last	Apps	Tries	Goals	Honours as a Lion	150
	George Buxton	HB	12/03/1887	26/12/1892	92	16	0		
	William Sabin	TQ	26/03/1887	28/03/1887	2	0	0		
	Albert Le Peton	TQ	28/03/1887	28/03/1887	1	0	0		
	Percy Brookshaw	F	11/04/1887	30/04/1888	5	0	0		
	Jim Slevin	TQ	18/04/1887	18/04/1887	1	2	0		
	Vic Slater	TQ	18/04/1887	18/04/1887	1	1	0		
	Billings	HB	18/04/1887	18/04/1887	1	0	0		
	Harry Eagles	F	18/04/1887	18/04/1887	1	2	0		
	W Higham	F	23/04/1887	23/04/1887	1	0	0		
Season 1887/88		**Position**	**Debut**	**Last**	**Apps**	**Tries**	**Goals**	**Honours as a Lion**	**150**
	BOB (ROBERT LEVER) SEDDON	F	03/09/1887	11/02/1888	14	4	0	T1888(19)(1g, 3t), NRU2, LRU3	1888
	Fair Turner	F	17/09/1887	21/04/1888	3	0	0		
	ARTHUR PAUL	FB	01/10/1887	04/02/1893	113	1	96	T1888(29)(15g), LRU3(5g)	1889
	Ned Bullough	F	15/10/1887	06/09/1890	11	3	0		
	Ted Worsley	FB	22/10/1887	27/04/1889	10	0	0		
	E Critchley	F	24/12/1887	24/12/1887	1	0	0		
	Robert Whitehead	TQ	31/12/1887	28/01/1888	2	0	0		
	Samuel Walsh	HB	31/12/1887	10/02/1890	22	1	0		
	Tom Hallam	F	02/01/1888	05/12/1896	241	19	0		
	Alfred Barrett	HB	12/03/1888	12/03/1888	1	0	0		
	Anthony Bennett	F	12/03/1888	12/03/1888	1	0	0		
	D Evans	F	12/03/1888	12/03/1888	1	0	0		
	SAM HALL	F	12/03/1888	02/01/1897	157	8	0	LRU1	
	Michael Mannion	F	12/03/1888	10/02/1890	2	0	0		
	William Winterbottom	FB/TQ	17/03/1888	03/10/1896	163	34	1		
	William Walsh	F	02/04/1888	02/04/1888	1	0	0		
	Simeon Grundy	TQ	09/04/1888	09/04/1888	1	0	0		
	T Pendlebury	F	21/04/1888	21/04/1888	1	0	0		
Season 1888/89		**Position**	**Debut**	**Last**	**Apps**	**Tries**	**Goals**	**Honours as a Lion**	**150**
	Percy Robertson	F	29/09/1888	29/09/1888	1	0	0		
	William Walker	F	08/10/1888	25/04/1892	101	5	0		
	John Seddon	TQ	20/10/1888	08/12/1888	5	0	0		
	William Donaldson	TQ	20/10/1888	17/11/1888	3	1	0		
	HAROLD (GH) MURRAY	TQ/F	03/11/1888	29/02/1896	186	29	0	LRU9	1896
	James Russell	HB	03/11/1888	03/11/1888	1	1	0		
	Fred Plumpton	TQ	26/11/1888	26/11/1888	1	0	0		
	William Wynard	TQ	01/12/1888	01/01/1889	2	0	0		
	William Greenhalgh	FB	08/12/1888	01/11/1890	9	0	0		
	Harry Mowatt	TQ	08/12/1888	15/12/1888	2	0	0		
	"Smiler" Ihaimaira Karaka	HB	08/12/1888	08/12/1888	1	0	0		
	Wiri Nehua	F	08/12/1888	08/12/1888	1	0	0		
	A Taylor	F	08/12/1888	23/02/1889	4	0	0		
	George Ogden	TQ	26/12/1888	24/01/1891	3	0	0		
	Henderson	F	26/12/1888	26/12/1888	1	0	0		
	Howard	F	26/12/1888	26/12/1888	1	0	0		
	one player unidentified	F	26/12/1888	n/a	1	0	0		
	Joseph Warbrick	F	01/01/1889	01/01/1889	1	0	0		
Season 1889/90		**Position**	**Debut**	**Last**	**Apps**	**Tries**	**Goals**	**Honours as a Lion**	**150**
	James Clarke	TQ	07/09/1889	07/09/1889	1	1	0		
	Alf Sharples	F	07/09/1889	16/04/1894	134	4	1		
	George Battersby	TQ	07/09/1889	28/09/1889	3	1	1		
	FRED LOMAX	F	28/09/1889	22/09/1894	112	4	0	LRU3	
	Henry Bailey	TQ	26/10/1889	26/10/1889	1	0	0		
	Arthur (AW) Smith	TQ	26/10/1889	22/03/1890	10	0	0		
	J Heywood	TQ	02/11/1889	02/11/1889	1	0	0		
	Arthur Chambers	F	02/11/1889	02/11/1889	1	0	0		
	J Sackfield	F	02/11/1889	01/11/1890	5	0	0		
	Matthew Wilson	TQ	09/11/1889	09/11/1889	1	0	0		
	Tom Okell	TQ	28/12/1889	22/03/1890	7	0	1		
	George Astall	F	11/01/1890	18/10/1890	24	1	0		
	Alfred Holker	F	11/01/1890	01/03/1890	3	1	0		
	Tom Nicholas	F	20/01/1890	10/02/1890	4	2	0		
	Walter Evans	F	25/01/1890	07/11/1896	196	1	0		
	Yates	F	25/01/1890	25/01/1890	1	0	0		
	Tom Bradburn	FB	15/02/1890	15/02/1890	1	0	0		
	Arthur Marsden	HB	22/02/1890	12/04/1890	2	0	0		
	James Atkinson	F	01/03/1890	01/03/1890	1	0	0		
	Joe Hotchkiss	F	01/03/1890	05/04/1894	22	2	0		
	Tom (JT) Haslam	FB	22/03/1890	25/04/1892	7	1	3		
	Peter Entwistle	TQ	22/03/1890	14/04/1894	4	0	0		
Season 1890/91		**Position**	**Debut**	**Last**	**Apps**	**Tries**	**Goals**	**Honours as a Lion**	**150**
	Roger Holroyd	F	06/09/1890	24/10/1891	6	0	0		
	James (JW) Roberts	F	06/09/1890	06/09/1890	1	1	0		
	GEORGE SHARPLES	F	04/10/1890	22/04/1895	161	6	3	LRU4	
	D Edge	TQ	01/11/1890	08/11/1890	2	0	0		
	Frank Green	TQ	15/11/1890	21/03/1891	17	2	1		
	William Baldwin	TQ	22/11/1890	27/12/1890	4	1	0		
	Charles Wardley	FB	06/12/1890	06/12/1890	1	0	0		
	Tom Coop	FB	10/12/1890	27/03/1894	2	0	1		
	Ashton	F	13/12/1890	13/12/1890	1	1	0		
	HERBIE BROCKBANK	HB	27/12/1890	16/04/1895	142	11	17	LRU3	1893

286	Paul Chapman	F	27/12/1890	11/02/1893	21	3	0		
287	Harrison	F	27/12/1890	27/12/1890	1	0	0		
288	Layfield	F	27/12/1890	27/12/1890	1	0	0		
289	Herbert Parkinson	F	27/12/1890	23/01/1892	3	0	0		
290	Robson	F	27/12/1890	27/12/1890	1	0	0		
291	John Randle	F	01/01/1891	01/01/1891	1	0	0		
292	C Jones	F	03/01/1891	10/01/1891	2	0	0		
n/a	*one player unidentified*	*F*	*03/01/1891*	*n/a*	*1*	*0*	*0*		
293	T Smith	F	10/01/1891	10/01/1891	1	0	0		
294	Jake (JT) Harris	HB	24/01/1891	16/04/1895	55	4	0		
295	W Sharples	F	24/01/1891	24/01/1891	1	0	0		
296/6	**BILLY PEARSON**	**TQ/HB**	**07/02/1891**	**18/11/1899**	**197**	**70**	**23**	**LRU3(1t)**	
297	B Powell	F	14/02/1891	04/04/1891	4	1	0		
298	Frank Miles	TQ	21/03/1891	21/3/91	1	0	0		
299	Tom Kent	F	23/04/1891	28/04/1891	2	2	0		
300	J Williams	FB	28/04/1891	12/04/1893	2	0	0		

HN	Season 1891/92	Position	Debut	Last	Apps	Tries	Goals	Honours as a Lion	
301	William Gill	F	14/11/1891	28/11/1891	2	0	0		
302	George Simpson	TQ	21/11/1891	20/02/1892	4	2	0		
303	Arthur Walsh	F	23/01/1892	02/10/1893	5	0	0		
304/7	**JACK LEWIS**	**TQ**	**27/02/1892**	**26/12/04**	**121**	**37**	**1**	**LRU5(2t)**	
305	Fred Ashton	TQ	12/03/1892	18/02/1893	4	2	0		

HN	Season 1892/93	Position	Debut	Last	Apps	Tries	Goals	Honours as a Lion	
306	Wilson	TQ	03/09/1892	03/09/1892	1	2	2		
307	John Rawlinson	TQ	14/01/1893	11/02/1893	4	2	0		
308	F James	F	23/01/1893	08/04/1895	5	0	0		
309/8	**JACK JOHNSON**	**F**	**25/02/1893**	**7/3/00**	**42**	**0**	**0**	**LRU1**	
310	George Hibbert	TQ	04/03/1893	04/03/1893	1	0	0		
311	Tom Sudlow	TQ	11/03/1893	15/03/1893	2	1	0		
312	Percy Lomax	TQ	25/03/1893	25/03/1893	1	0	0		
313	**FRED JONES**	**TQ**	**01/04/1893**	**17/12/1894**	**32**	**19**	**0**	**CHRU1**	
314	J Uttley	TQ	12/04/1893	12/04/1893	1	0	0		
315	J Hancock	F	12/04/1893	12/04/1893	1	0	0		
316/9	**JOHNNY GOODMAN**	**TQ**	**24/04/1893**	**19/2/01**	**1**	**1**	**0**		
317	James Gadd	TQ	29/04/1893	03/03/1894	3	0	0		
318	Arthur Ward	TQ	29/04/1893	29/04/1893	1	0	0		

HN	Season 1893/94	Position	Debut	Last	Apps	Tries	Goals	Honours as a Lion	
319	Richard Hosker	HB	02/09/1893	10/02/1894	25	2	0		
320	**HERBERT CASE**	**F**	**02/09/1893**	**15/09/1894**	**18**	**1**	**0**	**NRU1, LRU6**	
321	Andrew Knowles	F	02/09/1893	27/01/1894	15	1	0		
322	Frank Knowles	F	02/09/1893	11/04/1896	102	3	0		
323	James Stephens	FB	04/11/1893	05/01/1895	17	5	0		
324	John Berry	FB	23/12/1893	04/04/1896	45	0	0		
325	Charles Bowker	FB	25.12.1893	17/03/1894	3	1	0		
326/10	Bob Berry	F	01/01/1894	26/9/03	33	0	0		
327	Joe Berry	F	01/01/1894	19/04/1894	14	1	0		
328	George Hiley	F	27/01/1894	27/01/1894	1	0	0		
329	A Barratt	TQ	28/02/1894	19/04/1894	4	2	0		
330	W Berry	F	28/02/1894	08/04/1895	2	0	0		
331	George Berry	TQ	24/03/1894	02/03/1895	11	4	0		
332	James Beattie	F	24/03/1894	07/11/1894	15	0	0		
333	Tom Cleminson	F	27/03/1894	27/04/1895	50	3	1		
334	Robert Medley	F	27/03/1894	27/03/1894	1	1	0		
335	William Parlane	HB	05/04/1894	05/04/1894	1	0	0		
336	James Rangeley	F	05/04/1894	05/04/1894	1	0	0		
337	J Lawton	TQ	07/04/1894	07/04/1894	1	0	0		
338	James Seddon	FB	16/04/1894	12/09/1894	2	0	0		
339	Arthur Cooper	F	16/04/1894	16/04/1894	1	0	0		
340	Richard Buckley	F	19/04/1894	02/01/1895	8	0	0		
341/11	George Harris	F	19/04/1894	9/11/01	61	3	0		
342/12	**BOB TICKLE**	**F**	**19/04/1894**	**29/4/05**	**62**	**3**	**0**	**LRU1**	19

HN	Season 1894/95	Position	Debut	Last	Apps	Tries	Goals	Honours as a Lion	1
343	**GEORGE COOKSON**	**HB**	**08/09/1894**	**18/04/1896**	**41**	**4**	**0**	**LRU2(1t)**	
344	Walter Barrington	F	08/09/1894	22/04/1895	29	1	0		
345	Charles Crews	FB	12/09/1894	01/12/1894	15	0	0		
346	J Cooper	HB	12/09/1894	15/09/1894	2	0	0		
347	Richard Sharrocks	TQ	15/09/1894	15/09/1894	1	0	0		
348	E J Harvey	HB	15/09/1894	20/10/1894	3	0	0		
349/13	Henry Close	TQ	03/11/1894	03/10/1896	5	1	1		
350	John Tyldesley	TQ	10/11/1894	27/04/1895	24	3	0		
351	John Nowell	F	25/12/1894	25/12/1894	1	0	0		
352	Moses Hully	TQ	02/01/1895	07/03/1896	6	1	0		
353	Charles (CR) Jackson	F	02/01/1895	08/04/1895	2	0	0		
354/14	William Spruce	F	01/04/1895	24/10/1896	26	1	0		
355	**JACK SUNDERLAND**	**TQ**	**06/04/1895**	**18/04/1896**	**39**	**16**	**0**	**LRU1**	
356	J H Kelly	F	27/04/1895	09/11/1895	3	0	0		

HN	Season 1895/96	Position	Debut	Last	Apps	Tries	Goals	Honours as a Lion	19
357	Harold Ashton	TQ	21/09/1895	26/02/1896	10	1	1		
358	W Jackson	F	21/09/1895	14/12/1895	5	0	0		
359	**WILLIAM LANCASTER**	**F**	**21/09/1895**	**18/04/1896**	**30**	**2**	**0**	**LRU3**	
360/15	Percy Greenhalgh	F	28/09/1895	17/12/1898	31	4	0		

RUGBY UNION ERA

									150
16	William Kilner	F	19/10/1895	14/11/1896	29	4	0		
2	Dan Ashton	TQ	02/11/1895	08/02/1896	9	1	0		
3	James Parkinson	HB	02/11/1895	02/11/1895	1	0	0		
4	J Andrews	TQ	09/11/1895	15/04/1896	8	3	3		
5	John Harrell	TQ	16/11/1895	30/03/1896	20	0	1		
6	John Spinks	TQ	14/12/1895	26/02/1896	3	1	0		
7	TOM BLACKLOCK	F	26/12/1895	03/04/1896	13	0	0	CRU?	
8	GEORGE STEELE	F	26/12/1895	29/02/1896	10	1	0	CRU?	
9	James Sidebottom	HB	02/01/1896	21/03/1896	8	0	0		
0	A Smith	FB	02/01/1896	06/04/1896	4	1	0		
1	S Spence	F	02/01/1896	15/02/1896	2	0	0		
17	Ralph Makin	FB	04/01/1896	21/09/1896	6	0	0		
3	William Lazonby	F	08/02/1896	08/02/1896	1	0	0		
18	BOB VALENTINE	TQ	26/02/1896	24/2/08	3	0	0		1902
5	Ernest Taylor	F	26/02/1896	26/02/1896	1	0	0		
19	Frank Ainsworth	F	21/03/1896	26/11/1898	6	0	0		
7	John Rothwell	QF	28/03/1896	28/03/1896	1	0	0		

RUGBY LEAGUE ERA

N	Debut under Union era	Position	Debut	Last	Apps	Tries	Goals	Honours as a Lion	150
70	JIM VALENTINE	TQ/F	05/01/1884	16/3/01	130	39	57	L5(2g, 2t), RNU1	1900
27	Tom Hallam	F	02/01/1888	05/12/1896	2	0	0		
231	SAM HALL	F	12/03/1888	02/01/1897	15	0	0		
233	William Winterbottom	FB	17/03/1888	03/10/1896	1	0	0		
268	Walter Evans	F	25/01/1890	07/11/1896	10	0	0		
296	BILLY PEARSON	HB	07/02/1891	18/11/1896	75	10	6	L1, RNU1	1898
304	JACK LEWIS	W	27/02/1892	26/12/04	152	76	0		1901
309	JACK JOHNSON	F	25/02/1893	7/3/00	80	1	0	L4, RNU1	
316	JOHNNY GOODMAN	FB	24/04/1893	19/2/01	97	4	22	WE1	
326	Bob Berry	F	01/01/1894	26/9/03	55	0	0		
341	George Harris	F	19/04/1894	9/11/01	124	1	0		
342	BOB TICKLE	F	19/04/1894	29/4/05	190	2	0		1905
349	Henry Close	HB	03/11/1894	03/10/1896	1	0	0		
354	William Spruce	F	01/04/1895	24/10/1896	1	0	0		
360	Percy Greenhalgh	F	28/09/1895	17/12/1898	51	0	0		
361	William Kilner	F	19/10/1895	14/11/1896	10	0	0		
372	Ralph Makin	FB	04/01/1896	21/09/1896	4	0	0		
374	BOB VALENTINE	C	26/02/1896	25/4/03	95	36	10	L5(3g, 2t)	1902
	second spell	C	24/2/08	24/2/08	1	0	0		
376	Frank Ainsworth	F	21/03/1896	26/11/1899	24	1	0		

HN	Season 1896/97	Position	Debut	Last	Apps	Tries	Goals	Honours as a Lion	150
20	William Butler	C	05/09/1896	05/09/1896	1	0	0		
21	Frank Atherton	W	05/09/1896	13/03/1897	12	2	0		
22	William Hanson	HB	05/09/1896	05/12/1896	12	0	0		
23	Stephen Norton	F	05/09/1896	26/12/1896	11	0	0		
24	Stanley Ashworth	F	21/09/1896	21/09/1896	1	0	0		
25	John Leather	FB	26/09/1896	26/09/1896	1	0	0		
26	Phillip Wilkinson	FB	10/10/1896	10/10/1896	1	0	0		
27	Fred Crocker	C	24/10/1896	18/09/1897	26	4	0		
28	George Evans	HB	07/11/1896	07/11/1896	1	0	0		
29	John Sharples	F	07/11/1896	19/02/1899	10	0	0		
30	BOBBY MESSER	C	14/11/1896	27/9/02	144	48	12	L1, RNU1	1897
31	John Fearnley	HB	14/11/1896	05/12/1896	3	0	0		
32	Mansel Owen	F	14/11/1896	31/12/1898	47	2	0		
33	John Walker	F	28/11/1896	02/01/1897	7	0	0		
34	Fred Yeoman	F	28/11/1896	18/12/1897	26	0	0		
35	Fred Edwards	HB	12/12/1896	06/03/1897	6	1	0		
36	JOEY MORGAN	HB	12/12/1896	4/2/05	195	25	13	L1	1908
	second spell	HB	2/1/08	8/2/08	4	0	0		
37	CHARLIE POLLITT	F	12/12/1896	26/3/04	126	4	0	L2	
38	John Worthington	F	12/12/1896	16/09/1899	66	2	0		
39	Jim Shepherd	F	01/01/1897	10/12/1898	39	1	0		
40	Henry Todd	F	06/03/1897	06/03/1897	1	0	0		

HN	Season 1897/98	Position	Debut	Last	Apps	Tries	Goals	Honours as a Lion	150
41	Morgan Bevan	W	11/09/1897	25/02/1899	34	28	9		
42	Jack Selway	HB	23/10/1897	16/04/1898	16	3	0		
43	JACK EVANS (snr)	F	23/10/1897	13/10/06	251	28	33	L9(1t), RNU2(1t)	1903
44	OWEN BADGER	C	04/12/1897	05/04/1902	28	6	19	L1	
45	Jim Brooksbank	F	11/12/1897	11/12/1897	1	0	0		
46	William Davies	C	08/01/1898	08/01/1898	1	0	0		
47	JACK PRESTON	F	26/02/1898	26/3/04	142	6	75	L2	1910
	second spell	F	25/1/08	1/1/10	39	6	20		
48	Stanley Whittingham	FB	12/03/1898	12/03/1898	1	0	0		

HN	Season 1898/99	Position	Debut	Last	Apps	Tries	Goals	Honours as a Lion	150
49	Jim Reynolds	F	03/09/1898	27/1/00	26	1	0		
50	EVAN VIGORS	F	03/09/1898	1/4/07	125	7	0	L4	
51	Arthur Allen	HB	26/11/1898	28/01/1899	5	0	0		
52	VERNON HAMPSON	W	10/12/1898	30/4/04	145	64	8	L2(1t)	1899
	second spell	W	2/1/09	25/9/09	13	6	0		
	third spell	W	30/11/12	25/1/13	2	0	0		

HN	Name	Position	Debut	Last	Apps	Tries	Goals	Honours as a Lion	
53	Jim Thomas	F	17/12/1898	05/04/1899	2	0	0		
54	Charles Holmes	F	24/12/1898	15/9/00	37	2	0		
55	Jim Vickers	F	24/12/1898	18/03/1899	11	0	0		
56	Dick (GR) Jones	F	28/01/1899	11/3/05	78	0	0		
57	Arthur Ward	F	28/01/1899	05/04/1899	6	0	0		
58	Harry Wilson	F	28/01/1899	16/09/1899	11	0	0		
59	Alf Chorley	FB	11/02/1899	23/5/05	134	4	6		
60	**DAI DAVIES**	HB	03/04/1899	12/4/02	87	15	0	L3(1t), RNU1	
	second spell	HB	25/12/09	8/3/13	83	15	2	W1	
HN	**Season 1899/00**	**Position**	**Debut**	**Last**	**Apps**	**Tries**	**Goals**	**Honours as a Lion**	
61	Ben Murphy	F	06/09/1899	21/12/01	44	1	0		
62	Joe Taylor	TQ	06/09/1899	24/10/03	22	2	0		
63	Tom Pomfret	F	27/1/00	10/4/09	241	9	0		
64	Jack Watson	F	17/2/00	17/2/00	1	0	0		
65	Charles Worthington	FB	17/2/00	17/2/00	1	0	0		
66	Arthur Williamson	HB	17/3/00	27/10/06	51	4	0		
HN	**Season 1900/01**	**Position**	**Debut**	**Last**	**Apps**	**Tries**	**Goals**	**Honours as a Lion**	
67	Lawrence Clewes	F	27/10/00	27/10/00	1	0	0		
68	**BILLY WALLWORK**	TQ	14/11/00	10/4/11	273	79	30	L1	
69	Robert Eckersley	C	17/11/00	17/11/00	1	0	0		
70	John Blackburn	F	26/1/01	12/4/02	24	0	0		
71	Arthur Long	F	26/1/01	26/1/01	1	0	0		
72	Joe (J H) Cooper	W	9/2/01	10/10/03	46	27	0		
	second spell	W	11/2/05	11/2/05	1	0	0		
73	George (GH) Jones	W	16/3/01	28/9/01	5	1	0		
	second spell	W	16/4/06	2/1/08	43	10	9		
HN	**Season 1901/02**	**Position**	**Debut**	**Last**	**Apps**	**Tries**	**Goals**	**Honours as a Lion**	
74	**WALTER CHEETHAM**	F	2/9/01	1/12/06	161	7	0	L5	
75	**HARRY BARNETT**	W/F	14/9/01	10/4/11	273	47	2	L1	1
76	Fred Jackson (aka Jack Jones)	F	23/9/01	5/4/02	15	1	0		
77	David Traynor	C	28/9/01	16/3/04	12	0	2		
78	Lawrence Critch	HB	12/10/01	16/3/07	43	6	0		
79	Edward Yates	F	11/1/02	27/1/06	89	1	0		
80	Albert Valentine	C	3/3/02	17/2/12	163	33	5		
HN	**Season 1902/03**	**Position**	**Debut**	**Last**	**Apps**	**Tries**	**Goals**	**Honours as a Lion**	
81	Tom Samuel	HB	6/9/02	18/2/03	14	0	0		
82	William Yates	F	1/11/02	22/11/03	2	0	0		
83	Billy Dixon	FB	31/1/03	5/1/07	119	9	12		
84	Tom Oldfield	W	31/1/03	13/4/07	33	4	2		
85	Tom Hall	F	31/1/03	25/4/03	15	0	0		
86	Nicholas Fitzpatrick	F	4/4/03	11/4/03	2	0	0		
87	William Lowe	F	4/4/03	4/4/03	1	0	0		
HN	**Season 1903/04**	**Position**	**Debut**	**Last**	**Apps**	**Tries**	**Goals**	**Honours as a Lion**	
88	Denny Ryan	HB	5/9/03	24/10/03	4	0	0		
89	Jim Burrows	F	5/9/03	11/2/05	41	3	0		
90	Tom Ramsay	F	5/9/03	19/9/03	3	0	0		
91	Ben Booth	HB	12/9/03	12/9/03	1	0	0		
92	**BILLY SIMISTER**	F	26/9/03	24/9/10	215	23	0	L1	19
93	Jim Coletrup	F	3/10/03	3/4/09	80	1	0		
94	William Unsworth	HB	10/10/03	17/10/03	2	0	0		
95	Tom Burriss	W	17/10/03	2/9/05	2	0	0		
96	Richard Greenwood	W	21/11/03	21/11/03	1	0	0		
97	Arthur Booth	HB	21/11/03	20/4/07	69	13	2		
98	**TOMMY GARTRELL**	W/F	28/11/03	29/9/06	59	12	2	C1	19
	second spell	W/F	21/9/08	4/10/13	161	30	0		
99	Martin Burrows	TQ	28/11/03	20/2/04	11	0	0		
100	**JIMMY MOLYNEUX**	HB	12/12/03	27/1/06	44	1	7	CH2(1g)	
101	Joe Cooper	F	2/4/04	25/2/05	16	0	0		
102	Harry Jones	F	2/4/04	30/4/04	6	0	0		
103	John Brimley	FB	11/4/04	11/4/04	1	0	0		
104	William Griffin	TQ	11/4/04	23/1/09	56	13	0		
105	Billy Lloyd	F	23/4/04	10/4/09	143	10	0		
106	Fred Steele	F	30/4/04	7/1/05	6	0	0		
HN	**Season 1904/05**	**Position**	**Debut**	**Last**	**Apps**	**Tries**	**Goals**	**Honours as a Lion**	15
107	**JACK FLYNN**	B	3/9/04	21/4/06	61	4	21	C6	19
	second spell	B	28/1/11	18/10/13	18	3	0		
108	Jack Kewin	HB	3/9/04	21/11/08	49	3	1		
109	John Massey	F	12/11/04	15/9/06	9	3	0		
110	Charles Platt	F	14/1/05	14/1/05	1	0	0		
111	Harry Chadderton	C	4/2/05	16/12/06	6	0	1		
112	Robert Jones	F	4/2/05	18/3/05	8	0	0		
113	William Larkin	F	25/2/05	9/9/05	8	0	0		
114	Alf Morgan	TQ	8/3/05	17/12/10	35	3	0		
HN	**Season 1905/06**	**Position**	**Debut**	**Last**	**Apps**	**Tries**	**Goals**	**Honours as a Lion**	15
115	Tom Crowther	F	2/9/05	2/9/05	1	0	0		
116	Tom Abbott	W	7/10/05	11/11/05	4	1	0		
117	Herbert Williams	HB	7/10/05	7/10/05	1	0	0		
118	Edgar Hobson	F	28/10/05	5/10/07	56	2	9		
119	Enoch Blakeley	C	11/11/05	26/11/06	24	9	0		
120	**DAN DAVIES**	F	11/11/05	29/3/13	201	14	0	ONI1, L1	190
121	Charlie Woods	FB	18/11/05	9/1/09	16	0	19		

#	Name	Position	Debut	Last	Apps	Tries	Goals	Honours as a Lion	150
	Jim Maxwell	W	7/4/06	7/4/06	1	0	0		
	Season 1906/07	**Position**	**Debut**	**Last**	**Apps**	**Tries**	**Goals**	**Honours as a Lion**	**150**
	Charles Garside	HB	1/9/06	2/1/07	8	0	0		
	George Beach	W	13/10/06	8/12/06	3	0	0		
	Paul Bradley	W	10/11/06	26/11/06	3	0	0		
	George Cowell	HB	24/11/06	12/10/07	22	3	0		
	Will Preston	F	15/12/06	24/3/13	146	3	21		
	George Taylor	F	15/12/06	1/1/09	35	1	0		
	Llewellyn Thomas	W	1/1/07	23/2/07	10	2	0		
	Jack Fielding	FB	12/1/07	18/1/08	19	0	1		
	David Barlow	W	9/2/07	9/2/07	1	0	0		
	unofficial war-time spell	*W*	*17/11/17*	*17/11/17*	*1*	*0*	*0*		
	Sam Jones	W	20/4/07	20/4/07	1	0	0		1941
	Jim Groves	F	20/4/07	20/4/07	1	0	0		
	Season 1907/08	**Position**	**Debut**	**Last**	**Apps**	**Tries**	**Goals**	**Honours as a Lion**	**150**
	Richard Townson	FB	7/9/07	10/4/09	59	0	5		
	Tom Green	W	7/9/07	5/10/07	4	1	0		
	Tom Ford	C/HB	7/9/07	24/10/08	4	0	0		
	Lawrence Walsh	C	12/9/07	18/1/08	15	0	0		
	Harry Smith	F	12/9/07	12/10/07	6	0	0		
	James Barnes	F	21/9/07	21/9/07	1	0	0		
	Frank Daniels	F	21/9/07	2/1/08	3	0	0		
	Jim Downing	HB	5/10/07	7/12/07	7	0	0		
	Jack Rowley	F	5/10/07	27/12/20	15	1	0		
	unofficial war-time spell	*F*	*2/10/15*	*1/1/19*	*65*	*7*	*0*		
	Jim (JH) Smith	W	2/11/07	14/12/07	7	0	0		
	John Cunningham	HB	2/11/07	14/3/08	14	0	0		
	Harry Hopwood	FB/C	16/11/07	2/1/09	11	1	0		
	Alf Stephens	HB	21/12/07	26/9/08	14	3	0		
	Tom Rickers	F	2/1/08	7/11/08	11	0	0		
	Jim Wharton	W/HB	25/1/08	30/4/10	76	19	0		
	Tom Williams	C	1/4/08	10/9/08	3	0	0		
	Ebenezer Luckman	W	11/4/08	11/4/08	1	0	0		
	Season 1908/09	**Position**	**Debut**	**Last**	**Apps**	**Tries**	**Goals**	**Honours as a Lion**	**150**
	Sam Wallace	C	5/9/08	10/9/08	2	1	0		
	Jim Fairhurst	HB	5/9/08	8/3/13	84	26	8		
	unofficial war-time spell	*HB*	*15/12/17*	*1/1/18*	*3*	*2*	*1*		
	Richard Jones	HB	5/9/08	14/9/12	53	2	34		
	JACK BAILEY	**F**	**5/9/08**	**21/1/22**	**173**	**28**	**0**	L2(2t), TT1	1914
	unofficial war-time spell	*F*	*9/9/16*	*9/9/16*	*1*	*0*	*0*		
	Joe Vickers	F	5/9/08	16/1/09	13	0	0		
	Ellis Travis	F	21/9/08	21/9/08	1	0	0		
	Gordon Greatorex	F	10/10/08	2/10/09	3	0	0		
	Eric Young	C	31/10/08	23/1/11	58	5	0		
	Sam Morton	W	14/11/08	14/11/08	1	0	0		
	JIM POLLITT	**F**	**12/12/08**	**12/3/21**	**146**	**4**	**0**		
	unofficial war-time spell	*F*	*11/9/15*	*18/11/16*	*22*	*1*	*0*	*LL1*	
	Jack (JD) Wharton	C/HB	26/12/08	14/11/14	102	17	2		
	unofficial war-time spell	*C/HB*	*01/04/18*	*01/04/18*	*1*	*0*	*0*		
	John Byrne	F	26/12/08	2/1/09	3	0	0		
	Simon Hopkins	F	2/1/09	2/1/09	1	0	0		
	Tom Elwell	HB	16/1/09	16/1/09	1	0	0		
	William Kidd	C	30/1/09	13/2/09	2	1	0		
	Herbert Davies	W	6/2/09	18/2/11	47	19	6		
	William Hillen	FB	20/3/09	10/4/09	3	0	0		
	Harry Lythgoe	W	3/4/09	3/4/09	1	0	0		
	Season 1909/10	**Position**	**Debut**	**Last**	**Apps**	**Tries**	**Goals**	**Honours as a Lion**	**150**
	Gordon Thomas	FB	4/9/09	14/2/10	11	0	0		
	Jack Parker	C	4/9/09	25/1/13	92	14	3		
	Tom Neen	F	4/9/09	3/9/10	27	1	0		
	Dick Cullis	F	18/9/09	3/2/23	156	7	0		
	Robert Johnson	FB	25/9/09	15/2/13	41	0	6		
	unofficial war-time spell	*FB*	*17/03/17*	*17/03/17*	*1*	*0*	*0*		
	Elijah Williams	W	6/11/09	4/12/09	3	1	0		
	Albert Morris	W	11/12/09	22/3/13	77	21	31		
	Albert Jonas	F	18/12/09	30/4/10	9	0	0		
	Fred Riley	FB	1/1/10	3/10/10	2	0	0		
	Morgan Evans	C	15/1/10	7/10/11	16	3	0		
	Jim Blears	F	25/3/10	17/4/15	113	4	0		
	JIM (JE) "NOBBY" SMITH	**F**	**26/3/10**	**5/11/21**	**144**	**6**	**1**		
	unofficial war-time spell	*F*	*25/12/16*	*11/1/19*	*22*	*2*	*0*	*LL1*	
	Robert Flinn	F	2/4/10	2/4/10	1	0	0		
	Season 1910/11	**Position**	**Debut**	**Last**	**Apps**	**Tries**	**Goals**	**Honours as a Lion**	**150**
	Tom McVeigh	F	17/9/10	17/5/19	95	3	1		
	DAVID (DB) DAVIES	**F**	**1/10/10**	**30/12/11**	**37**	**8**	**0**	W3(1t)	
	Edward Griffiths	FB	15/10/10	24/2/12	46	0	59		
	Chris Randall	F	10/12/10	7/9/12	24	0	0		
	Fred Howard	W	10/4/11	21/10/11	7	2	0		
	Joe Bamford	W	18/4/11	10/2/12	7	3	0		
	unofficial war-time spell	*W*	*01/01/19*	*01/01/19*	*1*	*0*	*0*		

HN	Season 1911/12	Position	Debut	Last	Apps	Tries	Goals	Honours as a Lion	
188	Tom (TJ) Williams	C	2/9/11	23/9/11	3	0	0		
189	**DICK PRICE**	F	2/9/11	29/11/19	126	9	0	L2(1t)	
	unofficial war-time spell	*F*	*4/9/15*	*11/1/19*	*67*	*5*	*0*	*LL1*	
190	**JIMMY DAWSON**	C	14/10/11	1/11/24	187	31	26	L1	
	unofficial war-time spell	*C*	*4/9/15*	*26/12/18*	*63*	*13*	*6*	*LL1*	
191	Peter Frodsham	FB	1/11/11	21/4/19	75	0	1		
192	William Price	F	1/11/11	4/11/11	2	0	0		
193	Walter Sharples	F	1/11/11	9/4/21	117	6	0		
	unofficial war-time spell	*F*	*4/9/15*	*1/4/18*	*47*	*3*	*0*		
194	Jim Miller	W	4/11/11	4/11/11	1	0	0		
195	**TOM ANDERSON**	HB	11/11/11	27/11/20	102	11	14	TT1	
	unofficial war-time spell	*HB*	*4/9/15*	*26/12/18*	*35*	*6*	*10*		
196	Frank Markland	F	18/11/11	20/3/15	5	0	0		
	unofficial war-time spell	*F*	*4/9/15*	*4/11/16*	*23*	*1*	*0*		
197	**MATT RYDER**	FB/C	9/12/11	27/8/21	170	11	167	L2(3g)	2
	unofficial war-time spell	*FB/C*	*25/9/15*	*3/3/17*	*46*	*2*	*40*	*LL1*	
198	Fred Anderson	W	2/3/12	31/3/14	21	6	0		
HN	Season 1912/13	Position	Debut	Last	Apps	Tries	Goals	Honours as a Lion	
199	John Brookes	W	7/9/12	9/11/12	8	0	0		
200	**FRANK MOORES**	W	7/9/12	25/12/19	84	39	2	L2	2
	unofficial war-time spell	*W*	*28/4/17*	*28/4/17*	*1*	*0*	*0*		
201	William Bibby	W	16/11/12	18/1/13	7	2	0		
202	William Holland	W/HB	14/12/12	30/1/15	27	2	0		
203	Joe Hackett	HB	14/12/12	6/12/13	4	0	0		
204	Jim Grice	W	8/2/13	1/10/21	50	4	0		
	unofficial war-time spell	*W*	*21/4/17*	*21/4/17*	*1*	*0*	*0*		
205	Tom Wharton	W/HB	29/3/13	19/4/13	5	2	0		
206	Ernie Stephenson	W	29/3/13	19/4/13	4	0	0		
207	George Crabtree	FB	5/4/13	13/12/13	9	0	0		2
208	Tom Riley	F	5/4/13	16/4/13	3	0	0		
HN	Season 1913/14	Position	Debut	Last	Apps	Tries	Goals	Honours as a Lion	
209	Billy Leah	C	6/9/13	4/1/15	44	5	3		
210	Peter Heaton	HK	27/9/13	2/4/15	29	2	0		
	unofficial war-time spell	*HK*	*4/9/15*	*2/10/15*	*4*	*1*	*0*		
211	Harold Whitehead	TQ	1/11/13	4/10/19	11	2	1		
	unofficial war-time spell	*TQ*	*2/11/18*	*2/11/18*	*1*	*0*	*0*		
212	Jack Daley	F	22/11/13	13/3/15	33	1	0		1?
213	**HARRY WORSLEY**	F	22/11/13	18/10/24	201	20	1	L3	
	unofficial war-time spell	*F*	*11/9/15*	*16/3/18*	*13*	*2*	*0*	*LL1*	
214	Jack Winstanley	W	13/12/13	1/2/19	7	0	0		
	unofficial war-time spell	*W*	*4/9/15*	*11/1/19*	*84*	*24*	*1*		
215	Jim Irish	HB	27/12/13	17/5/19	6	0	0		
HN	Season 1914/15	Position	Debut	Last	Apps	Tries	Goals	Honours as a Lion	1
216	Tom Kilgariff	HB	12/9/14	5/12/14	10	3	0		
	unofficial war-time spell	*HB*	*4/3/16*	*28/4/17*	*18*	*3*	*0*		
217	Horace Boardman	W	3/10/14	18/9/20	53	9	0		
	unofficial war-time spell	*W*	*4/9/15*	*16/3/18*	*40*	*4*	*0*		
218	Jimmy Mee	F	26/12/14	25/10/19	20	0	0		
	unofficial war-time spell	*F*	*4/9/15*	*11/1/19*	*51*	*8*	*0*		
219	**JACK HOLDEN**	F	4/1/15	21/4/19	10	0	0		
	unofficial war-time spell	*F*	*4/9/15*	*27/4/18*	*55*	*4*	*0*	*LL1*	
220	John Blackledge	FB/W	16/1/15	16/1/15	1	0	0		
	unofficial war-time spell	*FB/W*	*4/9/15*	*25/3/16*	*4*	*0*	*0*		
221	Frank Raynor	W	23/1/15	9/4/21	38	10	0		
222	Jack Dean	C	6/2/15	15/2/19	12	3	2		
	unofficial war-time spell	*C*	*2/10/15*	*26/1/18*	*55*	*6*	*0*		
223	Harry Crudden	F	20/2/15	27/2/15	2	0	0		
	unofficial war-time spell	*F*	*23/9/16*	*27/4/18*	*12*	*0*	*0*		
	War Years (unofficial)								
HN	Season 1915-16	Position	Debut	Last	Apps	Tries	Goals	Honours as a Lion	1?
W	*Peter Evans*	*F*	*4/9/15*	*1/4/18*	*21*	*2*	*0*		
W	*Herbert Jackson*	*F*	*12/2/16*	*19/2/16*	*2*	*0*	*0*		
W	*Harold Wagstaff*	*C*	*21/4/16*	*21/4/16*	*1*	*0*	*0*		
HN	Season 1916-17	Position	Debut	Last	Apps	Tries	Goals	Honours as a Lion	1?
W	*David Price*	*F*	*9/9/16*	*14/4/17*	*17*	*0*	*0*		
W	*Tommy Gostridge*	*F*	*21/10/16*	*27/4/18*	*3*	*0*	*0*		
W	*Frank Hardman*	*F*	*21/10/16*	*21/10/16*	*1*	*0*	*0*		
W	*Ernie Cullis*	*W*	*28/10/16*	*28/10/16*	*1*	*0*	*0*		
W	*Joe Williamson*	*W*	*28/10/16*	*3/11/17*	*14*	*1*	*0*		
W	*John Duggan*	*F*	*3/3/17*	*6/10/17*	*4*	*0*	*0*		
W	*Edward Roberts*	*FB*	*24/3/17*	*1/4/18*	*15*	*0*	*0*		
W	*Jim Brannen*	*F*	*28/4/17*	*28/4/17*	*1*	*0*	*0*		
W	*Walter Ferguson*	*F*	*28/4/17*	*28/4/17*	*1*	*0*	*0*		
W	*Sam Higham*	*F*	*28/4/17*	*28/4/17*	*1*	*0*	*0*		
W	*Walter Clegg*	*HB*	*5/5/17*	*5/5/17*	*1*	*0*	*0*		
HN	Season 1917-18	Position	Debut	Last	Apps	Tries	Goals	Honours as a Lion	150?
W	*Jim Carey*	*HB*	*15/9/17*	*11/1/19*	*26*	*3*	*10*		
W	*Albert Sanderson*	*C/HB*	*10/11/17*	*24/11/17*	*2*	*0*	*0*		
W	*Frank Smith*	*C*	*17/11/17*	*17/11/17*	*1*	*0*	*0*		

RUGBY LEAGUE ERA

		Position	Debut	Last	Apps	Tries	Goals	Honours as a Lion	150
	Jim Douglas	W	17/11/17	17/11/17	1	0	0		
	Jim Starkey	HB	17/11/17	17/11/17	1	0	0		
	Sam Stretford	F	17/11/17	17/11/17	1	0	0		
	Jim Wall	F	17/11/17	17/11/17	1	0	0		
	Jim Whittle	C	24/11/17	15/12/17	3	0	0		
	Joe Carr	F	24/11/17	24/11/17	1	0	0		
	Billy Yarwood	F	24/11/17	15/12/17	3	0	0		
	John Moores	FB	15/12/17	12/1/18	3	0	0		
	Joe Dunphy	HB	12/1/18	12/1/18	1	0	0		
	Henry Williams	F	12/1/18	26/1/18	2	0	0		
	Walter Thomas	C	26/1/18	26/1/18	1	0	0		
	Jim Sayers	HB	26/1/18	26/1/18	1	0	0		
	John McGuiness	F	23/2/18	1/4/18	3	1	0		
	William Pinnington	F	29/3/18	29/3/18	1	0	0		
	Jack Armstrong	F	27/4/18	27/4/18	1	1	0		
	Jim Crank	F	27/4/18	16/11/18	2	0	0		
	Ralph Openshaw	F	27/4/18	16/11/18	2	0	0		
	Season 1918-19	**Position**	**Debut**	**Last**	**Apps**	**Tries**	**Goals**	**Honours as a Lion**	**150**
	Alf Rourke	F	2/11/18	7/12/18	4	0	0		
	Jim Goulding	FB/C	16/11/18	23/11/18	2	0	0		
	Tom Clark	F	16/11/18	11/1/19	6	0	0		
	Robert Hall	W	7/12/18	7/12/18	1	0	0		
	Ernie Clark	C	11/1/19	11/1/19	1	0	0		
	Season 1919	**Position**	**Debut**	**Last**	**Apps**	**Tries**	**Goals**	**Honours as a Lion**	**150**
24	John Dawson	FB	18/1/19	8/2/19	4	0	0		
	unofficial war-time spell	FB	15/9/17	11/1/19	7	0	1		
25	Jack Edge	W	18/1/19	18/1/19	1	0	0		
	unofficial war-time spell	W	11/1/19	11/1/19	1	0	0		
26	**CHRIS BROCKBANK**	W	18/1/19	1/1/31	272	136	28	E1, L2, TT1(1t)	1927
	unofficial war-time spell	W	29/3/18	11/1/19	11	3	0		
27	Billy Talbot	C/HB	18/1/19	5/3/21	33	1	10		
	unofficial war-time spell	C/HB	25/9/15	11/1/19	70	8	38		
28	**HENRY BLEWER**	HK	18/1/19	9/5/31	392	17	2	L1	1922
	unofficial war-time spell	HK	9/9/16	11/1/19	51	4	0		
29	Harold Bowker	F	18/1/19	4/12/20	14	1	0		
	unofficial war-time spell	F	25/12/16	11/1/19	16	3	0		
30	**JACK YORKE**	F	18/1/19	8/1/21	40	1	0	L2	
31	George Eccles	C	25/1/19	1/3/19	4	0	0		
32	Albert Howarth	HB	25/1/19	17/5/19	8	1	0		
	unofficial war-time spell	HB	23/2/18	23/11/18	8	1	3		
33	Tom Edsforth	W/HB	8/2/19	15/2/19	2	0	0		
34	Billy Moss	F	8/2/19	29/12/23	69	9	0		
	unofficial war-time spell	F	9/9/16	1/1/19	19	1	0		
35	Harry Priestley	F	8/2/19	8/2/19	1	0	0		
36	Edward Dawson	W	15/2/19	15/2/19	1	0	0		
	unofficial war-time spell	C	25/12/16	25/12/16	1	0	0		
37	Fred Hill	C	8/3/19	19/4/19	4	0	0		
38	Tom Jones	W	15/3/19	18/4/19	3	0	0		
39	**HARRY HALL**	W	22/3/19	29/3/19	2	0	0		
	unofficial war-time spell	W	4/9/15	1/1/19	86	24	0	LL1(1t)	
40	Harold Norrey	W	19/4/19	16/10/20	37	13	0		
41	Bill Darbyshire	HB	14/5/19	1/1/20	12	1	0		
HN	**Season 1919/20**	**Position**	**Debut**	**Last**	**Apps**	**Tries**	**Goals**	**Honours as a Lion**	**150**
242	Mackenzie Boswell	W	13/9/19	18/10/19	4	2	0		
243	Robert McCreery	SH	20/9/19	20/9/19	1	0	0		
244	Tommy "Totty" (TL) Smith	W	25/10/19	26/11/23	136	49	1		
245	John Boardman	C	1/1/20	3/1/20	2	0	0		
246	Harry Hughes	FB	1/1/20	3/1/20	2	0	0		
247	**BRYN EVANS**	SH	17/1/20	29/2/36	467	102	0	GB10, T1928(11)(1t) & 1932(9)(2t), E4(1t), L21(1t), TT3(1t)	1931
248	Stan Howarth	SR/LF	24/1/20	13/4/25	116	22	1		
249	Jim Maguire	W	24/1/20	24/1/20	1	0	0		
HN	**Season 1920/21**	**Position**	**Debut**	**Last**	**Apps**	**Tries**	**Goals**	**Honours as a Lion**	**150**
250	Bob Spruce	W	18/9/20	12/4/24	25	5	0		
251	Wilf Summerville	HB	2/10/20	19/4/24	5	1	0		
252	Tommy Mee	SO	9/10/20	9/10/20	1	0	0		
253	**HECTOR HALSALL**	C	6/11/20	22/2/30	369	55	17	GB1, L2, NRL1	1928
254	Albert Jenkins	SO	6/11/20	8/9/28	146	29	25		1920
255	Billy Britton	FB	19/2/21	25/2/22	20	1	14		
256	**JACK EVANS (jnr)**	C	19/2/21	17/9/32	276	99	27	GB3(2t), T1928(3)(1t), E5(1t), L11(4t), TT1	1925
257	Harold Unsworth	PF	26/2/21	21/4/23	67	2	0		
258	Hector Holt	SH	2/4/21	2/4/21	1	0	0		
HN	**Season 1921/22**	**Position**	**Debut**	**Last**	**Apps**	**Tries**	**Goals**	**Honours as a Lion**	**150**
259	**FRANK EVANS**	W	27/8/21	22/10/30	341	195	1	GB4(3t), T1924(10)(10t), W7(7t), ONI2(1t), GM1(1t), TT1(1t)	1924
260	Harry Powell	SR/LF	27/8/21	16/10/26	102	14	0		
261	Jimmy Arnold	HB	10/9/21	20/1/23	8	0	0		
262	Tom O'Neill	SH	12/11/21	12/11/21	1	0	0		
263	Billy Price	HK	12/11/21	20/1/23	20	0	0		
264	**BILLO REES**	SO	3/12/21	21/10/33	360	38	2	GB11(2t), T1928(13)(3t), W6, ONI2, GM2, TT1	1933
265	Jack Pearson	FB	31/12/21	18/4/33	207	5	132		
266	Albert Morgan	SR	14/1/22	21/10/22	4	1	0		

#	Name	Position	Debut	Last	Apps	Tries	Goals	Honours as a Lion	
267	Jim Knott	LF	14/1/22	14/1/22	1	0	0		
268	Jim Turner	HK	25/2/22	2/4/34	131	2	0		
269	Alf Pardon	W	22/4/22	1/4/29	39	6	0		
HN	**Season 1922/23**	**Position**	**Debut**	**Last**	**Apps**	**Tries**	**Goals**	**Honours as a Lion**	
270	Joe Marsh	SR	28/10/22	6/1/23	6	1	0		
271	Stan Pearson	C	13/1/23	13/1/23	1	0	0		
272	**MILLER STRONG**	**PF**	**3/2/23**	**3/10/34**	**348**	**12**	**1**	C21	
273	Jack Butters	LF	24/2/23	26/12/25	26	6	0		
HN	**Season 1923/24**	**Position**	**Debut**	**Last**	**Apps**	**Tries**	**Goals**	**Honours as a Lion**	
274	John Fisher	SR	22/9/23	6/9/24	10	0	0		
275	William Beaver	W	29/9/23	29/3/24	6	2	0		
276	Albert Atkinson	SH	29/9/23	2/1/33	82	11	0		
277	Tom McCormick	PF	6/10/23	19/2/27	24	1	1		
278	Bert Morris	PF	17/11/23	9/5/31	301	16	377		
279	Arnold Ashton	C	1/1/24	1/1/24	1	0	0		
280	Bob (RE) Williams	FB	12/4/24	17/10/25	21	0	1		
HN	**Season 1924/25**	**Position**	**Debut**	**Last**	**Apps**	**Tries**	**Goals**	**Honours as a Lion**	
281	Jack Entwistle	W	30/8/24	27/9/24	5	6	0		
282	**HARRY ENTWISTLE**	**SR**	**30/8/24**	**9/2/29**	**128**	**9**	**0**	L3	
283	**FRED BESWICK**	**LF**	**27/9/24**	**11/5/35**	**396**	**83**	**6**	L5(2g, 1t)	
284	Tom Halliwell	SR	1/11/24	17/11/28	130	28	0		
285	Wilf Sulway	C/PF	8/11/24	31/3/34	191	25	0		
286	William (WH) Price	FB	29/11/24	29/8/25	22	0	0		
287	Peter Taylor	SR	17/1/25	17/1/25	1	0	0		
288	Jack Fairhurst	HK	7/2/25	17/11/25	36	1	0		
289	John Entwistle	PF/SR	13/4/25	19/1/29	4	0	0		
HN	**Season 1925/26**	**Position**	**Debut**	**Last**	**Apps**	**Tries**	**Goals**	**Honours as a Lion**	
290	Tom King	SR	7/11/25	1/1/26	3	0	0		
291	Ivor Jones	FB	26/12/25	15/1/27	6	0	0		
292	Ivor (IC) Davies	W	26/12/25	27/2/26	11	1	0		
293	Elwyn Leigh	FB/W	3/3/26	28/3/31	43	5	0		
294	William Paisley	SO	14/4/26	14/4/26	1	0	0		
HN	**Season 1926/27**	**Position**	**Debut**	**Last**	**Apps**	**Tries**	**Goals**	**Honours as a Lion**	
295	Richard Coles	SR	30/10/26	30/10/26	1	0	0		
296	Albert Grimshaw	PF/SR	6/11/26	21/4/37	35	4	4		
297	Syd Phillips	W	4/12/26	20/4/27	2	1	0		
298	Dick Cracknell	SR	5/2/27	18/4/30	126	49	2		
299	**HAROLD "Chick" EVANS**	**C/SO**	**28/3/27**	**18/2/39**	**399**	**94**	**16**	L1, NRL1(1t), TT1	
300	Billy Young	FB	16/4/27	22/9/28	16	0	15		
301	**MARTIN HODGSON**	**SR**	**16/4/27**	**25/12/40**	**473**	**39**	**870**	GB16(8g), T1932(13)(13g, 2t) & 1936(14)(58g, 3t), E9(14g), C29(17g, 4t), LL1(2g, 1t), NRL1, TT1(1t)	
302	**FRED BUTTERS**	**LF**	**16/4/27**	**11/5/40**	**351**	**70**	**0**	GB2, T1932(1)(1t), E1, L15(3t), NRL1(1t), TT2	
HN	**Season 1927/28**	**Position**	**Debut**	**Last**	**Apps**	**Tries**	**Goals**	**Honours as a Lion**	
303	Frank Buckingham	W	18/2/28	7/11/36	172	69	0		
HN	**Season 1928/29**	**Position**	**Debut**	**Last**	**Apps**	**Tries**	**Goals**	**Honours as a Lion**	
304	Archie Mansfield	C	27/10/28	20/4/31	8	2	0		
305	**JOE WRIGHT**	**PF**	**3/11/28**	**17/11/45**	**419**	**14**	**7**	GB1, T1932(15)(3t), E3, C19(2t), TT2	
306	**BOBBY SCOTT**	**FB**	**8/12/28**	**23/1/37**	**337**	**9**	**127**	C9(1g)	
HN	**Season 1929/30**	**Position**	**Debut**	**Last**	**Apps**	**Tries**	**Goals**	**Honours as a Lion**	
307	Ivor (IJ) Davies	W/SO	5/10/29	22/4/30	19	5	0		
308	Jim Cheetham	LF	21/12/29	24/3/34	17	3	0		
309	Hughie Salmon	SH	21/4/30	14/4/33	18	2	0		
HN	**Season 1930/31**	**Position**	**Debut**	**Last**	**Apps**	**Tries**	**Goals**	**Honours as a Lion**	
310	**GEORGE WHITTAKER**	**C**	**30/8/30**	**21/4/34**	**132**	**55**	**0**	Y4(2t)	
311	Vic Redmonds	W	6/9/30	6/9/30	1	0	0		
312	Stan Woodall	SR	20/9/30	31/10/36	63	6	0		
313	**JACK KENNY**	**W**	**6/12/30**	**18/9/37**	**229**	**112**	**0**	E1, L2, NRL1(1t)	19
314	John Jones	W	24/1/31	3/4/37	66	22	0		
HN	**Season 1931/32**	**Position**	**Debut**	**Last**	**Apps**	**Tries**	**Goals**	**Honours as a Lion**	
315	**TOMMY ARMITT**	**HK**	**29/8/31**	**19/10/46**	**355**	**25**	**6**	GB8, T1936(8), E10(1t), L13(1t), LL1, NRL3, TT1	19
316	Tommy (TW) Shaw	C	17/10/31	7/5/46	92	25	1		
317	Albert Hogan	C	6/2/32	17/4/33	19	9	0		
318	Dick Green	C/SO	2/4/32	26/4/39	155	29	0		194
319	Joe Sullivan	LF	20/4/32	5/11/38	69	18	0		
320	Billy (W) Shaw	SR	23/4/32	2/4/34	56	7	0		
HN	**Season 1932/33**	**Position**	**Debut**	**Last**	**Apps**	**Tries**	**Goals**	**Honours as a Lion**	
321	**JACK STODDART**	**PF/SR**	**1/10/32**	**28/4/51**	**368**	**18**	**0**	C6(1t)	194
322	**JIM MCGREGOR**	**W**	**15/2/33**	**26/10/35**	**63**	**16**	**0**	C7, NRL1(1t)	
323	Robert Brydon	C	15/2/33	18/4/33	2	1	0		
324	**TOMMY HOLLAND**	**SH**	**18/4/33**	**25/5/40**	**109**	**20**	**0**	NRL1(3t)	194
HN	**Season 1933/34**	**Position**	**Debut**	**Last**	**Apps**	**Tries**	**Goals**	**Honours as a Lion**	
325	William Moore	FB	28/10/33	9/12/33	2	0	0		
326	Billy Trew	SO	28/10/33	1/9/34	24	2	0		
327	Sam Lee	HK	28/10/33	16/10/37	29	0	27		
	second spell	HK	9/5/42	9/5/42	1	0	0		
328	Bob Spruce	SR	3/2/34	7/5/46	99	8	0		
329	Tudor Evans	SO	17/3/34	24/3/34	2	0	0		
HN	**Season 1934/35**	**Position**	**Debut**	**Last**	**Apps**	**Tries**	**Goals**	**Honours as a Lion**	156
330	Arthur Hickman	TQ	25/8/34	2/5/42	165	45	0		194
331	**GOMER HUGHES**	**PF**	**25/8/34**	**10/5/47**	**293**	**16**	**0**	W3, W1*	193

RUGBY LEAGUE ERA

		Position	Debut	Last	Apps	Tries	Goals	Honours as a Lion	
32	Jack McGurk	W/SO	22/9/34	2/11/46	136	24	15		
33	Hector Dugdale	HB	16/2/35	8/2/36	2	0	0		
HN	**Season 1935/36**	**Position**	**Debut**	**Last**	**Apps**	**Tries**	**Goals**	**Honours as a Lion**	**150**
34	**BRUCE HOOTEN**	**W**	**2/11/35**	**4/4/38**	**71**	**21**	**1**	**C3(1t)**	
35	Harold Lloyd	SR	1/2/36	1/2/36	1	0	0		
36	Frank Bowyer	HB/LF	8/2/36	11/1/47	138	18	5		
HN	**Season 1936/37**	**Position**	**Debut**	**Last**	**Apps**	**Tries**	**Goals**	**Honours as a Lion**	**150**
37	Trevor Jones	C	3/10/36	18/3/39	37	5	0		
38	George Millar	PF	31/10/36	31/10/36	1	0	0		
39	**HAROLD PALIN**	**FB/SR**	**2/1/37**	**7/6/47**	**82**	**6**	**16**	**L2**	
40	Viv Warry	TQ	2/1/37	16/4/49	200	59	0		
41	Randall Lewis	C	9/1/37	26/4/47	206	74	0		1945
42	Peter Barnes	FB	6/2/37	19/4/41	109	7	23		
43	Jim Dempsey	SH	28/3/37	30/8/39	42	14	0		
44	Weston Evans	C	1/5/37	1/5/37	1	0	0		
45	**JOE KNOWLES**	**SR**	**1/5/37**	**1/3/52**	**184**	**21**	**1**	**L1(1t)**	**1952**
HN	**Season 1937/38**	**Position**	**Debut**	**Last**	**Apps**	**Tries**	**Goals**	**Honours as a Lion**	**150**
46	Trevor Jenkins	W	25/9/37	25/8/45	37	6	0		
47	Tom Halsall	HK	13/11/37	9/11/38	9	0	0		
48	Fletcher Stoddart	SO	22/1/38	13/10/45	16	9	0		
HN	**Season 1938/39**	**Position**	**Debut**	**Last**	**Apps**	**Tries**	**Goals**	**Honours as a Lion**	**150**
349	Cledwyn Williams	SR	27/8/38	25/5/40	18	2	0		
350	Tony Town	W	10/9/38	26/10/40	8	0	0		
351	Herbert Wallwork	PF	1/10/38	20/4/46	11	0	0		
352	Bob Whittaker	HK	5/11/38	29/3/48	20	0	0		
353	Bill Hopkin	W	12/11/38	3/10/46	59	28	0		
354	Tommy Havard	C	11/2/39	11/2/39	1	0	0		
HN	**Season 1939/40**	**Position**	**Debut**	**Last**	**Apps**	**Tries**	**Goals**	**Honours as a Lion**	**150**
355	Tommy Bartram	FB/SO	2/9/39	10/10/45	42	12	9		
356	Eddie (EG) Turner	FB/W	30/9/39	1/10/49	115	25	51		
357	Fred Garner	PF/SR	30/9/39	14/1/50	147	16	0		
358	Bert Roughley	LF	7/10/39	24/1/48	10	0	0		
359	George Crossland	W	2/3/40	21/8/48	31	14	0		
360	Tom Preston	PF	16/3/40	5/10/40	6	0	0		
HN	**Season 1940/41**	**Position**	**Debut**	**Last**	**Apps**	**Tries**	**Goals**	**Honours as a Lion**	**150**
361	Vic Woodend	HK	7/9/40	7/9/40	1	0	0		
362	Jim Davies	HK	21/9/40	10/9/47	59	1	0		
363	Jim Yates	C	28/9/40	26/1/46	16	1	8		
364	Eddie Marsden	C/SO	19/10/40	25/9/48	15	7	0		
365	Charles Brown	SR	26/10/40	16/5/42	10	1	0		
366	Jack Bateman	SH	2/11/40	2/11/40	1	0	0		
367	Jim McGurk	SR	2/11/40	15/9/45	7	0	0		
368	Harry Edden	SR	14/12/40	14/12/40	1	0	0		
HN	**Season 1941/42**	**Position**	**Debut**	**Last**	**Apps**	**Tries**	**Goals**	**Honours as a Lion**	**150**
369	Hector Thomas	PF	25/4/42	16/5/42	4	0	0		
370	Walter Brown	SR	25/4/42	9/5/42	3	0	0		
371	Dennis Hartley	W	9/5/42	9/5/42	1	0	0		
372	Bert Day	HK	16/5/42	16/5/42	1	0	0		
HN	**Season 1945/46**	**Position**	**Debut**	**Last**	**Apps**	**Tries**	**Goals**	**Honours as a Lion**	**150**
373	Jeremy Lowe	FB	25/8/45	27/4/46	24	1	23		
374	Peter Evans	SO	25/8/45	25/8/45	1	0	0		
375	Jack Ducker	SR	25/8/45	22/11/47	44	3	0		
376	Cyril Cavanagh	SR	25/8/45	18/5/46	18	1	0		
377	William Lowe	SH	1/9/45	22/9/45	4	0	0		
378	John (JG) Schofield	W	8/9/45	23/3/46	23	9	0		
379	Don Morley	W/SO	15/9/45	22/12/45	4	1	0		
380	Fred Howarth	TQ	22/9/45	13/10/45	5	1	0		
381	George Turner	SH	13/10/45	27/12/52	75	5	0		
382	Jack Burgess	SR/LF	3/11/45	17/5/47	2	0	0		
383	Bob Rainsbury	FB	24/11/45	24/11/45	1	0	0		
384	Melvyn Fry	W	24/11/45	19/10/46	7	3	0		
385	Ken Turner	C	24/11/45	23/9/50	105	35	6		
386	Harold Green	W	22/12/45	29/12/45	2	0	0		
387	Jack Thomas	SO	2/2/46	20/4/46	4	0	0		
388	Dennis Parfitt	SH	9/3/46	20/4/46	6	0	0		
389	Chris Wharton	SO	16/3/46	23/3/46	2	0	0		
390	Reg Mycock	LF	23/3/46	3/4/48	4	0	1		
391	Les Fogerty	W	06/04/46	27/4/46	5	1	0		
392	Kenneth Venn	LF	10/4/46	31/8/46	7	0	1		
393	Jack (JT) Schofield	PF	19/4/46	5/9/53	85	3	0		
394	George Taylor	C	1/5/46	12/3/49	33	4	0		
HN	**Season 1946/47**	**Position**	**Debut**	**Last**	**Apps**	**Tries**	**Goals**	**Honours as a Lion**	**150**
395	Norman Hodgkinson	SR	5/10/46	17/10/53	32	0	0		
396	Ken Winkworth	C	2/11/46	10/9/55	212	60	4		
397	Billy Williams	W	2/11/46	10/4/48	53	22	0		
398	Alan Roper	SH	2/11/46	18/10/47	36	1	0		
399	Joe Warham	SO	7/12/46	23/10/48	58	11	0		
400	Jim Syddall	LF	7/12/46	30/8/47	17	1	0		
401	**RALPH MORGAN**	**FB**	**11/1/47**	**4/10/52**	**151**	**8**	**327**	**W3(2g)**	**1946**
402	**FRANK OSMOND**	**HK**	**25/1/47**	**6/10/56**	**305**	**12**	**0**	**GB1*, T1950(10)(4t), W14**	**1950**

403	Walter Evans	SO	7/4/47	23/8/47	6	1	0		
404	**BOB (RWT) JONES**	SR	12/4/47	25/8/48	41	8	2	W2(1t)	19
HN	Season 1947/48	Position	Debut	Last	Apps	Tries	Goals	Honours as a Lion	1
405	Billy Riley	SH	3/9/47	28/10/50	67	10	6		
406	Ron Tucker	LF	20/9/47	23/4/49	60	2	1		
407	Ernie Mills	C	11/10/47	11/10/47	1	0	1		
408	**CHARLIE ARMITT**	SR	18/10/47	11/4/53	144	31	3	E1, L1	19
409	Ken Birkett	W	25/10/47	22/8/53	33	11	0		
410	Jim Myers	C	29/11/47	14/9/49	48	15	0		
411	Bill Rudge	PF	31/1/48	23/10/48	11	0	0		
HN	Season 1948/49	Position	Debut	Last	Apps	Tries	Goals	Honours as a Lion	1
412	Ernest Eccleston	W	28/8/48	23/4/49	15	5	0		
413	Cyril Moran	SO	28/8/48	7/2/53	146	43	0		
414	Billy Lowe	SH	30/8/48	14/9/49	19	5	1		
415	Tommy Holder	LF	30/8/48	29/9/56	220	21	0		
416	Andrew Daley	W	25/9/48	27/11/48	10	3	0		
417	Dick Atherton	PF	2/10/48	23/2/52	91	1	0		
418	Lawrie McLoughlin	HK	23/10/48	9/9/53	21	0	0		
419	Chris Coburn	W	11/12/48	8/4/50	51	26	0		
420	Vince Kenny	C/SO	15/1/49	20/10/51	53	9	0		
421	Harry Welsh	C	29/1/49	1/5/54	113	32	0		
422	**ALBERT BLAN**	FB/SO/LF	9/4/49	27/5/64	447	75	744	E1, L5(12g, 3t)	19
HN	Season 1949/50	Position	Debut	Last	Apps	Tries	Goals	Honours as a Lion	15
423	Hubert Hirst	W	20/8/49	2/12/50	31	9	0		
424	Les Woods	SR	20/8/49	28/9/57	237	14	0		
425	Ron Taylor	PF	14/9/49	24/9/49	2	0	0		
426	**REES THOMAS**	SH	17/9/49	1/9/56	203	14	0	W1*	19
	second spell	SH	19/12/59	27/4/60	15	1	0		
427	**OWEN PHILLIPS**	PF	31/12/49	5/3/55	112	4	0	W6, CN1	19
428	Colin Syddall	LF	31/12/49	31/12/49	1	0	0		
HN	Season 1950/51	Position	Debut	Last	Apps	Tries	Goals	Honours as a Lion	15
429	Russell Burn	W	19/8/50	17/2/54	74	35	1		
430	Jackie Blan	HK/SR	19/8/50	26/12/52	45	5	0		
431	**PETER NORBURN**	W/SR	26/8/50	30/3/64	440	166	0	E1(4t), L4(1t), NRL1, TT1(1t)	19
432	Jack Lowe	C	23/9/50	26/12/53	16	1	2		
433	Tom Nuttall	C	25/12/50	23/4/51	2	0	0		
434	Arthur Sugden	SR	25/12/50	25/12/50	1	0	1		
435	John Hardiman	W	10/3/51	23/9/53	26	6	0		
436	Fred Lowe	SO	17/3/51	27/9/52	9	0	0		
437	Tom Walls	SH	17/3/51	28/4/51	5	0	0		
438	Frank Price	SR	14/4/51	1/3/52	27	2	0		
439	Evan Lewis	C	21/4/51	24/5/51	3	1	6		
HN	Season 1951/52	Position	Debut	Last	Apps	Tries	Goals	Honours as a Lion	150
440	Eddie Billington	PF	3/11/51	16/4/60	115	6	0		
441	Reg Senior	C	24/11/51	17/9/55	79	11	0		
442	Roy Sulway	LF	25/12/51	25/12/51	1	0	0		
443	Eric Jevons	W	26/12/51	28/8/54	42	12	0		
444	Bert Scott	PF	26/1/52	13/4/57	17	0	0		
445	Harold Lea	SR	8/3/52	18/9/54	56	5	0		
HN	Season 1952/53	Position	Debut	Last	Apps	Tries	Goals	Honours as a Lion	150
446	George Greenacre	SH	23/8/52	20/4/53	10	0	0		
447	Eddie Cheetham	SR	10/9/52	20/4/57	72	9	0		
448	Tommy Stott	C	4/10/52	18/12/54	51	7	52		
449	Derek Bellard	C	25/10/52	25/12/52	5	2	2		
450	**GEORGE PARKINSON**	C/SO	26/12/52	22/3/66	457	114	3	L4(2t), TT2, ES1	1958
451	**GORDON HAYNES**	LF	13/4/53	11/4/59	128	19	0	GB1*, NRL1	1956
452	Bill Hunt	HK	20/4/53	12/11/55	36	0	0		
453	Eric Glover	SH	22/4/53	7/11/53	13	2	0		
HN	Season 1953/54	Position	Debut	Last	Apps	Tries	Goals	Honours as a Lion	150
454	Johnny Lawrenson	FB	15/8/53	4/12/54	41	5	17		
455	Gordon Hardman	W	12/9/53	12/1/57	40	21	0		
456	Bill McGowan	PF	10/10/53	13/8/60	52	3	0		
457	Jack Tonge	SR	7/11/53	23/4/55	38	6	0		
458	William Brant	PF	5/12/53	5/12/53	1	0	0		
459	Ted Hulme	W	6/4/54	25/12/54	9	0	8		
460	**ARNOLD THOMPSON**	PF	6/4/54	27/3/64	192	17	0	NRL1	
461	Derek Parton	SO	16/4/54	11/1/58	8	2	0		
462	Chris Thompson	HK	16/4/54	19/4/54	3	0	0		
HN	Season 1954/55	Position	Debut	Last	Apps	Tries	Goals	Honours as a Lion	150
463	Gerry Doughty	W	25/8/54	5/3/60	111	54	0		
464	Alan Easterbrook	SR	25/8/54	2/1/56	45	2	0		
465	Frank Pritchard	PF	4/9/54	4/9/54	1	0	0		
466	Colin Pearson	SR	6/9/54	30/10/54	3	1	0		
467	Cliff Berry	W	18/9/54	2/1/60	113	70	0		
468	**BRIAN CRITCHLEY**	C	30/10/54	23/4/60	150	50	0	FS1	
469	**KEN GOWERS**	FB	20/11/54	21/4/73	601	55	970	GB14(21g), T1966(12)(53g), E1, L12(27g), NRL1, ES1	1973
470	Albert Cartwright	SH	27/12/54	9/3/66	213	19	0		1954
HN	Season 1955/56	Position	Debut	Last	Apps	Tries	Goals	Honours as a Lion	150
471	Harry Atkinson	PF	20/8/55	3/9/55	3	0	0		
472	Jack Tobin	FB	17/9/55	12/4/58	82	1	241		
473	Brian Greenhalgh	W	17/9/55	8/9/56	9	3	0		

No.	Name	Position	Debut	Last	Apps	Tries	Goals	Honours as a Lion	Year
4	Hopkin Morgan	C/SR	24/9/55	16/11/57	55	9	0		
5	Peter Smethurst	C/SR	19/11/55	2/9/61	99	28	0		
6	Jim Tynan	SH	27/12/55	27/12/55	1	0	0		
7	Jim Stevenson	HK	14/1/56	21/1/56	2	0	0		
8	Graham Hilton	W	10/3/56	13/2/57	13	1	0		
9	KEN ROBERTS (snr)	PF/SR	10/3/56	23/4/63	201	33	19	L1	1959
40	Alan Fish	SR	2/4/56	2/4/56	1	0	0		
N	**Season 1956/57**	**Position**	**Debut**	**Last**	**Apps**	**Tries**	**Goals**	**Honours as a Lion**	**150**
81	Fred Hardman	W	8/9/56	8/9/56	1	1	0		
82	TREVOR ROBERTS	HK	29/9/56	24/8/64	239	12	0	L4(1t)	1957
83	Dennis Wallwork	LF	26/1/57	16/1/60	3	1	0		
84	Les Worthington	SR	2/2/57	2/2/57	1	0	0		
85	Bill Peel	C	2/3/57	28/9/57	13	2	0		
86	Jim Hope	LF	16/3/57	27/8/66	43	8	0		
87	Dick Wood	W	23/3/57	23/3/57	1	1	0		
88	Malcolm Beaver	W	13/4/57	4/1/58	11	1	0		
89	Alex Smethurst	W	15/4/57	22/4/57	3	0	0		
90	Vince Smith	SR	20/4/57	29/4/61	100	6	0		
91	Lionel Robson	FB	22/4/57	4/4/58	17	0	42		
N	**Season 1957/58**	**Position**	**Debut**	**Last**	**Apps**	**Tries**	**Goals**	**Honours as a Lion**	**150**
92	Harold Lamb	PF	14/9/57	21/9/60	91	10	0		
93	Gordon Curran	SR	14/9/57	23/11/57	3	0	0		
94	Billy Mather	C	5/10/57	30/3/59	50	14	0		
95	Rodney Addy	HK	5/10/57	22/2/58	3	0	0		
96	Brian Vierod	W	12/10/57	23/11/57	6	2	0		
97	Alan Worsley	W	25/12/57	21/2/59	23	13	0		
98	Frank Wallwork	W	18/1/58	22/2/58	3	1	0		
N	**Season 1958/59**	**Position**	**Debut**	**Last**	**Apps**	**Tries**	**Goals**	**Honours as a Lion**	**150**
99	DAI MOSES	PF	16/8/58	11/3/61	88	6	0	W1*	
00	JOHNNY STOPFORD	W	11/11/58	7/4/69	298	195	1	GB12(7t), T1966(15)(1g, 16t), L5(1t)	1964
01	Bernard McMahon	W	15/11/58	11/3/63	84	53	16		
02	Geoff Maddock	W	3/1/59	30/3/59	4	3	0		
03	Malcolm Cummings	SR	3/1/59	13/1/70	181	11	0		
04	Eric Jackson	SH	28/2/59	14/3/59	2	0	0		
05	Alan Armstrong	PF	28/2/59	14/3/59	3	0	0		
06	Dick Leece	HK	28/2/59	28/9/60	24	0	0		
N	**Season 1959/60**	**Position**	**Debut**	**Last**	**Apps**	**Tries**	**Goals**	**Honours as a Lion**	**150**
507	Mike McGillicuddy	C	15/8/59	7/4/62	35	10	0		
508	Harold O'Boyle	FB	5/9/59	1/12/62	47	5	11		
509	ALAN BUCKLEY	C	9/1/60	24/3/74	466	192	3	GB7(1t), T1966(13)(4t), E1, L10(1g, 2t)	1974
510	Ken McGregor	W	9/1/60	4/4/64	21	4	0		
511	Dennis Ayres	C	6/2/60	29/4/61	46	12	0		
512	John Speed	W	11/4/60	2/1/67	224	79	0		1962
HN	**Season 1960/61**	**Position**	**Debut**	**Last**	**Apps**	**Tries**	**Goals**	**Honours as a Lion**	**150**
513	Bill Bretherton	PF	17/9/60	15/12/62	69	5	2		
514	Tony Dyson	SH	28/9/60	5/11/66	9	0	0		
515	Bob Fleet	C	28/1/61	18/4/70	329	87	0		1969
	second spell	C	9/3/74	26/9/76	47	3	0		
HN	**Season 1961/62**	**Position**	**Debut**	**Last**	**Apps**	**Tries**	**Goals**	**Honours as a Lion**	**150**
516	Dick Bonser	SR	26/8/61	2/2/66	71	6	0		
517	Harold Bate	PF	28/8/61	25/11/73	262	9	1		
518	RON MORGAN	PF/SR	7/10/61	27/5/64	90	18	0	GB2, W1*, Y1(1t)	1961
519	Frank Halliwell	FB/C	18/11/61	18/5/64	60	10	0		
520	Derek Clarke	HK	20/1/62	19/9/70	228	20	0		1970
521	Harold Lill	PF	31/1/62	22/9/62	12	2	0		
522	Ken Halliwell	PF	16/12/61	7/9/67	183	13	10		
523	Barry Gettins	W	21/4/62	28/4/62	3	1	0		
HN	**Season 1962/63**	**Position**	**Debut**	**Last**	**Apps**	**Tries**	**Goals**	**Honours as a Lion**	**150**
	Brian Robinson	FB/SO	18/8/62	13/1/74	87	4	6		
525	GRAHAM WILLIAMS	SH	1/9/62	29/11/68	179	62	9	L6(1t)	1967
526	Dennis Gordon	SH	3/10/62	13/11/65	4	0	0		
527	BARRY SIMPSON	SR	6/10/62	8/8/71	189	7	0	L3(1t)	1965
528	Frank Eckersley	TQ	15/12/62	2/1/67	19	2	0		
529	Colin Smith	HK	22/12/62	7/5/66	41	2	0		
530	Graham Rees	SR	9/3/63	22/11/67	154	35	0		
HN	**Season 1963/64**	**Position**	**Debut**	**Last**	**Apps**	**Tries**	**Goals**	**Honours as a Lion**	**150**
531	DAVE ROBINSON	LF	21/3/64	10/1/70	177	30	0	12GB(1t), T1966(17)(4t), E1, L6(3t), GB(24)1	1966
	second spell	LF	8/2/76	6/3/77	26	2	0		
532	Ken Tighe	SH	11/4/64	22/4/67	31	1	0		
HN	**Season 1964/65**	**Position**	**Debut**	**Last**	**Apps**	**Tries**	**Goals**	**Honours as a Lion**	**150**
533	Derek Hurt	PF/LF	29/8/64	24/9/66	62	2	0		
534	Derek Whitehead	FB/W	3/10/64	19/4/68	99	22	260		
535	BILLY "DAZ" DAVIES	C/SO	3/10/64	1/1/72	204	69	0	GB1, E1, L2	1968
536	Dave Harries	W	17/10/64	27/8/66	16	3	0		
537	Ted Bonner	SR	7/11/64	24/8/66	10	1	0		
538	John Isaac	HK	21/11/64	22/4/66	15	1	0		
539	Warren Jenkins	PF	6/2/65	22/3/66	7	0	0		
540	Frank Hutton	SR/LF	13/2/65	23/12/73	124	17	0		
541	Cliff Potts	PF	27/3/65	24/4/65	6	0	3		
542	Bill Hiscox	C	6/4/65	13/4/65	3	0	0		
543	Reg Williams	W	17/4/65	25/9/70	63	22	0		

RUGBY LEAGUE ERA

HN	Season 1965/66	Position	Debut	Last	Apps	Tries	Goals	Honours as a Lion	
544	Austin Rhodes	SO	21/8/65	16/12/67	92	9	14		
545	John Gomersall	TQ	27/10/65	13/12/72	224	84	0		
HN	**Season 1966/67**	**Position**	**Debut**	**Last**	**Apps**	**Tries**	**Goals**	**Honours as a Lion**	
546	Bernard Scott	PF	9/9/66	23/8/69	93	5	0		
547	George Swanston	W	18/2/67	2/3/68	11	2	4		
548	**TERRY CRAMANT**	**SR**	**27/3/67**	**30/10/71**	**46**	**4**	**0**	**L1**	
	second spell	SR	8/9/74	22/12/74	6	0	0		
HN	**Season 1967/68**	**Position**	**Debut**	**Last**	**Apps**	**Tries**	**Goals**	**Honours as a Lion**	3
549	Tony Stephens	SR	18/8/67	20/2/68	24	1	0		
550	**PETER KENNY**	**HB**	**23/8/67**	**5/11/72**	**164**	**54**	**39**	**L1(1t)**	1
551	Granville Hoyle	SR	9/9/67	17/11/73	72	23	0		
552	Jeff Price	W	23/9/67	10/10/70	54	16	0		
553	John Stevens	HK	7/10/67	4/11/67	5	0	0		
554	**GRAHAM MACKAY**	**PF**	**7/10/67**	**3/4/72**	**102**	**9**	**0**	**C2**	
555	Peter Goddard	PF	28/10/67	23/2/68	17	0	1		
556	Graham Wood	HK	17/1/68	24/10/69	22	4	0		
557	John Carey	HK	13/4/68	27/3/71	17	0	0		
HN	**Season 1968/69**	**Position**	**Debut**	**Last**	**Apps**	**Tries**	**Goals**	**Honours as a Lion**	1
558	Mick Philbin	W/SH	2/9/68	26/11/72	79	29	1		
559	**BILL HOLLIDAY**	**PF/SR**	**7/9/68**	**21/10/72**	**94**	**5**	**59**	**C2(4g, 1t)**	19
560	Les Atkinson	HB	29/11/68	1/4/79	143	21	0		
561	**ROD SMITH**	**SR**	**17/1/69**	**19/8/73**	**156**	**20**	**0**	**C3**	
562	Kevin Whittle	SR	15/3/69	28/8/77	180	18	0		19
HN	**Season 1969/70**	**Position**	**Debut**	**Last**	**Apps**	**Tries**	**Goals**	**Honours as a Lion**	1
563	Steve Dainty	SO	13/9/69	17/10/76	78	15	0		
564	Don Preston	W	18/10/69	24/11/74	77	28	0		
565	Jim Cadman	FB	1/1/70	27/12/71	36	3	41		
566	Tom Young	PF/SR	1/1/70	2/9/79	132	8	0		
567	Lol Lowe	PF	17/1/70	20/4/78	90	10	0		
568	Tony Pratt	W	31/1/70	13/1/74	52	23	0		
HN	**Season 1970/71**	**Position**	**Debut**	**Last**	**Apps**	**Tries**	**Goals**	**Honours as a Lion**	1
569	Bill Pattinson	SR/LF	8/8/70	7/1/73	69	12	3		
	second spell	SR/LF	17/8/75	24/4/77	36	0	0		
570	Barry Philbin	LF	22/8/70	15/12/73	86	14	0		
571	Derek Jones	C	22/8/70	20/1/76	4	0	0		
572	Billy "Rufus" Hill	C	7/9/70	26/2/72	9	0	0		
573	Ian Entwistle	HK	30/9/70	9/4/72	38	4	0		
574	Dennis Hughes	W	30/9/70	21/9/71	8	0	0		
575	Cliff Williams	SH	8/10/70	13/4/71	16	0	0		
576	**BOB FLEAY**	**W**	**23/10/70**	**10/10/76**	**211**	**88**	**0**	**ONC1**	19
577	Duncan Walton	SR	6/11/70	19/10/75	3	0	0		
578	Dennis Murray	PF/SR	26/12/70	21/4/73	37	2	0		
579	Dave Winnard	HK	26/12/70	8/8/71	3	0	0		
580	**DICK EVANS**	**HK**	**9/1/71**	**27/2/77**	**195**	**2**	**4**	**W3, L6**	19
581	Gordon Lewis	C	23/1/71	12/9/71	19	8	0		
582	**ALBERT HALSALL**	**PF**	**6/2/71**	**13/12/72**	**45**	**1**	**0**	**L2**	
HN	**Season 1971/72**	**Position**	**Debut**	**Last**	**Apps**	**Tries**	**Goals**	**Honours as a Lion**	15
583	Stan Gittins	FB	16/1/72	19/8/73	32	0	9		
	second spell	FB	1/4/79	1/4/79	1	0	0		
584	Brian Heaton	SR	13/2/72	24/4/77	30	0	0		
585	Les Bolton	SO/LF	9/4/72	26/12/78	110	12	0		197
	second spell	SO/LF	13/9/81	23/10/83	65	13	1		
HN	**Season 1972/73**	**Position**	**Debut**	**Last**	**Apps**	**Tries**	**Goals**	**Honours as a Lion**	154
586	John Cooke	C	20/8/72	1/5/79	185	51	83		
587	Mick Doorey	LF	20/8/72	7/4/74	14	1	0		
588	Paul Jackson	W	15/9/72	2/2/75	90	32	80		
589	Bernard Swift	W	29/10/72	29/10/72	1	1	0		
590	Graham Evans	C	12/11/72	25/1/76	94	29	0		
591	Geoff Thompson	PF	12/11/72	12/11/72	1	0	0		
592	Tony Connolly	W	18/11/72	26/8/74	15	2	0		
593	Ray "Chico" Hopkins	SH	3/12/72	3/3/74	30	5	0		
594	Dave Hallas	FB	26/12/72	26/12/72	1	0	0		
595	John Houghton	FB	14/1/73	1/10/78	46	3	37		
596	**BRIAN BUTLER**	**PF**	**14/1/73**	**6/4/75**	**62**	**2**	**0**	**W2, ONC3**	
597	Ken Green	SH	21/1/73	25/9/77	101	17	1		
598	Mick Henighan	SR	27/1/73	25/4/76	114	42	1		
599	Paul Armitage	PF	18/3/73	3/5/85	79	2	0		
600	Les Green	SR	21/4/73	9/1/77	8	0	0		
HN	**Season 1973/74**	**Position**	**Debut**	**Last**	**Apps**	**Tries**	**Goals**	**Honours as a Lion**	150
601	Jim Brady	LF	5/9/73	9/2/75	20	7	0		
602	Geoff Hilton	PF	16/9/73	1/1/74	8	0	0		
603	Bob Bruen	C/SH	25/11/73	3/1/82	77	5	0		
604	Ken Hindley	FB	27/1/74	9/1/77	57	2	152		
605	Phil Evans	SO	27/1/74	27/1/74	1	0	0		
HN	**Season 1974/75**	**Position**	**Debut**	**Last**	**Apps**	**Tries**	**Goals**	**Honours as a Lion**	150
606	Jeff Whiteside	W	1/9/74	19/10/75	24	3	0		
607	Vic Lawton	SR	1/9/74	9/12/79	58	1	0		
608	Steve Phythian	PF	1/10/74	16/8/81	64	2	0		
609	Tommy Highton	SR	14/3/75	17/4/83	96	11	0		

HN	Season 1975/76	Position	Debut	Last	Apps	Tries	Goals	Honours as a Lion	150
10	Ian Holland	W	31/8/75	14/11/76	42	10	2		
11	Tommy Davies	W/SO	31/8/75	13/4/80	63	11	0		
12	Kel Earl	PF	21/9/75	1/2/81	112	19	0		
13	John McCabe	SO	5/10/75	5/10/75	1	0	0		
14	Dave Chisnall	PF	5/10/75	25/4/76	24	0	0		
15	Graeme Johns	FB	2/11/75	17/12/78	63	10	104		
16	Colin Dickman	SR	16/11/75	22/2/76	11	0	0		
17	Bob Jolly	HK	14/12/75	21/10/79	55	5	0		
18	Steve Wardle	W	26/12/75	6/3/79	4	0	1		
19	Phil Ward	C	8/2/76	11/12/77	40	6	0		
HN	Season 1976/77	Position	Debut	Last	Apps	Tries	Goals	Honours as a Lion	150
20	Chris McGreal	SR	22/8/76	26/9/76	4	0	0		
21	Dave Potts	W	5/9/76	11/3/79	75	32	0		
22	Ian Wallis	W	10/10/76	27/12/76	7	2	0		
23	Trevor Darby	SR	17/10/76	17/10/76	1	0	0		
24	Colin Simkins	C	24/10/76	26/10/76	2	0	0		
25	Ken Andersson	C	2/1/77	12/4/78	30	3	0		
26	Alan Derbyshire	HK/SR	2/1/77	6/12/87	198	26	5		1985
27	John Gorton	FB	23/1/77	21/8/83	108	13	228		1980
28	Jimmy O'Neill	SO	23/1/77	25/9/77	19	5	2		
29	John Swann	SR	20/2/77	11/9/77	10	0	0		
30	Brian Sutton	HK	6/3/77	15/4/79	17	1	0		
31	Jimmy Arnold	SH	1/4/77	2/1/78	9	2	9		
32	Wilf Cantillon	PF	24/4/77	24/4/77	1	0	0		
HN	Season 1977/78	Position	Debut	Last	Apps	Tries	Goals	Honours as a Lion	150
33	Alva Drummond	W	28/8/77	25/8/82	70	16	0		
34	Keith Ashcroft	PF	28/8/77	20/4/78	27	0	1		
35	John Harrison	HK	28/8/77	6/4/80	7	0	0		
36	Kevin O'Loughlin	FB/LF	28/8/77	4/12/83	168	29	3		1979
37	Terry Cassidy	SO	8/9/77	4/2/79	33	7	0		
38	Alan Rowley	PF	8/9/77	8/9/77	1	0	0		
	second spell	PF	14/3/82	9/5/82	13	0	0		
	third spell	PF	21/8/83	2/10/83	8	0	0		
39	Doug Davies	SR	27/11/77	26/12/78	22	0	0		
40	John Davies	W	8/1/78	10/2/80	28	8	0		
41	Tony Peters	LF	5/2/78	13/4/83	106	30	0		
42	Glen Crehan	W	24/3/78	1/5/79	26	9	0		
43	Allan Doran	PF	2/4/78	30/8/81	41	4	0		
HN	Season 1978/79	Position	Debut	Last	Apps	Tries	Goals	Honours as a Lion	150
44	Denis Ashcroft	PF	20/8/78	6/3/79	18	1	0		
	second spell	PF	31/8/80	2/10/83	82	6	0		
45	John Derbyshire	PF	3/9/78	9/5/82	8	0	1		
46	Brian Gomm	PF	8/10/78	1/5/79	9	0	0		
47	Steve Hindley	W	26/12/78	20/1/80	36	7	0		
48	Adrian Foster	SH	21/1/79	2/9/79	17	4	1		
49	Ken Roberts Jr	SR	21/1/79	22/9/82	14	1	0		
50	Dave McAtee	SO	1/4/79	2/9/79	10	2	0		
51	Dave Woods	C	22/4/79	31/8/80	12	5	0		
HN	Season 1979/80	Position	Debut	Last	Apps	Tries	Goals	Honours as a Lion	150
52	Gary Fletcher	SR	19/8/79	3/2/80	22	4	0		
53	David Watkins	FB/C	2/9/79	10/2/80	20	2	28		
54	Peter Clarke	HK	2/9/79	6/1/80	13	0	0		
55	Gordon Graham	C	9/9/79	20/9/81	39	9	0		
56	Alan Riding	FB	16/9/79	23/9/79	2	0	0		
57	Dave Nicholson	SR	16/9/79	19/4/81	31	8	0		
58	Alan Grice	PF	2/10/79	23/1/83	84	4	0		
59	John Mellor	SH	14/10/79	26/12/82	78	21	3		
60	Dave Carsley	W	26/10/79	4/4/82	6	2	0		
61	Terry McGovern	SO	4/11/79	2/3/80	13	4	0		
62	Kevin Simpson	SH	11/11/79	9/12/79	3	0	0		
63	Chris Middlehurst	HK	13/1/80	27/9/81	25	5	0		
64	Alan Taylor	HB	27/1/80	19/4/81	34	7	0		
65	DANNY WILSON	C/SO	2/3/80	1/1/88	180	62	49	W4(3g, 1t)	1981
66	Gerald Cordle	W	2/3/80	2/3/80	1	1	0		
67	Tony Cooper	SR	9/3/80	13/9/81	37	2	0		
68	Charlie Bundy	W	9/3/80	13/4/80	3	0	0		
HN	Season 1980/81	Position	Debut	Last	Apps	Tries	Goals	Honours as a Lion	150
69	Dean Evans	TQ	31/8/80	6/9/80	2	1	0		
70	Green Vigo	W	19/10/80	21/8/82	52	28	0		
71	Kevin Taylor	HK	16/11/80	16/11/80	1	0	0		
72	Wayne Rutene	SO	23/11/80	15/2/81	12	2	0		
	second spell	SO	14/10/84	10/3/85	8	1	0		
73	Keith Gaskell	LF	14/12/80	14/12/80	1	0	0		
74	John Clough	SR	1/2/81	14/12/82	56	17	0		
75	Jeff Brown	C/SR	22/2/81	17/5/87	99	26	0		
76	PAUL MELLOR	FB	22/2/81	6/1/91	91	10	94	GB(C)1(4g, 1t)	1982
77	Brian Higgins	HK	8/3/81	5/1/86	57	9	1		
78	Uri Stondin	W	15/3/81	29/3/81	2	0	0		

HN	Season 1981/82	Position	Debut	Last	Apps	Tries	Goals	Honours as a Lion	1
679	Alan Fairhurst	SO	16/8/81	20/4/84	55	12	24		
680	Mike Peers	SR/LF	6/9/81	18/9/83	37	5	3		
681	Steve Breheny	PF	13/9/81	7/11/82	20	2	0		
682	Norman Turley	SR	29/11/81	7/2/82	7	1	3		
683	Alan Ratcliffe	FB/C	6/12/81	17/5/87	168	38	0		
684	Darryl Pierce	SR	19/1/82	27/11/83	30	6	0		
685	Ken Jones	W	7/2/82	12/4/87	136	56	310		
686	Terry Clark	PF	28/2/82	23/10/83	38	3	0		
687	Martin Lee	SH	14/3/82	5/2/89	148	75	3		19
688	Bob Irving	PF	14/3/82	1/4/83	25	10	0		
689	Colin Mercer	SH	25/4/82	12/4/83	3	0	0		
HN	Season 1982/83	Position	Debut	Last	Apps	Tries	Goals	Honours as a Lion	1
690	Clive Hunter	C	29/8/82	19/1/86	85	23	0		
691	Dave Sutton	W	22/9/82	4/9/83	29	9	0		
692	Sean Connor	C	22/9/82	2/2/86	44	7	2		
693	Billy Lomax	PF	21/11/82	1/1/87	65	1	0		
694	Willie Johnson	SH	21/11/82	31/1/88	31	6	0		
695	**LES HOLLIDAY**	LF	14/12/82	4/10/87	131	29	18	C1(1t)	19
	second spell	LF	20/8/95	27/7/97	51	10	10		
696	Steve Walsh	PF	2/1/83	13/4/86	32	1	0		
697	Dennis Boyd	LF	30/1/83	6/2/83	2	0	0		
698	Geoff Munro	W	6/3/83	27/3/83	4	3	0		
699	Carl Crawshaw	W	1/4/83	12/4/83	4	0	0		
700	Mark Rowbottom	SR	4/4/83	7/12/86	68	11	0		
701	Paul Hunter	FB	12/4/83	12/4/83	1	0	0		
702	Steve Turner	C	12/4/83	12/4/83	1	0	1		
703	Eric Wiliams	HK	12/4/83	12/4/83	1	0	0		
704	Mike Hazeldene	C	12/4/83	12/4/83	1	0	0		
HN	Season 1983/84	Position	Debut	Last	Apps	Tries	Goals	Honours as a Lion	15
705	Bob Twist	C	21/8/83	23/4/84	2	0	0		
706	Derek Bate	W	28/8/83	10/12/89	185	119	0		198
707	Gary Arrowsmith	PF	11/9/83	26/12/85	53	1	0		
708	Tommy Gittins	SR	14/9/83	30/10/83	5	0	0		
709	Alex Melling	HK	25/9/83	28/11/93	198	24	0		199
710	Gary Hitchens	HK	23/10/83	3/3/85	3	0	0		
711	Steve Snape	C	5/2/84	11/10/92	216	49	3		198
712	Dave Maloney	W	15/2/84	10/9/89	35	4	0		
713	Mick Coates	SR	19/2/84	19/2/84	1	0	0		
714	Mark Viller	FB	4/3/84	7/1/90	117	23	40		
715	John Allen	SR	11/3/84	29/9/92	152	12	0		198
716	Steve Tomlinson	W	20/4/84	20/4/84	1	1	4		
717	Steve Whittle	SO	29/4/84	20/4/86	3	1	0		
HN	Season 1984/85	Position	Debut	Last	Apps	Tries	Goals	Honours as a Lion	156
718	John Stapleton	SR	1/9/84	27/11/85	20	8	2		
719	Dave Barrett	PF	1/9/84	1/11/92	3	0	0		
720	**ANDY RIPPON**	FB/W	7/10/84	12/4/89	65	6	104	GB(21)1	
721	Ian Thomson	PF	14/10/84	23/1/85	5	1	0		
722	Rod Haslam	HK	10/3/85	3/5/85	9	1	0		
723	Alan Hodkinson	PF	24/3/85	22/9/85	9	0	0		
HN	Season 1985/86	Position	Debut	Last	Apps	Tries	Goals	Honours as a Lion	156
724	Paul Topping	FB/C	30/8/85	22/4/90	138	28	270		198
725	Mike Holliday	SR	30/8/85	4/10/87	42	7	0		
726	Mark Hudson	SR/LF	30/8/85	29/10/89	3	0	0		
727	John Horrocks	SR	4/9/85	14/5/89	40	4	0		
728	Tony Hewitt	SH	22/9/85	31/1/90	90	24	0		
729	Andrew Geere	C	6/10/85	6/10/85	1	0	0		
730	Terry Scott	W	20/10/85	20/1/91	55	21	0		
731	Paddy Tuimavave	SR	20/10/85	31/3/86	18	3	0		
	second spell	SR	22/11/87	10/1/88	7	1	0		
732	Mark Sheals	PF/SR	20/10/85	17/4/88	45	2	0		
	second spell	PF/SR	3/9/89	22/4/90	28	8	0		
	third spell	PF/SR	27/8/95	7/9/97	55	5	0		
733	**FRANK CASSIDY**	SO	27/10/85	12/11/89	65	22	3	GB(21)2	
734	Joe Grima	PF	3/11/85	1/1/88	47	6	0		
735	Frank Mooney	PF	3/11/85	19/11/89	60	2	0		
736	Terry Wright	PF	22/12/85	27/3/89	20	0	0		
737	Tex Evans	TQ	2/2/86	28/2/88	46	24	0		
738	Roby Muller	PF	2/2/86	6/3/88	52	8	0		
739	Gary Ainsworth	HK	28/3/86	1/1/90	100	38	0		
740	Malcolm Swann	SR	22/4/86	22/4/86	1	0	0		
HN	Season 1986/87	Position	Debut	Last	Apps	Tries	Goals	Honours as a Lion	150
741	Mark Bourneville	W	2/11/86	16/11/86	3	1	0		
742	Mark Meadows	SR	26/12/86	17/4/88	26	5	0		
HN	Season 1987/88	Position	Debut	Last	Apps	Tries	Goals	Honours as a Lion	150
743	Dave McFarland	PF	18/10/87	27/12/87	8	0	0		
744	Ian Skeech	SR/LF	22/11/87	25/8/96	106	20	0		1998
745	Scott Ranson	W	13/12/87	6/1/92	129	69	0		1990
746	John Percival	LF	27/12/87	1/1/88	2	0	0		
747	Bryan Gelling	PF	1/1/88	19/2/89	30	2	0		

	Name	Position	Debut	Last	Apps	Tries	Goals	Honours as a Lion	150
48	Darren Abram	C	10/1/88	17/1/88	2	0	0		
49	Tommy Frodsham	SO	10/1/88	14/5/89	37	19	0		
	second spell	SO	17/3/91	21/4/91	5	4	0		
50	Neil Frazer	PF	17/1/88	9/10/88	16	0	0		
51	Bernard Bibby	SH	24/1/88	24/1/88	1	0	0		
52	Andy Brown	PF	31/1/88	11/9/88	3	0	0		
53	Gary Forber	SR	14/2/88	8/3/89	12	0	0		
	second spell	SR	5/2/95	12/3/95	4	0	0		
54	Roy Howarth	LF	20/3/88	5/2/89	14	0	0		
HN	**Season 1988/89**	**Position**	**Debut**	**Last**	**Apps**	**Tries**	**Goals**	**Honours as a Lion**	**150**
55	Stuart Wakefield	C	28/8/88	16/10/88	4	0	0		
56	Gary Bond	SH	28/8/88	2/10/88	5	0	0		
57	John Wood	PF	28/8/88	9/10/88	7	0	0		
58	Tony Kinsey	SR	28/8/88	28/9/88	4	0	2		
59	Ian Connor	PF/SR	11/9/88	26/2/89	15	3	0		
	second spell	PF/SR	25/1/95	4/2/96	29	6	0		
60	Mike Kuiti	LF	9/10/88	26/2/89	18	1	16		
61	Steve O'Neill	PF	23/10/88	24/9/89	31	3	7		
62	John Myler	LF	30/10/88	17/1/90	31	4	81		
63	Willie Tangira	TQ	6/11/88	26/2/89	12	4	0		
64	Dennis Smith	PF	27/11/88	27/3/89	7	0	0		
65	Morvin Edwards	FB	11/12/88	26/2/89	10	5	0		
66	Ian Pickavance	TQ/SR	12/2/89	18/4/93	95	24	0		1992
	second spell	C/SR	26/12/99	2/7/00	26	3	0		
67	Barry Ashall	SH	12/4/89	17/4/92	46	7	22		
	second spell	SH	6/3/94	8/1/95	17	6	2		
HN	**Season 1989/90**	**Position**	**Debut**	**Last**	**Apps**	**Tries**	**Goals**	**Honours as a Lion**	**150**
768	Darren Bloor	SH	3/9/89	5/11/89	7	0	0		
769	Joe Natoli	PF	3/9/89	3/9/89	1	0	0		
770	Tony Morrison	SR	3/9/89	20/4/92	72	10	0		1991
	second spell	SR	31/3/96	19/5/96	7	2	0		
771	Shane Tupaea	SR	3/9/89	21/4/91	61	19	0		
772	Andy Pucill	PF	3/9/89	20/4/92	94	7	2		
773	John Berry	W	17/9/89	24/9/89	2	0	0		
774	Gary Sutton	C	24/9/89	22/10/89	5	0	0		
775	Mike Hancock	SH	1/10/89	20/1/91	10	1	0		
776	Les Chadwick	PF	1/10/89	31/1/90	8	2	0		
777	Phil Capewell	SR	8/10/89	22/4/90	20	2	0		
778	Ralph Linton	C	15/10/89	31/1/90	10	3	0		
779	Vince McCue	C	29/10/89	3/12/89	3	1	0		
780	Steve Jackson	SH	29/10/89	4/4/91	6	1	0		
781	Joe Ropati	C	19/11/89	1/4/91	45	18	5		
782	Barry Peters	C	17/1/90	14/2/93	32	6	0		
783	Terry Flanagan	LF	17/1/90	8/4/90	12	3	0		
784	Keith Holden	SH	21/1/90	25/3/90	7	1	0		
785	Ronel Zenon	SH	21/1/90	21/1/90	1	0	0		
786	Logan Edwards	LF	11/2/90	29/3/91	28	13	0		
787	Gary Peacham	C	18/3/90	21/4/91	26	14	0		
788	Carl Partington	PF	18/3/90	15/3/92	17	0	0		
789	Keith Waterworth	SH	8/4/90	8/4/90	1	0	1		
790	Julian Hudson	W	13/4/90	26/12/91	9	0	0		
791	Jacent Rabbitt	SR	16/4/90	12/1/92	8	0	0		
792	Joe Graziano	HK	22/4/90	1/11/92	10	2	0		
HN	**Season 1990/91**	**Position**	**Debut**	**Last**	**Apps**	**Tries**	**Goals**	**Honours as a Lion**	**150**
793	Chris Johnson	FB	26/8/90	4/4/91	15	2	46		
794	Tim Street	PF	26/8/90	21/4/91	14	4	0		
795	John Kerr	SO	26/8/90	12/4/92	10	4	0		
796	Steve Topping	W	16/9/90	18/11/90	3	0	3		
797	Danny Griffiths	SO	11/11/90	22/12/91	16	2	0		
798	Peter Subritzky	LF	25/11/90	7/4/91	11	2	1		
799	Emon Ratu	TQ	16/12/90	18/4/93	55	9	4		
800	Jason Clark	PF	9/1/91	2/10/94	9	0	0		
801	Brian Best	W	27/1/91	24/4/94	26	8	0		
802	Tony McNichol	W	3/2/91	3/3/91	4	1	0		
803	Gary Murdock	SH	17/2/91	3/3/91	3	0	0		
804	Steve Herbert	PF	24/2/91	21/4/91	7	0	0		
805	Ian Daintith	SO	24/2/91	29/9/92	15	0	2		
806	Chris Wilkinson	FB	17/3/91	13/12/92	44	3	81		
807	Phil Boucher	W	4/4/91	4/4/91	1	1	0		
808	Martin Leyland	W	14/4/91	4/10/92	14	5	0		
809	**PAUL KENNETT**	C	21/4/91	18/9/94	71	12	0	W1	
HN	**Season 1991/92**	**Position**	**Debut**	**Last**	**Apps**	**Tries**	**Goals**	**Honours as a Lion**	**150**
810	Chris O'Sullivan	SO	1/9/91	26/12/91	11	1	1		
811	Neil Clawson	PF	1/9/91	15/12/91	10	0	0		
812	Mark Lowry	SR	1/9/91	26/12/91	15	1	0		
813	Craig Bellamy	HB	8/9/91	26/12/91	14	0	0		
814	John Fairbank	SR	8/9/91	8/9/91	1	0	0		
815	Steve Garner	HK	22/9/91	4/10/92	29	9	0		
816	Glen Prince	C/SR	13/10/91	22/1/95	70	4	0		
817	Joe Faimalo	SR	6/1/92	15/3/92	5	0	0		

HN	Name	Position	Debut	Last	Apps	Tries	Goals	Honours as a Lion	
818	Darren Whitfield	SR	19/1/92	1/11/92	17	1	0		
819	Shane Ngataki	PF	19/1/92	2/2/92	2	0	0		
820	Richard Irving	TQ	16/2/92	30/8/92	11	0	0		
821	Paul Kay	SH	16/2/92	26/2/95	46	2	0		
822	Tony Barrow	PF	16/2/92	11/2/01	243	25	0		20
823	Carl Cooper	SR	16/2/92	6/11/94	7	0	0		
824	Simon Longstaff	LF	16/2/92	28/10/92	13	1	0		
825	Paul Roberts	W	22/3/92	29/3/92	2	0	0		
826	Danny Whittle	LF	12/4/92	19/2/95	47	2	0		
HN	**Season 1992-93**	Position	Debut	Last	Apps	Tries	Goals	Honours as a Lion	1
827	Simon Ashcroft	W	30/8/92	1/8/99	203	120	0		19
828	Mark Welsby	FB	30/8/92	6/2/00	195	62	1		19
829	Chris Parr	PF	30/8/92	28/3/93	19	1	0		
830	Ronnie Duane	LF	30/8/92	14/3/93	17	2	0		
831	Craig Errington	HB	27/9/92	1/10/95	60	18	102		
832	Craig Hibberd	C/SO	29/9/92	27/12/92	8	1	0		
833	John Machon	PF	11/10/92	1/11/92	3	0	0		
834	Darren Barker	C	1/11/92	1/11/92	1	0	0		
835	Adrian Earner	PF	15/11/92	7/9/97	77	1	0		
836	Ian Smith	PF	22/11/92	21/3/93	11	0	0		
837	Neil Massey	C	6/1/93	17/1/93	4	0	0		
838	Andy Crehan	PF	10/1/93	21/2/93	3	0	0		
839	Darryl Rogers	C	27/1/93	7/2/93	2	0	0		
840	Hugh Waddell	PF	7/3/93	18/4/93	8	0	0		
841	Barry Ledger	W	14/3/93	27/11/94	46	13	9		
842	Tony Humphries	PF	28/3/93	10/1/96	81	8	0		
843	Gary Welsby	SH	12/4/93	12/4/93	1	0	0		
HN	**Season 1993-94**	Position	Debut	Last	Apps	Tries	Goals	Honours as a Lion	19
844	Stuart Turner	C	29/8/93	11/12/94	22	8	0		
845	Paul Gartland	HK	29/8/93	11/7/99	65	23	102		
846	Chris Ashurst	PF	29/8/93	27/11/94	25	2	0		
847	Dave Marsh	C/LF	29/8/93	7/9/97	82	4	0		
848	Paul Barrow	SR	5/9/93	10/12/95	39	11	0		
	second spell	SR	1/2/98	2/7/00	70	15	0		
849	John Maxwell	SR	19/9/93	14/11/93	6	2	0		
850	Shane Hansen	SR	26/9/93	16/10/94	26	4	0		
851	Shaun O'Bryan	HB	26/9/93	27/2/94	20	4	4		
852	Paul Lord	W	3/10/93	2/4/95	51	21	0		
853	Paul Danes	SH	31/10/93	24/4/94	25	3	0		
854	Dave Hartill	W	31/10/93	12/5/96	11	0	0		
855	Steve Allinson	SR	13/3/94	26/3/95	6	0	0		
	second spell	SR	16/5/99	16/5/99	1	0	0		
856	Steve Ellis	FB	20/3/94	20/3/94	1	0	2		
857	Richard Clayton	FB	27/3/94	6/11/94	7	2	0		
858	Keith Atkinson	SR	1/4/94	4/4/94	2	0	0		
859	Steve Warburton	C	12/4/94	6/11/94	8	1	0		
860	Eddie Tinsley	C	17/4/94	24/4/94	2	0	0		
861	Vinnie Baines	SH	24/4/94	9/4/95	5	1	0		
HN	**Season 1994-95**	Position	Debut	Last	Apps	Tries	Goals	Honours as a Lion	150
862	Andy Purcell	SO	21/8/94	23/4/95	23	5	0		
863	**GAVIN PRICE-JONES**	TQ/SR	4/9/94	23/5/99	138	44	37	W2(1t)	199
864	Carl McCabe	HK	11/9/94	7/9/97	63	6	0		
	second spell	HK	31/1/99	22/8/99	19	3	0		
865	Jimmy Evans	TQ	18/9/94	1/7/01	139	25	11		
866	Brett Clark	SH	13/11/94	29/1/95	11	6	0		
867	Ben Olsen	SR	13/11/94	26/12/94	6	1	0		
868	Dameion Pickles	C	18/12/94	22/1/95	5	2	0		
869	Mark Hudspith	FB	26/12/94	17/4/95	16	12	31		
	second spell	FB	2/4/03	2/4/03	1	0	0		
870	Dave Chrimes	SR	25/1/95	10/1/96	33	8	0		
871	Dave Tanner	SO	5/2/95	10/1/96	32	6	5		
872	John Gunning	SO	9/4/95	14/4/95	27	5	19		
873	Neil Measures	SR	9/4/95	23/4/95	3	0	0		
HN	**Season 1995-96**	Position	Debut	Last	Apps	Tries	Goals	Honours as a Lion	150
874	**JASON ROACH**	W	20/8/95	25/8/96	45	43	3		2004
	second spell	W	26/12/99	2/7/00	28	16	0		
	third spell	W	9/12/01	27/8/04	66	35	0	S4(1t)	
875	Martin Birkett	C	20/8/95	27/7/97	51	15	50		
876	Peter Cannon	SH	20/8/95	6/9/98	71	19	1		
	second spell	SH	14/4/02	8/8/04	63	20	0		
877	Shaun Moran	SR	15/11/95	19/11/95	2	0	0		
878	Wesley Else	FB	26/11/95	7/9/97	6	3	3		
879	Kevin Fox	SH	29/11/95	28/3/97	9	0	0		
880	Mike Edwards	LF	3/1/96	4/2/96	5	1	0		
881	Willie Wolfgramm	SO	14/1/96	25/8/96	22	15	0		
882	Talite Liava'a	SR	14/1/96	16/8/96	19	7	0		
883	Mark Bolton	TQ	21/1/96	21/1/96	1	1	0		
	second spell	TQ	15/2/04	23/5/04	12	4	0		

	Season 1996	Position	Debut	Last	Apps	Tries	Goals	Honours as a Lion	150
4	Mark Riley	SH	31/3/96	20/7/97	45	30	0		1996
5	LEO CASEY	PF	31/3/96	20/7/97	44	3	0	l2	
6	Brett Rodger	C	5/4/96	8/4/96	2	1	0		
7	Greg Pearce	C/SR	14/4/96	6/7/97	37	4	150		
8	Steve Gibson	FB	19/5/96	30/3/97	18	7	0		
9	Colin Armstrong	PF/SR	30/6/96	30/3/97	18	0	0		
	Season 1997	**Position**	**Debut**	**Last**	**Apps**	**Tries**	**Goals**	**Honours as a Lion**	**150**
0	Jason Walker	C	26/1/97	28/3/97	6	0	0		
1	Marlon Gardiner	W	26/1/97	28/3/97	7	5	0		
2	Davide Longo	SO	26/1/97	4/3/98	29	14	2		
3	Gareth Adams	SR	26/1/97	23/8/98	47	11	0		
4	Wes Rogers	SR	26/1/97	11/7/99	53	4	11		
	second spell	SR	29/6/03	21/5/06	53	3	0		
5	Andy Craig	C	9/2/97	6/9/98	59	27	9		
	second spell		2/1/00	2/7/00	26	16	2		
6	Sean Casey	LF	9/2/97	2/7/00	103	38	14		2000
7	Andy Coley	SR	23/3/97	26/3/00	64	20	0		
8	John McAtee	SH	28/3/97	28/3/97	1	0	0		
9	Matt Knowles	PF/SR	20/4/97	30/8/98	35	6	0		
	second spell	PF/SR	26/12/99	9/6/00	23	2	0		
0	Tommy Hodgkinson	LF	20/4/97	6/9/98	38	2	0		
1	Jimmy Veikoso	C	11/5/97	6/9/98	37	9	0		
2	Dave McComas	W	27/7/97	21/2/99	12	1	0		
3	Damien Cleary	SH	27/7/97	29/8/99	32	9	0		
4	Ryan Stazicker	SR/LF	27/7/97	13/5/01	41	4	0		
	second spell	SR/LF	2/5/02	20/6/04	6	1	0		
	Season 1998	**Position**	**Debut**	**Last**	**Apps**	**Tries**	**Goals**	**Honours as a Lion**	**150**
5	IAN WATSON	SH	1/2/98	2/7/00	92	22	166	W9	2013
	second spell	SH	13/2/05	23/4/06	36	7	8		
	third spell	SH	7/2/10	22/6/14	111	10	6		
6	Steve Gartland	SO	8/2/98	26/3/00	64	19	164		
7	Paul Hulme	SR	15/3/98	6/9/98	19	1	0		
8	Ian Blease	PF/SR	5/4/98	29/8/99	48	3	0		
9	Phil Cushion	PF/SR	10/4/98	19/9/04	131	15	0		
0	George Mann	PF	13/5/98	6/9/98	17	4	0		
	Season 1999	**Position**	**Debut**	**Last**	**Apps**	**Tries**	**Goals**	**Honours as a Lion**	**150**
11	Paul Stevens	C	31/1/99	25/4/99	6	1	0		
12	Marlon Billy	W	31/1/99	2/7/00	51	16	0		2008
	second spell	W	13/2/05	13/9/09	119	72	0		
13	Cliff Eccles	PF	31/1/99	29/8/99	24	4	0		
14	Steve Taylor	PF	31/1/99	30/5/99	10	2	0		
15	Darren Williams	W	14/2/99	14/2/99	1	0	0		
16	Gerrod Killeen	SR	21/2/99	21/2/99	1	0	0		
17	Howard Hill	C	7/3/99	29/8/99	26	6	0		
18	Martin Gleeson	C	7/3/99	7/3/99	1	0	0		
19	Richard Henare	W	14/3/99	2/7/00	36	23	0		
20	Paul Smith	SR	18/4/99	1/7/01	70	35	0		
	second spell	SR	7/2/10	19/5/10	12	5	0		
21	Matt Bateman	C	23/5/99	1/7/01	55	21	0		
22	Jason Hunter	SR	13/6/99	11/7/99	6	1	0		
23	RICHIE EYRES	SR	13/6/99	29/8/99	11	3	0	W2	
24	Mick Nanyn	C	8/8/99	20/9/02	82	40	152		1999
	second spell	C	5/7/13	3/5/15	32	12	69		
25	Gareth Norman	C	22/8/99	22/8/99	1	0	0		
26	Jake Johnstone	W	29/8/99	29/8/99	1	2	0		
	second spell	W	15/2/04	4/4/04	4	0	0		
	Season 2000	**Position**	**Debut**	**Last**	**Apps**	**Tries**	**Goals**	**Honours as a Lion**	**150**
27	Phil Coussons	C	26/12/99	2/7/00	28	18	0		
28	Paul Loughlin	C	26/12/99	1/7/01	29	11	2		
29	Chris Highton	HK	26/12/99	25/6/00	21	1	0		
30	Jon Neill	PF	2/1/00	24/2/02	36	0	0		
31	Sean Furey	SO/HK	9/1/00	1/7/01	32	4	0		
32	Wayne English	FB	1/2/00	5/7/09	226	97	0		2009
33	Craig Randall	SR	5/3/00	18/6/00	16	5	0		
34	Steve Barrow	SR	1/5/00	21/5/00	3	2	0		
	Season 2001	**Position**	**Debut**	**Last**	**Apps**	**Tries**	**Goals**	**Honours as a Lion**	**150**
35	Ade Meade	W	3/12/00	13/4/03	50	9	0		
36	Phil Veivers	SO/LF	3/12/00	1/7/01	21	5	0		
37	Kelvin Peet	SH	3/12/00	11/2/01	7	1	0		
38	Rob Barraclough	HK	3/12/00	9/5/04	79	11	0		2003
39	Lee Hansen	PF	3/12/00	8/6/03	66	2	0		2002
40	John Paul Doherty	PF	3/12/00	24/6/01	25	5	1		
41	Andy Cheetham	TQ	3/12/00	15/6/03	34	13	0		
42	Paul Crossland	PF	3/12/00	18/2/01	4	1	0		
43	Rob Russell	C/LF	17/12/00	25/9/05	83	14	21		
44	Nick Camman	W	17/12/00	3/6/01	12	0	0		
45	Lee Hudson	W	31/12/00	7/9/03	63	27	0		
46	Phil Waring	SH	31/12/00	10/6/01	22	2	3		
47	Carlo Napolitano	SR	31/12/00	6/5/01	16	3	0		
48	Danny Butler	C	18/2/01	22/6/03	37	1	0		

HN		Position	Debut	Last	Apps	Tries	Goals	Honours as a Lion	
949	Mike Loughlin	SR	4/3/01	13/6/04	44	3	0		
950	Dale Holdstock	SR	4/3/01	20/9/02	43	7	0		
951	Chris Newall	LF	8/4/01	9/6/02	23	0	0		
952	Rob Gallagher	SO	6/5/01	31/8/03	53	4	3		
953	Ian Lewis	SR	27/5/01	24/6/01	5	0	0		
954	Gareth Chambers	SR	3/6/01	9/6/02	13	2	0		
955	Mike Woods	W	10/6/01	17/3/02	15	7	0		
956	Wayne Jackman	FB	10/6/01	9/12/01	3	0	0		
HN	**Season 2002**	**Position**	**Debut**	**Last**	**Apps**	**Tries**	**Goals**	**Honours as a Lion**	
957	Stuart Dickinson	C	9/12/01	21/7/02	7	1	0		
958	Jason Johnson	SO	9/12/01	23/3/03	22	8	0		
959	Craig Dean	SH	9/12/01	20/9/02	30	6	8		
960	Andy Leathem	PF	9/12/01	4/5/03	38	1	0		
961	Karl Fitzpatrick	SH/LF	9/12/01	21/4/02	16	6	1		
962	Steve Gee	SR	9/12/01	9/12/01	1	0	0		
963	Adam Hughes	FB	9/12/01	26/5/02	12	0	0		
964	Alan Shea	SR	9/12/01	21/4/03	31	2	0		
965	Craig Wingfield	SR	9/12/01	15/8/04	64	6	12		
966	Anthony Murray	SO	20/1/02	17/5/03	3	0	0		
967	Dean Conway	HB	20/1/02	20/1/02	1	0	0		
968	Hugh Thorpe	TQ	10/2/02	14/8/05	75	23	0		
969	Gareth Pratt	SR	17/3/02	2/6/02	4	0	0		
970	Dave Gibbons	HK	14/4/02	8/9/02	15	1	0		
971	Dave Ellison	SR	16/6/02	20/7/03	31	7	0		
972	Mike Whiteside	PF	21/6/02	20/9/02	13	0	0		
973	Jamie Stenhouse	C	5/7/02	20/9/02	12	8	0		
974	Peter Shaw	W	21/7/02	20/9/02	4	0	0		
975	Matt Mahoney	SR	25/8/02	20/9/02	5	1	0		
HN	**Season 2003**	**Position**	**Debut**	**Last**	**Apps**	**Tries**	**Goals**	**Honours as a Lion**	1
976	Phil Hassan	C	19/1/03	7/9/03	22	3	0		
977	Chris Hough	SH	19/1/03	7/9/03	29	6	98		2
	second spell	SH	28/7/06	16/9/07	28	6	23		
978	**SIMON KNOX**	PF	19/1/03	7/9/03	32	7	0	S2	
979	Kris Smith	SO/LF	19/1/03	8/10/06	71	12	33		
980	Chris Roe	PF	19/1/03	31/8/03	25	1	0		
981	Danny Turner	HB	19/1/03	2/2/03	3	0	0		
982	**KRIS TASSELL**	C	26/1/03	7/9/03	22	12	0	W3(1t)	
983	Grant Bithell	HB	23/2/03	15/2/04	16	6	0		
984	Mark Ashton	HB	9/3/03	22/6/03	3	0	0		
985	David Ogden	PF	2/4/03	2/4/03	1	0	0		
986	Mick Durham	LF	13/4/03	4/5/03	4	0	0		
987	James Lomax	SR	18/4/03	10/8/03	6	1	0		
988	Liam Owen	PF	8/6/03	15/6/03	2	0	0		
989	Mike Saunders	FB	22/6/03	17/8/03	4	0	0		
990	Srfraz Patel	PF	22/6/03	16/7/06	39	7	2		
991	Danny Tyres	PF	22/6/03	24/8/03	8	0	0		
992	Andy Gorski	SR	17/8/03	7/9/03	4	1	0		
	second spell	SR	15/7/11	14/4/12	13	5	0		
993	Danny Barton	SR	17/8/03	7/9/03	4	1	0		
	second spell	SR	1/5/05	14/8/05	11	0	0		
994	Greg McAvoy	W	24/8/03	24/8/03	1	0	0		
HN	**Season 2004**	**Position**	**Debut**	**Last**	**Apps**	**Tries**	**Goals**	**Honours as a Lion**	19
995	**CHRIS MAYE**	C	1/2/04	18/9/05	49	38	3	I2	
996	Dave Llewellyn	C	1/2/04	13/8/06	33	9	0		
997	Chris Irwin	W	1/2/04	10/7/05	30	15	0		
998	Warren Ayres	HB	1/2/04	21/8/05	45	6	40		
999	Paul Ashton	SH	1/2/04	19/9/04	17	2	38		
1000	Tau Liku	PF	1/2/04	13/6/04	15	0	0		
1001	**IAN SINFIELD**	SR	1/2/04	8/10/06	76	13	0	S3	
	second spell	SR	28/3/10	28/3/10	1	0	0		
1002	Ian Hodson	LF	1/2/04	8/3/06	29	6	0		
	second spell	LF	24/2/08	30/3/08	5	0	0		
1003	Danny Heaton	PF	1/2/04	20/6/10	67	15	0		
1004	Rob Whittaker	PF	15/2/04	9/4/06	52	1	0		
1005	Chris Brett	SR	7/3/04	25/7/04	3	0	0		
1006	Neil Hayden	SH	21/3/04	25/3/05	7	0	0		
1007	Mick Coates	SO	4/4/04	14/5/06	57	13	5		
1008	Craig Kay	SH	4/4/04	4/4/04	1	0	0		
1009	Mark Pembroke	PF	4/4/04	11/7/04	6	0	0		
1010	Alan Kilshaw	SR	9/5/04	9/5/04	1	0	0		
1011	Lee Gardner	PF	11/7/04	3/4/05	13	2	0		
1012	Danny Tyrrell	W	25/7/04	5/9/04	4	2	0		
1013	Andrew Wallace	PF	25/7/04	25/7/04	1	0	0		
1014	Darren Speakman	PF	22/8/04	25/3/05	4	0	0		
1015	Steve Warburton	W	5/9/04	19/9/04	3	0	0		
HN	**Season 2005**	**Position**	**Debut**	**Last**	**Apps**	**Tries**	**Goals**	**Honours as a Lion**	15
1016	Stuart Oldham	32	13/2/05	10/9/06	32	9	0		
1017	Lee Philip Patterson	C	13/2/05	25/9/05	30	20	0		
1018	Paul Southern	PF	13/2/05	31/7/05	18	2	0		
	second spell	PF	15/2/09	3/5/10	15	2	0		
1019	**PHIL JOSEPH**	HK	13/2/05	25/9/05	29	11	1	W3	

#	Name	Position	Debut	Last	Apps	Tries	Goals	Honours as a Lion	
	second spell	LF	7/2/10	21/8/11	41	22	0		
20	Lee Marsh	SO/LF	13/2/05	16/9/07	69	34	220		2005
21	Ben Cramant	C	18/2/05	25/3/05	3	0	0		
22	Andy Crabtree	HK	6/3/05	10/9/06	27	1	4		
23	Ian Parry	PF	1/5/05	8/10/06	43	7	0		
24	Matt Leigh	SR	12/6/05	14/8/05	7	1	0		
25	Phil Anderton	SH	10/7/05	14/8/05	2	0	0		
26	Alex Muff	C	14/8/05	2/9/05	2	0	0		
27	Craig Farrimond	SR	14/8/05	12/8/07	22	2	0		
N	**Season 2006**	**Position**	**Debut**	**Last**	**Apps**	**Tries**	**Goals**	**Honours as a Lion**	**150**
28	Andy Saywell	W	12/2/06	13/9/09	83	67	0		
29	Dave Alstead	C	12/2/06	8/10/06	26	8	0		
30	Richard Marshall	PF	12/2/06	8/7/07	32	1	0		
31	Liam McGovern	SH	12/2/06	17/8/08	78	13	107		
32	Jordan James	SR	12/2/06	2/4/06	6	0	0		
	second spell	SR	1/3/15	4/10/15	28	3	0		
33	Martin Moana	SO/LF	12/2/06	13/9/09	112	45	0		2007
34	Dave Newton	PF	12/2/06	4/7/10	80	5	0		
35	Mike Stout	C/SR	12/2/06	3/9/06	20	7	0		
36	Dave Ashton	C	19/2/06	5/8/07	25	11	0		
37	**CHRIS MORLEY**	SR	19/2/06	17/2/08	50	7	0	W1	
38	Kieron Hersnip	SR	26/2/06	17/4/06	6	0	0		
39	Darren Woods	C	23/4/06	20/5/97	27	28	0		
40	Paul Alcock	SR	23/4/06	19/8/07	27	9	0		
41	Bruce Johnson	PF	23/4/06	9/4/11	105	16	0		
42	Dave Cunliffe	SR	30/4/06	26/5/06	4	0	0		
43	Kyle Neal	PF	30/4/06	14/5/06	3	0	0		
44	Danny Aboushakra	PF	11/6/06	17/6/07	15	0	0		
45	Steve McCurrie	PF	11/6/06	12/8/07	20	2	0		
46	Phil Wood	HK	18/6/06	26/7/09	77	25	0		
47	Dean Rhodes	C	2/7/06	2/7/06	1	0	0		
48	Tama Wakelin	W	28/7/06	2/8/06	2	1	0		
N	**Season 2007**	**Position**	**Debut**	**Last**	**Apps**	**Tries**	**Goals**	**Honours as a Lion**	**150**
49	Sean Conway	C	11/2/07	18/2/07	2	0	0		
50	Gareth Hayes	PF	11/2/07	5/9/09	60	8	0		
51	Craig Ashall	LF	11/2/07	13/9/09	61	15	2		
52	Rob Line	PF	11/2/07	23/8/08	51	8	0		
53	Mike Smith	SR	11/2/07	28/6/08	29	3	0		
54	John Walker	SR	11/2/07	11/3/07	3	2	0		
55	Desai Williams	W	18/2/07	5/9/07	13	7	0		
56	Adam Sharples	PF	18/2/07	25/2/07	2	0	0		
57	Mark Brocklehurst	C	25/2/07	9/9/07	14	4	0		
58	Matty Bryers	SR	25/2/07	16/3/08	15	0	0		
59	Ben Williamson	C	25/3/07	22/6/08	13	3	0		
60	Mark Ogden	SO	22/4/07	27/5/07	5	1	2		
61	Kash Watkins	C	7/5/07	27/5/07	3	1	0		
	second spell	C	16/2/14	18/4/14	8	3	0		
62	Dean Gorton	C	27/5/07	16/8/09	41	11	0		
63	David Bates	PF	27/5/07	23/8/08	19	5	0		
64	Chris Hull	SO	10/6/07	27/6/10	49	12	0		
65	Jay Duffy	SH	21/7/07	16/9/07	8	2	0		
66	Rob Draper	SR	19/8/07	16/9/07	5	0	0		
67	Adam Bowman	C	2/9/07	20/7/08	6	0	0		
HN	**Season 2008**	**Position**	**Debut**	**Last**	**Apps**	**Tries**	**Goals**	**Honours as a Lion**	**150**
68	Ritchie Hawkyard	FB	1/2/08	4/10/15	168	49	53		2015
69	Gary Hulse	SH	1/2/08	1/8/10	68	13	0		
70	Rob Ball	PF	1/2/08	15/6/08	16	2	0		
71	Neil Rigby	LF	1/2/08	21/8/11	78	10	0		
72	Gary Sykes	HK/LF	1/2/08	17/8/08	24	5	5		
73	Chris Tyrer	PF	1/2/08	9/4/11	36	1	0		
74	Darren Bamford	FB/C	10/2/08	14/3/10	36	2	0		
75	Barry Hamilton	W	10/2/08	5/3/11	26	6	0		
76	Darren Gibson	SR	10/2/08	12/7/08	16	3	0		
77	Chris Brand	C	29/2/08	11/5/08	5	2	8		
78	Ryan Mirfield	W	29/2/08	16/3/08	2	0	0		
79	Adam Bibey	PF	9/3/08	3/4/09	5	0	0		
80	Richard Jones	PF	13/4/08	5/5/08	2	0	0		
81	Chris Frodsham	SH	5/5/08	4/5/09	16	2	1		
82	Paul Raftery	PF	8/6/08	22/6/08	3	0	0		
83	Paul Crook	SH	22/6/08	5/9/09	8	0	9		
84	Dayne Donoghue	C/SR	28/6/08	12/7/08	3	1	0		
85	Dave York	SR	9/7/08	23/8/08	4	0	0		
86	Mike Wainwright	SR	20/7/08	13/9/09	25	3	0		
HN	**Season 2009**	**Position**	**Debut**	**Last**	**Apps**	**Tries**	**Goals**	**Honours as a Lion**	**150**
1087	Dave Hull	C	15/2/09	19/5/10	30	15	0		
1088	Carl Sneyd	C	15/2/09	16/4/10	30	12	88		
1089	Alex McClurg	HK	15/2/09	28/3/10	17	2	0		
1090	Tommy Grundy	SR	15/2/09	23/5/10	26	8	0		
1091	Matty Ashe	C	11/3/09	4/5/09	5	1	0		
1092	Graham Holroyd	SO	22/3/09	23/5/10	27	6	27		
1093	Richard Lopag	W	17/5/09	5/9/09	7	0	0		
1094	Craig Littler	W	28/6/09	5/7/09	2	0	0		

SUMMER ERA

HN	Season 2010	Position	Debut	Last	Apps	Tries	Goals	Honours as a Lion	
1095	Gavn Dodd	FB/C	7/2/10	2/9/12	65	44	113		
1096	Rob Foxen	W	7/2/10	2/9/12	55	32	0		
1097	Sam Reay	C	7/2/10	2/9/12	39	7	0		
1098	Dana Wilson	PF	7/2/10	2/9/11	44	12	0		2
1099	Andy Isherwood	SR	7/2/10	4/7/10	22	6	0		
1100	Aaron Smith	LF	7/2/10	5/3/10	6	0	0		
1101	Lee Wingfield	SR	17/2/10	14/4/12	47	15	0		2
1102	Tony Stewart	C	21/2/10	10/7/11	18	3	0		
1103	Neil Cherryholme	PF	25/4/10	20/6/10	8	1	0		
1104	Mick Govin	C/SH	3/5/10	19/5/10	3	0	0		
	second spell	C/SH	11/4/05	13/9/15	15	4	0		
1105	Wayne Corcoran	HK	3/5/10	23/5/10	3	1	0		
1106	Saqib Murtza	SR	23/5/10	23/5/10	1	0	0		
1107	Simon Burkinshaw	C	30/5/10	11/7/10	6	1	0		
1108	Richard Flooks	W	30/5/10	2/9/11	24	11	5		
1109	Darren Hawkyard	SR	30/5/10	19/7/15	122	36	0		
1110	**ALEX HURST**	**W**	6/6/10	2/9/12	26	11	0	S3(1g, 1t)	
	second spell	W	19/4/15	19/4/15	1	0	0		
1111	Danny Meekin	PF	13/6/10	2/9/12	29	2	0		
1112	Andy Ainscough	SR	20/6/10	22/8/10	8	0	0		
1113	Anthony Mullaly	PF	4/7/10	22/8/10	6	2	0		
1114	Craig Harvey	SO	11/7/10	22/08/20109	5	4	0		
	second spell	SO	28/4/13	1/9/13	15	7	18		
1115	Dale Cuniffe	SR	11/7/10	2/9/12	53	23	0		
1116	Joe Fitzpatrick	PF	1/8/10	21/8/11	8	3	0		
HN	**Season 2011**	Position	Debut	Last	Apps	Tries	Goals	Honours as a Lion	1
1117	Dean Thompson	C	4/2/11	3/7/11	11	8	0		
1118	Martin Ainscough	SO	4/2/11	4/8/13	74	36	0		
	second spell	SO	13/7/14	7/9/14	7	3	0		
1119	Mike Morrison	PF	4/2/11	21/9/12	45	2	0		2
	second spell	PF	16/2/14	12/6/16	69	5	0		
1120	Karl Ashall	SH/HK	4/2/11	2/9/12	46	10	1		
1121	Neil Holland	PF	4/2/11	13/6/13	45	5	0		
1122	Ian Mort	FB/W	4/2/11	2/9/12	41	29	175		
	second spell	FB/W	5/7/15	6/9/15	6	6	24		
1123	Mark Smith	HK	4/2/11	1/9/13	77	4	0		
1124	Carl Forber	HB	13/2/11	3/4/11	3	0	0		
1125	Tommy Gallagher	SR	13/2/11	2/9/11	13	5	0		
	second spell	SR	1/3/15	4/10/15	22	8	1		
1126	Richard Mervill	PF	27/2/11	20/3/11	2	0	0		
1127	Lee James Paterson	LF	9/4/11	9/4/11	1	0	0		
1128	Warren Thompson	PF	17/4/11	2/9/11	15	2	0		
HN	**Season 2012**	Position	Debut	Last	Apps	Tries	Goals	Honours as a Lion	1
1129	Adam Higson	C	19/2/12	24/6/12	15	10	0		
1130	Tom Armstrong	C	19/2/12	2/9/12	25	13	0		
1131	Kevin Penny	W	19/2/12	1/9/13	40	19	2		20
	second spell	W	16/2/14	7/9/14	14	12	0		
1132	Chaz I'Anson	LF	19/2/12	1/9/13	37	6	0		
1133	David Mills	PF	19/2/12	1/9/13	46	5	0		
1134	Carl Forster	P/LF	11/3/12	19/8/12	12	0	0		
	second spell	PF	7/2/16	26/2/16	4	0	0		
1135	Scott Hale	SR	11/3/12	22/4/13	5	1	0		
1136	Dave McConnell	HK	25/3/12	14/4/12	2	0	0		
1137	Glenn Riley	PF	22/4/12	7/9/14	40	0	0		
1138	Chris Clarke	SR	29/4/12	2/6/13	13	1	0		
1139	Adam Walker	PF	6/5/12	1/7/12	7	2	0		
HN	**Season 2013**	Position	Debut	Last	Apps	Tries	Goals	Honours as a Lion	19
1140	Gene Ormsby	W	3/2/13	4/5/14	19	2	0		
1141	Ryan Shaw	C	3/2/13	23/6/13	18	9	38		
1142	James Mendieka	C/SO	3/2/13	1/9/13	17	11	0		
1143	Andy Ballard	W	3/2/13	17/2/13	3	0	0		
1144	Jack Morrison	PF	3/2/13	19/4/15	22	2	0		
1145	Paul Wood	PF	3/2/13	30/3/14	3	1	0		
1146	James Laithwaite	SR	3/2/13	21/7/13	9	1	0		
1147	**JOSH BARLOW**	SR/LF	3/2/13	current	84	13	0	S7	
1148	Danny Bridge	SR	3/2/13	7/9/14	22	1	0		
1149	Liam Hulme	LF	3/2/13	18/4/14	19	0	0		
1150	Tyrone McCarthy	P/SR	3/2/13	4/8/13	11	0	0		
1151	Jordan Burke	FB	10/2/13	7/9/14	32	5	0		
1152	Dan Birkett	W	10/2/13	10/2/13	1	1	0		
1153	Gareth O'Brien	HB	10/2/13	22/6/14	15	2	42		
1154	Brad Dwyer	HK	10/2/13	7/9/14	19	8	0		
1155	Ben Currie	SR	17/2/13	30/3/14	3	5	0		
1156	Gavin Bennion	PF	23/2/13	7/9/14	17	2	0		
1157	Chris Bridge	C	3/3/13	3/3/13	1	0	0		
1158	Rhys Williams	W	10/3/13	1/9/13	16	9	0		
1159	Rhys Evans	C	17/3/13	23/3/14	7	2	0		
1160	Matt Sarsfield	SR	28/4/13	1/9/13	16	8	0		
	second spell	SR	5/2/17	current					
1161	Jack Cooper	PF	28/4/13	9/3/14	11	2	0		

No	Name	Position	Debut	Last	Apps	Tries	Goals	Honours as a Lion	150	
62	Lee Briers	SO	2/5/13	2/5/13	1	1	0			
63	Adrian Morley	PF	19/5/13	19/5/13	1	0	0			
64	Samir Tahraoui	PF	9/6/13	1/9/13	10	2	0			
65	Mark Thomas	SR	9/6/13	11/5/14	10	1	0			
66	James Brown	PF/LF	13/6/13	7/9/14	39	4	0			
67	Ben Harrison	LF	14/7/13	14/7/13	1	0	0			
	Season 2014	**Position**	**Debut**	**Last**	**Apps**	**Tries**	**Goals**			150
68	Joe Worthington	W	16/2/14	11/5/14	6	1	0			
69	Liam Fishwick	SO	16/2/14	9/3/14	3	0	0			
70	Luke Menzies	PF	16/2/14	10/8/14	25	4	0			
71	Andy Ackers	HK	16/2/14	4/10/15	56	26	0			
72	Anthony Bowman	C/SO	16/2/14	29/6/14	11	6	0			
73	Zach Johnson	PF	16/2/14	27/7/14	23	1	0			
	second spell	PF	24/4/16	14/8/16	9	0	0			
74	Chris Riley	W	2/3/14	2/3/14	1	0	0			
75	Danny Halliwell	C/SR	2/3/14	18/4/14	6	1	0			
76	Freddie Walker	W	9/3/14	17/8/14	16	2	0			
77	Ben Warrilow	W	16/3/14	17/8/14	7	2	0			
78	Lewis Hulme	HB/HK	16/3/14	7/9/14	18	1	0			
79	Anthony England	PF	30/3/14	30/3/14	1	0	0			
80	Jacque Peet	C	30/3/14	7/9/14	16	1	8			
81	Chris Atkin	FB/SH	6/4/14	current	76	41	198			
82	Joe Philbin	SR	26/4/14	25/5/14	3	1	0			
83	Steve Lewis	TQ	26/4/14	1/6/14	5	1	0			
84	Andy Thornley	C/SR	4/5/14	current	53	3	0			
85	Ed Barber	C/SR	1/6/14	31/8/14	13	9	0			
86	Martin Aspinwall	LF	8/6/14	22/6/14	3	0	0			
87	Steve Maden	W	22/6/14	22/6/14	1	0	0			
88	Ryan Maneely	HK	29/6/14	29/6/14	1	0	0			
	Season 2015	**Position**	**Debut**	**Last**	**Apps**	**Tries**	**Goals**	**Honours as a Lion**		150
89	Shaun Robinson	W	1/3/15	current	59	31	0			
90	**STUART LITTLER**	C	1/3/15	18/9/16	55	24	0	I2(1g)		2016
91	Chris Rothwell	C	1/3/15	4/10/15	27	12	0			
92	**BEN WHITE**	SO	1/3/15	current	58	26	15	G1(1t)		
93	Jimmy Rowland	SH	1/3/15	13/9/15	9	3	3			
94	**RHODRI LLOYD**	C/SR	1/3/15	4/10/15	12	10	0			
	second spell	C/SR	14/2/16	current	24	9	0	W2(1t)		
95	Grant Beecham	SR	1/3/15	6/9/15	22	9	0			
96	Connor Dwyer	SR	1/3/15	current	49	12	0			
97	Ben Austin	PF	1/3/15	current	50	2	0			
98	Rob Lever	SR/LF	1/3/15	current	59	8	0			
99	Aaron Lloyd	SH	1/3/15	4/10/15	20	5	0			
200	Andy Ball	C/SR	3/4/15	14/6/15	6	1	0			
201	Matt Gardner	TQ/SR	7/4/15	31/5/15	7	3	0			
	second spell	TQ/SR	6/3/17	current						
202	Mike Butt	FB/W	17/5/15	current	27	15	0			
203	Keith Holden	HK	31/5/15	14/6/15	2	0	0			
204	Harry Aaronson	W	14/6/15	13/9/15	4	6	0			
205	Tom Thackray	SR	28/6/15	23/8/15	4	0	0			
	Season 2016	**Position**	**Debut**	**Last**	**Apps**	**Tries**	**Goals**			150
206	Greg Wilde	C	7/2/16	14/2/16	2	0	2			
207	Greg Scott	W	7/2/16	19/3/16	5	3	0			
208	Matty Beharrell	SH	7/2/16	18/9/16	26	2	3			
209	Liam Hood	HK	7/2/16	5/3/16	4	0	0			
210	Jordan Hand	PF	7/2/16	current	25	0	0			
211	Corbyn Kilday	SR	7/2/16	28/3/16	4	1	0			
212	Anthony Nicholson	HK	7/2/16	current	15	1	0			
213	Kieran Hyde	FB	14/2/16	22/5/16	5	0	0			
214	Macauley Hallett	C	20/2/16	18/9/16	25	17	0			
215	Stephen Nash	PF	20/2/16	17/7/16	10	0	0			
216	Liam Marshall	W	5/3/16	18/9/16	22	20	0			
217	Vila Halafihi	HK	13/3/16	19/6/16	5	1	0			
218	Gabriel Fell	FB	3/4/16	17/7/16	11	4	0			
219	Andy Bracek	PF	1/5/16	current	16	0	0			
220	Dan Fleming	PF	22/5/16	18/9/16	10	1	0			
221	Jake Shorrocks	HB	5/6/16	5/6/16	1	0	0			
222	Nick Gregson	SR	5/6/16	5/6/16	1	1	0			
223	Kyle Shelford	LF	12/6/16	12/6/16	1	0	0			
224	Luke Waterworth	HK	26/6/16	18/9/16	12	1	0			
	second spell	HK	26/2/17	current						
225	Tommi Hughes	W	24/7/16	24/7/16	1	0	0			
226	Jake Emmitt	PF	7/8/16	18/9/16	7	0	0			
	Season 2017	**Position**	**Debut**	**Last**	**Apps**	**Tries**	**Goals**			150
227	Jack Murphy	FB	5/2/17	current						
228	Chris Hankinson	C	5/2/17	current						
229	Liam Forsyth	C	5/2/17	current						
230	Tom Davies	W	5/2/17	current						
231	Grant Gore	SO	5/2/17	current						
232	Sean Kenny	HK	5/2/17	current						
233	Anthony Bate	PF	5/2/17	current						
234	Oliver Davies	SR	12/2/17	current						
235	Jack Higginson	C	19/2/17	current						
236	Romain Navarette	PF	19/2/17	current						
237	Adam Jones	SR	11/3/17	current						

KEY TO FIELD POSITIONS

Full-back	FB
Winger	W
Centre	C
Three-quarter	TQ
Stand-off	SO
Scrum-half	SH
Half-back	HB
Back	B
Prop-forward	PF
Hooker	HK
Second-row	SR
Loose-forward	LF
Forward	F
Not known	n/k

KEY TO HONOURS

Rugby Union Era	Abbv
England	ERU
Scotland	SRU
Australia/NZ Tourist in 1888	T1888
North	NRU
Rest of England	ROERU
North of England	NERU
Lancashire	LRU
Cumberland	CRU
Cheshire	CHRU

Rugby League Era	Abbv
Great Britain	GB
Australia/NZ Tourist	T(year)
Tour Trial	TT
England	E
Wales	W
Other Nationalities (Int)	ONI
Ireland	I
Scotland	S
Germany	G
Combined Nations	CN
English Services	ES
GB Under 24s	GB(24)
GB Under 21s	GB(21)
GB Colts	GB(C)
Lancashire	L
Lancashire League	LL
Cumberland/Cumbria	C
Yorkshire	Y
Cheshire	CH
Westmorland	WE
Glamorgan & Monmouth	GM
Other Nationalities (County)	ONC
(Northern) RL XIII	NRL
Rest of Northern Union	RNU
unofficial Test status	*

RU	NU/RL	A
	1204	Aaronson, Harry
	116	Abbott, Tom
	1044	Aboushakra, Danny
	748	Abram, Darren
	1171	Ackers, Andy
	893	Adams, Gareth
	495	Addy, Rodney
	1112	Ainscough, Andy
	1118	Ainscough, Martin
376	19	Ainsworth, Frank
	739	Ainsworth, Gary
102		Ainsworth, J
	1040	Alcock, Paul
	51	Allen, Arthur
180		Allen, Fred
	715	Allen, John
	855	Allinson, Steve
	1029	Alstead, Dave
	198	Anderson, Fred
	195	Anderson, Tom
	625	Andersson, Ken
	1025	Anderton, Phil
364		Andrews, J
	599	Armitage, Paul
	408	Armitt, Charlie
	315	Armitt, Tommy
	505	Armstrong, Alan
	889	Armstrong, Colin
	W	Armstrong, Jack
	1130	Armstrong, Tom
	261	Arnold, Jimmy
	631	Arnold, Jimmy
	707	Arrowsmith, Gary
	767	Ashall, Barry
	1051	Ashall, Craig
	1120	Ashall, Karl
	644	Ashcroft, Denis
	634	Ashcroft, Keith
	827	Ashcroft, Simon
	1091	Ashe, Matty
284		Ashton
	279	Ashton, Arnold
161		Ashton, C
362		Ashton, Dan
	1036	Ashton, Dave
305		Ashton, Fred
357		Ashton, Harold
	984	Ashton, Mark
	999	Ashton, Paul
18*		Ashton, Richard
	846	Ashurst, Chris
	24	Ashworth, Stanley
	1186	Aspinwall, Martin
265		Astall, George
	417	Atherton, Dick
	21	Atherton, Frank
	1181	Atkin, Chris
	276	Atkinson, Albert
196		Atkinson, Cornelius
	471	Atkinson, Harry
272		Atkinson, James
	858	Atkinson, Keith
	560	Atkinson, Les
	1197	Austin, Ben
	511	Ayres, Dennis
	998	Ayres, Warren

RU	NU/RL	B
	44	Badger, Owen
160		Bagshaw, Joe
257		Bailey, Henry
	154	Bailey, Jack
	861	Baines, Vinnie
281		Baldwin, William
	1200	Ball, Andy
	1070	Ball, Rob
	1143	Ballard, Andy
	1074	Bamford, Darren
	187	Bamford, Joe
35*		Banks, James
156		Banks, Tom
	1185	Barber, Ed
	834	Barker, Darren
9		Barker, Ted
	131	Barlow, David
19*		Barlow, James
	1147	Barlow, Josh
	139	Barnes, James
	342	Barnes, Peter
	75	Barnett, Harry
	938	Barraclough, Rob
329		Barratt, A
228		Barrett, Alfred
	719	Barrett, Dave
344		Barrington, Walter
	848	Barrow, Paul
	934	Barrow, Steve
	822	Barrow, Tony
	993	Barton, Danny
	355	Bartram, Tommy
	1233	Bate, Anthony
	706	Bate, Derek
	517	Bate, Harold
	366	Bateman, Jack
	921	Bateman, Matt
	1063	Bates, David
255		Battersby, George
	124	Beach, George
332		Beattie. James
	488	Beaver, Malcolm
	275	Beaver, William
	1195	Beecham, Grant
	1208	Beharrell, Matty
	813	Bellamy, Craig
	449	Bellard, Derek
229		Bennett, Anthony
	1156	Bennion, Gavin
326	10	Berry, Bob
	467	Berry, Cliff
331		Berry, George
327		Berry, Joe
324		Berry, John
	773	Berry, John
330		Berry, W
	801	Best, Brian
	283	Beswick, Fred
125		Beswick, Ted
	41	Bevan, Morgan
	751	Bibby, Bernard
	201	Bibby, William
	1079	Bibey, Adam
216		Billings
	440	Billington, Eddie
	912	Billy, Marlon
198		Birch, Joe
	1152	Birkett, Dan
	409	Birkett, Ken
	875	Birkett, Martin
	983	Bithel, Grant
135		Blackburn, Fred
	70	Blackburn, John
	220	Blackledge, John
367		Blacklock, Tom
	119	Blakeley, Enoch
	422	Blan, Albert
	430	Blan, Jackie
	179	Blears, Jim
103		Blears, Richard
	908	Blease, Ian
	228	Blewer, Henry
	768	Bloor, Darren
	217	Boardman, Horace
	245	Boardman, John
	585	Bolton, Les
	881	Bolton, Mark
	756	Bond, Gary

RU	NU/RL	Name
		B *continued*
	537	Bonner, Ted
	516	Bonser, Dick
	97	Booth, Arthur
	91	Booth, Ben
	242	Boswell, Mackenzie
	807	Boucher, Phil
	741	Bourneville, Mark
3		Bowers, James
325		Bowker, Charles
	229	Bowker, Harold
	1067	Bowman, Adam
	1172	Bowman, Anthony
157		Bowring, J
	336	Bowyer, Frank
	697	Boyd, Dennis
	1219	Bracek, Andy
270		Bradburn, Tom
	125	Bradley, Paul
	603	Brady, Jim
	1077	Brand, Chris
	W	Brannen, Jim
	458	Brant, William
	681	Breheny, Steve
	513	Bretherton. Bill
	1005	Brett, Chris
	1157	Bridge, Chris
	1148	Bridge, Danny
109		Brierley, John
	1162	Briers, Lee
	103	Brimley, John
	255	Britton, Billy
	226	Brockbank, Chris
285		Brockbank, Herbie
	1057	Brocklehurst, Mark
	199	Brookes, John
10		Brooks
	45	Brooksbank, Jim
213		Brookshaw, Percy
	752	Brown, Andy
	365	Brown, Charles
	1166	Brown, James
	675	Brown, Jeff
	370	Brown, Walter
	602	Bruen, Bob
	323	Brydon, Robert
	1058	Bryers, Matty
	303	Buckingham, Frank
	509	Buckley, Alan
340		Buckley, Richard
222		Bullough, Ned
145		Bumby, Walter
	668	Bundy, Charlie
	382	Burgess, Jack
	1151	Burke, Jordan
	1107	Burkinshaw, Simon
	429	Burn, Russell
	95	Burriss, Tom
	89	Burrows, Jim
	99	Burrows, Martin
	596	Butler, Brian
	948	Butler, Danny
	20	Butler, William
	1202	Butt, Mike
	302	Butters, Fred
	273	Butters, Jack
204		Buxton, Charlie
210		Buxton, George
209		Buxton, John
	162	Byrne, John
RU	NU/RL	**C**
	565	Cadman, Jim
	944	Camman, Nick
	876	Cannon, Peter
	632	Cantillon, Wilf
	777	Capewell, Phil
	W	Carey, Jim
	557	Carey, John
	W	Carr, Joe
	659	Carsley, Dave
	470	Cartwright, Albert
320		Case, Herbert
	885	Casey, Leo
	896	Casey, Sean
	733	Cassidy, Frank
	637	Cassidy, Terry
	376	Cavanagh, Cyril
	111	Chadderton, Harry
	776	Chadwick, Les
117		Chadwick, W
260		Chambers, Arthur
	954	Chambers, Gareth
286		Chapman, Paul
	941	Cheetham, Andy
	447	Cheetham, Eddie
148		Cheetham, Jim
	308	Cheetham, Walter
	74	Cheetham, Walter
	1103	Cherryholme, Neil
	614	Chisnall, Dave
	59	Chorley, Alf
	870	Chrimes, Dave
	866	Clark, Brett
	W	Clark, Ernie
	800	Clark, Jason
	686	Clark, Terry
	W	Clark, Tom
	1138	Clarke, Chris
	520	Clarke, Derek
254		Clarke, James
	654	Clarke, Peter
	811	Clawson, Neil
	857	Clayton, Richard
205		Clayton, Tom
	903	Cleary, Damien
20*		Clegg, Tom
	W	Clegg, Walter
333		Cleminson, Tom
	67	Clewes, Lawrence
349	13	Close, Henry
	674	Clough, John
	713	Coates, Mick
	1007	Coates, Mick
	419	Coburn, Chris
	295	Coles, Richard
	93	Coletrup, Jim
	897	Coley, Andy
	592	Connolly, Tony
	759	Connor, Ian
	692	Connor, Sean
	967	Conway, Dean
	1049	Conway, Sean
144		Cooke, Billy
197		Cooke, Herbert
	586	Cooke, John
343		Cookson, George
283		Coop, Tom
339		Cooper, Arthur
	823	Cooper, Carl
346		Cooper, J
	1161	Cooper, Jack
	101	Cooper, Joe
	72	Cooper, Joe (JH)
	667	Cooper, Tony
	1105	Corcoran, Wayne
	666	Cordle, Gerald
179		Coulthwaite, Tom
	927	Coussons, Phil
	126	Cowell, George
126		Cowper,
	1022	Crabtree, Andy
	207	Crabtree, George
	298	Cracknell, Dick
	895	Craig, Andy
	1021	Cramant, Ben
	548	Cramant, Terry

EVERY LION - IN ALPHABETICAL ORDER

RU	NU/RL	C continued
	W	Crank, Jim
699		Crawshaw, Carl
838		Crehan, Andy
642		Crehan, Glen
345		Crews, Charles
	78	Critch, Lawrence
	468	Critchley, Brian
224		Critchley, E
	27	Crocker, Fred
	1083	Crook, Paul
	359	Crossland, George
	942	Crossland, Paul
184		Crossley, J
104		Crossley, James
	115	Crowther, Tom
	223	Crudden, Harry
	172	Cullis, Dick
	W	Cullis, Ernie
	503	Cummings, Malcolm
	1115	Cuniffe, Dale
	1042	Cunliffe, Dave
	143	Cunningham, John
	493	Curran, Gordan
	1155	Currie, Ben
	909	Cushion, Phil

RU	NU/RL	D
	805	Daintith, Ian
	563	Dainty, Steve
	416	Daley, Andrew
	212	Daley, Jack
	853	Danes, Paul
	145	Daniels, Frank
	623	Darby, Trevor
	241	Darbyshire, Bill
	535	Davies, Billy "Daz"
	60	Davies, Dai
	120	Davies, Dan
	183	Davies, David (DB)
	639	Davies, Doug
	166	Davies, Herbert
	291	Davies, Ivor (IC)
	307	Davies, Ivor (IJ)
	362	Davies, Jim
	640	Davies, John
	1234	Davies, Oliver
	1230	Davies, Tom (Wigan)
	611	Davies, Tommy
	46	Davies, William
	236	Dawson, Edward
	190	Dawson, Jimmy
224		Dawson, John

RU	NU/RL	(D/E)
372		Day, Bert
959		Dean, Craig
222		Dean, Jack
343		Dempsey, Jim
15*		Denwood, J
626		Derbyshire, Alan
645		Derbyshire, John
158		Dickenson, Walter
957		Dickinson, Stuart
616		Dickman, Colin
167		Distin, Harry
	83	Dixon, Billy
	1095	Dodd, Gavin
	940	Doherty, John Paul
240		Donaldson, William
	1084	Donoghue, Dayne
	587	Doorey, Mick
	643	Doran, Allan
21*		Dorning, Arthur (AH)
22*		Dorning, H
2		Dorning, John
16*		Dorning, Radcliffe
	463	Doughty, Gerry
	W	Douglas, Jim
	140	Downing, Jim
	1066	Draper, Rob
	633	Drummond, Alva
	830	Duane, Ronnie
	375	Ducker, Jack
	1065	Duffy, Jay
	333	Dugdale, Hector
	W	Duggan, John
	W	Dunphy, Joe
	986	Durham, Mick
	1154	Dwyer, Brad
	1196	Dwyer, Connor
	514	Dyson, Tony

RU	NU/RL	E
217		Eagles, Harry
	612	Earl, Kel
	835	Earner, Adrian
	464	Easterbrook, Alan
	913	Eccles, Cliff
	231	Eccles, George
	412	Eccleston, Ernie
	528	Eckersley, Frank
	69	Eckersley, Robert
	368	Edden, Harry
279		Edge, D
	225	Edge, Jack
	233	Edsforth, Tom
	35	Edwards, Fred

RU	NU/RL	(E/F)
	786	Edwards, Logan
	880	Edwards, Mike
	765	Edwards, Morvin
165		Ellarby, W
	856	Ellis, Steve
	971	Ellison, Dave
	878	Else, Wesley
	164	Elwell, Tom
112		Emery, William
	1226	Emmitt, Jake
	1179	England, Anthony
	932	English, Wayne
	282	Entwistle, Harry
	573	Entwistle, Ian
	281	Entwistle, Jack
	289	Entwistle, John
275		Entwistle, Peter
	831	Errington, Craig
	247	Evans, Bryn
230		Evans, D
	669	Evans, Dean
	580	Evans, Dick
	259	Evans, Frank
	28	Evans, George
	590	Evans, Graham
	299	Evans, Harold "Chick"
	256	Evans, Jack jnr
	43	Evans, Jack snr
	865	Evans, Jimmy
	178	Evans, Morgan
	W	Evans, Peter
	374	Evans, Peter
	605	Evans, Phil
	1159	Evans, Rhys
	737	Evans, Tex
	329	Evans, Tudor
268	5	Evans, Walter
	403	Evans, Walter
	344	Evans, Weston
11		Evans, William
	923	Eyres, Richie

RU	NU/RL	F
	817	Faimolo, Joe
	814	Fairbank, John
	679	Fairhurst, Alan
	288	Fairhurst, Jack
	152	Fairhurst, Jim
8		Farr, Edward (EL)
23*		Farr, Henry (HP)
24*		Farr, Herbert (HF)
25*		Farr, Tom (TS)
	1027	Farrimond, Craig

RU	NU/RL	F continued
	1027	Farrimond, Craig
	31	Fearnley, John
	1218	Fell, Gabriel
	W	Ferguson, Walter
185		Fielding, J
	130	Fielding, Jack
	480	Fish, Alan
	274	Fisher, John
	1169	Fishwick, Liam
	1116	Fitzpatrick, Joe
	961	Fitzpatrick, Karl
	86	Fitzpatrick, Nicholas
	783	Flanagan, Terry
	576	Fleay, Bob
	515	Fleet, Bob
	1220	Fleming, Dan
	652	Fletcher, Gary
118		Fletcher, J
	181	Flinn, Robert
	1108	Flooks, Richard
	107	Flynn, Jack
	391	Fogerty, Les
	1124	Forber, Carl
	753	Forber, Gary
	136	Ford, Tom
	1134	Forster, Carl
	1229	Forsyth, Liam
	648	Foster, Adrian
	879	Fox, Kevin
	1096	Foxen, Rob
	750	Frazer, Neil
	1081	Frodsham, Chris
	191	Frodsham, Peter
	749	Frodsham, Tommy
	384	Fry, Mel
	931	Furey, Sean

RU	NU/RL	G
317		Gadd, James
	952	Gallagher, Rob
	1125	Gallagher, Tommy
	891	Gardiner, Marlon
	1011	Gardner, Lee
	1201	Gardner, Matt
	357	Garner, Fred
	815	Garner, Steve
	123	Garside, Charles
	845	Gartland, Paul
	906	Gartland, Steve
	98	Gartrell, Tommy
	673	Gaskell, Keith
	962	Gee, Steve

RU	NU/RL	
	729	Geere, Andrew
	747	Gelling, Bryan
	523	Gettins, Barry
	970	Gibbons, Dave
	1076	Gibson, Darren
	888	Gibson, Steve
301		Gill, William
	583	Gittins, Stan
	708	Gittins, Tommy
	918	Gleeson, Martin
119		Glossop, CJ
	453	Glover, Eric
	555	Goddard, Peter
	545	Gomersall, John
	646	Gomm, Brian
316	9	Goodman, Johnny
	526	Gordon, Dennis
	1231	Gore, Grant
	992	Gorski, Andy
	1062	Gorton, Dean
	627	Gorton, John
	W	Gostridge, Tommy
	W	Goulding, Jim
	1104	Govin, Mick
	469	Gowers, Ken
	655	Graham, Gordon
	792	Graziano, Joe
	157	Greatorex, Gordon
	318	Green, Dick
280		Green, Frank
	386	Green, Harold
	597	Green, Ken
	600	Green, Les
	135	Green, Tom
	446	Greenacre, George
	473	Greenhalgh, Brian
360	15	Greenhalgh, Percy
245		Greenhall, William
	96	Greenwood, Richard
	1222	Gregson, Nick
	657	Grice, Alan
	204	Grice, Jim
	104	Griffin, William
	797	Griffiths, Danny
	184	Griffiths, Edward
	734	Grima, Joe
	296	Grimshaw, Albert
	133	Groves, Jim
235		Grundy, Simeon
	1090	Grundy, Tommy
	872	Gunning, John

RU	NU/RL	H
	203	Hackett, Joe
	1217	Halafihi, Vila
	1135	Hale, Scott
	239	Hall, Harry
	W	Hall, Robert
231	3	Hall, Sam
	85	Hall, Tom
227	2	Hallam, Tom
	594	Hallas, Dave
	1214	Hallett, Macauley
	1175	Halliwell, Danny
	519	Halliwell, Frank
	522	Halliwell, Ken
	284	Halliwell, Tom
	582	Halsall, Albert
	253	Halsall, Hector
	347	Halsall, Tom
	1075	Hamilton, Barry
	52	Hampson, Vernon
315		Hancock, J
	775	Hancock, Mike
	1210	Hand, Jordan
	1228	Hankinson, Chris
	939	Hansen, Lee
	850	Hansen, Shane
	22	Hanson, William
	435	Hardiman, John
	W	Hardman, Frank
	481	Hardman, Fred
	455	Hardman, Gordon
206		Hardman, Tom
365		Harrell, John
	536	Harries, Dave
341	11	Harris, George
294		Harris, Jake (JT)
193		Harris, James (JH)
287		Harrison
191		Harrison, Arthur
	1167	Harrison, Ben
	635	Harrison. John
	854	Hartill, Dave
	371	Hartley, Dennis
	1114	Harvey, Craig
348		Harvey, EJ
	722	Haslam, Rod
274		Haslam, Tom (JT)
	976	Hassan, Phil
	354	Havard, Tommy
	1109	Hawkyard, Darren
	1068	Hawkyard, Richie
129		Haworth, James

RU	NU/RL	H continued
	1006	Hayden, Neil
	1050	Hayes, Gareth
	451	Haynes, Gordon
	704	Hazeldine, Mike
	584	Heaton, Brian
	1003	Heaton, Danny
	210	Heaton, Peter
	919	Henare, Richard
251		Henderson
	598	Henighan, Mick
	804	Herbert, Steve
	1038	Hersnip, Kieron
	728	Hewitt, Tony
259		Heywood, J
	832	Hibberd, Craig
310		Hibbert, George
	330	Hickman, Arthur
	677	Higgins, Brian
	1235	Higginson, Jack
	W	Higham, Sam
218		Higham, W
	929	Highton, Chris
	609	Highton, Tommy
	1129	Higson, Adam
328		Hiley, George
	572	Hill, Billy "Rufus"
	237	Hill, Fred
	917	Hill, Howard
	167	Hillen, William
	601	Hilton, Geoff
	478	Hilton, Graham
	604	Hindley, Ken
	647	Hindley, Steve
	423	Hirst, Hubert
	542	Hiscox, Bill
	710	Hitchens, Gary
	118	Hobson, Edgar
	395	Hodgkinson, Norman
	900	Hodgkinson, Tommy
	301	Hodgson Martin
	723	Hodkinson Alan
	1002	Hodson, Ian
	317	Hogan, Albert
	219	Holden, Jack
	784	Holden, Keith
	1203	Holden, Keith
	415	Holder, Tommy
	950	Holdstock, Dale
266		Holker, Alfred
	610	Holland, Ian
	1121	Holland, Neil

RU	NU/RL	
	324	Holland, Tommy
	202	Holland, William
	559	Holliday, Bill
	695	Holliday, Les
	725	Holliday, Mike
	54	Holmes, Charles
	1092	Holroyd, Graham
276		Holroyd, Roger
	258	Holt, Hector
	1209	Hood, Liam
	334	Hooten, Bruce
116		Hope, Albert
139		Hope, Harry
208		Hope, James
	486	Hope, Jim
140		Hope, Robert
171		Hopewell, Charles
	353	Hopkin, Bill
	593	Hopkins, Ray "Chico"
	163	Hopkins, Simon
	144	Hopwood, Harry
132		Horley, Charlie
	727	Horrocks, John
319		Hosker, Richard
273		Hotchkiss, Joe
154		Hotchkiss, Nat
	977	Hough, Chris
	595	Houghton, John
252		Howard
	186	Howard, Fred
	232	Howarth, Albert
136		Howarth, Billy
	380	Howarth, Fred
155		Howarth, L
17*		Howarth, Nathan
	754	Howarth, Roy
	248	Howarth, Stan
	551	Hoyle, Granville
	790	Hudson, Julian
	945	Hudson, Lee
	726	Hudson, Mark
	869	Hudspith, Mark
	963	Hughes, Adam
	574	Hughes, Dennis
	331	Hughes, Gomer
199		Hughes, H
	246	Hughes, Harry
	1225	Hughes, Tommi
	1064	Hull, Chris
	1087	Hull, Dave
352		Hully, Moses
	1178	Hulme, Lewis

RU	NU/RL	
	1149	Hulme, Liam
	907	Hulme, Paul
	459	Hulme, Ted
	1069	Hulse, Gary
	842	Humphries, Tony
	452	Hunt, Bill
	690	Hunter, Clive
	922	Hunter, Jason
	701	Hunter, Paul
130		Hunter, Tom
	1110	Hurst, Alex
201		Hurst, Jack
	533	Hurt, Derek
	540	Hutton, Frank
	1213	Hyde, Keiran

RU	NU/RL	I
247		Ihtmairi, J
	215	Irish, Jim
	688	Irving, Bob
	820	Irving, Richard
	997	Irwin, Chris
	538	Isaac, John
	1099	Isherwood, Andy

RU	NU/RL	J
	956	Jackman, Wayne
353		Jackson, Charles (CR)
	504	Jackson, Eric
	76	Jackson, Fred (aka Jack Jones)
	W	Jackson, Herbert
137		Jackson, Noah
	588	Jackson, Paul
	780	Jackson, Steve
358		Jackson, W
143		James, E
308		James, F
	1032	James, Jordan
105		Jeanes, Jim
	254	Jenkins, Albert
	346	Jenkins, Trevor
	539	Jenkins, Warren
	443	Jevons, Eric
	615	Johns, Graeme
127		Johnson
	1041	Johnson, Bruce
	793	Johnson, Chris
309	8	Johnson, Jack
	958	Johnson, Jason
	173	Johnson, Robert
	694	Johnson, Willie
	1173	Johnson, Zach
	926	Johnstone, Jake

EVERY LION - IN ALPHABETICAL ORDER

RU	NU/RL	J continued
	617	Jolly, Bob
	176	Jonas, Albert
	1237	Jones, Adam
	404	Jones, Bob (RWT)
292		Jones, C
108		Jones, Charles
	571	Jones, Derek
	56	Jones, Dick (GR)
313		Jones, Fred
	73	Jones, George (GH)
	102	Jones, Harry
	290	Jones, Ivor
168		Jones, J
	314	Jones, John
	685	Jones, Ken
	153	Jones, Richard
	1080	Jones, Richard
	112	Jones, Robert
	132	Jones, Sam
	238	Jones, Tom
	337	Jones, Trevor
	1019	Joseph, Phil

RU	NU/RL	K
	1008	Kay, Craig
152		Kay, Edward
110		Kay, L
	821	Kay, Paul
356		Kelly, JH
	809	Kennett, Paul
	313	Kenny, Jack
	550	Kenny, Peter
	1232	Kenny, Sean
	420	Kenny, Vince
299		Kent, Tom
151		Kenyon, James
181		Kenyon, John
194		Kenyon, Tom
	795	Kerr, John
	108	Kewin, Jack
	165	Kidd, William
	1211	Kilday, Corbyn
	216	Kilgariff, Tom
	916	Killeen, Gerrod
361	16	Kilner, William
	1010	Kilshaw, Alan
	292	King, Tom
192		Kinnish, William
	758	Kinsey, Tony
138		Kneen, Tom
	267	Knott, Jim
321		Knowles, Andrew

RU	NU/RL	
36*		Knowles, Arthur
322		Knowles, Frank
	345	Knowles, Joe
	899	Knowles, Matt
	978	Knox, Simon
	760	Kuiti, Mike

RU	NU/RL	L
	1146	Laithwaite, James
	492	Lamb, Harold
359		Lancaster, William
	1132	L'Anson, Chaz
	113	Larkin, William
	454	Lawrenson, Johnny
337		Lawton, J
	607	Lawton, Vic
288		Layfield
373		Lazonby, William
212		Le Peton, Albert
	445	Lea, Harold
	209	Leah, Billy
	960	Leathem, Andy
	25	Leather, John
	841	Ledger, Barry
	687	Lee, Martin
6		Lee, Richard
	327	Lee, Sam
	506	Leece, Dick
	293	Leigh, Elwyn
	1024	Leigh, Matt
	1198	Lever, Rob
	439	Lewis, Evan
	581	Lewis, Gordon
	953	Lewis, Ian
304	7	Lewis, Jack
	341	Lewis, Randall
	1183	Lewis, Steve
	808	Leyland, Martin
	883	Liava'a, Talite
	1000	Liku, Tau
	521	Lill, Harold
172		Lindley, Squire
	1052	Line, Rob
	778	Linton, Ralph
	1094	Littler, Craig
	1190	Littler, Stuart
	996	Llewellyn, Dave
	1199	Lloyd, Aaron
	105	Lloyd, Billy
	335	Lloyd, Harold
	1194	Lloyd, Rhodri
	693	Lomax, Billy
256		Lomax, Fred

RU	NU/RL	
	987	Lomax, James
312		Lomax, Percy
	71	Long, Arthur
	892	Longo, Davide
14		Longshaw, Harry
1		Longshaw, Walter
	824	Longstaff, Simon
	1093	Lopag, Richard
195		Lord, James
	852	Lord, Paul
	949	Loughlin, Mike
	928	Loughlin, Paul
	414	Lowe, Billy
	436	Lowe, Fred
	432	Lowe, Jack
	373	Lowe, Jeremy
	567	Lowe, Lol
	87	Lowe, William
	377	Lowe, William
	812	Lowry, Mark
	150	Luckman, Ebenezer
	168	Lythgoe, Harry

RU	NU/RL	M
	833	Machon, John
	554	Mackay, Graham
	502	Maddock, Geoff
	1187	Maden, Steve
	249	Maguire, Jim
	975	Mahoney, Matt
372	17	Makin, Ralph
	712	Maloney, Dave
	1188	Maneely, Ryan
	910	Mann, George
232		Mannion, Michael
	304	Mansfield, Archie
	196	Markland, Frank
131		Marr, Neil
271		Marsden, Arthur
	364	Marsden, Eddie
	847	Marsh, Dave
124		Marsh, James
188		Marsh, Jimmy
	270	Marsh, Joe
	1020	Marsh, Lee
176		Marsh, William
	1216	Marshall, Liam
	1030	Marshall, Richard
146		Mason, W
	109	Massey, John
	837	Massey, Neil
	494	Mather, Billy
	122	Maxwell, Jim

RU	NU/RL	M continued
	849	Maxwell, John
	995	Maye, Chris
	650	McAtee, Dave
	898	McAtee, John
	994	McAvoy, Greg
	864	McCabe, Carl
	613	McCabe, John
	1150	McCarthy, Tyrone
	1089	McClurg, Alex
	902	McComas, Dave
	1136	McConnell, Dave
	277	McCormick, Tom
	243	McCreery, Robert
	779	McCue, Vince
	1045	McCurrie, Steve
	743	McFarland, Dave
	507	McGillicuddy, Mike
	1031	McGovern, Liam
	661	McGovern, Terry
	456	McGowan, Billy
	620	McGreal, Chris
	322	McGregor, Jim
	510	McGregor, Ken
	W	McGuiness, John
	332	McGurk, Jack
	367	McGurk, Jim
	418	McLoughlin, Lawrie
	501	McMahon, Bernard
	802	McNichol, Tony
	182	McVeigh, Tom
150		Meach, G
	935	Meade, Ade
	742	Meadows, Mark
	873	Measures, Neil
334		Medley, Robert
	218	Mee, Jimmy
	252	Mee, Tommy
	1111	Meekin, Danny
	709	Melling, Alex
	658	Mellor, John
	676	Mellor, Paul
	1142	Mendieka, James
	1170	Menzies, Luke
	689	Mercer, Colin
	1126	Mervill, Richard
	30	Messer, Bobby
	663	Middlehurst, Chris
298		Miles, Frank
	338	Millar, George
	194	Miller, Jim
26*		Mills

RU	NU/RL	
	1133	Mills, David
	407	Mills, Ernie
34*		Mills, Joe
	1078	Mirfield, Ryan
	1033	Moana, Martin
	100	Molyneux, Jimmy
	735	Mooney, Frank
	325	Moore, William
	200	Moores, Frank
	W	Moores, John
	413	Moran, Cyril
	877	Moran, Shaun
	266	Morgan, Albert
	114	Morgan, Alf
	474	Morgan, Hopkin
	36	Morgan, Joey
	401	Morgan, Ralph
	518	Morgan, Ron
	1163	Morley, Adrian
	1037	Morley, Chris
	379	Morley, Don
37*		Morley, E
	175	Morris, Albert
	278	Morris, Bert
4		Morris, Thomas (AT)
202		Morris, Tom
	1144	Morrison, Jack
	1119	Morrison, Mike
27*		Morrison, Tom
	770	Morrison, Tony
	1122	Mort, Ian
	159	Morton, Sam
	499	Moses, Dai
	234	Moss, Billy
246		Mowatt, Harry
	1026	Muff, Alex
	1113	Mulally, Anthony
	738	Muller, Roby
200		Munro
	698	Munro, Geoff
	803	Murdock, Gary
28*		Murgatroyd
	61	Murphy, Ben
	1227	Murphy, Jack
	966	Murray, Anthony
	578	Murray, Dennis
241		Murray, Harold (GH)
183		Murray, Jimmy (JH)
	1106	Murtza, Saqib
	390	Mycock, Reg
	410	Myers, Jim
	762	Myler, John

RU	NU/RL	N
	924	Nanyn, Mick
	947	Napolitano, Carlo
	1215	Nash, Stephen
	769	Natoli, Joe
	1236	Navarette, Romain
	1043	Neal, Kyle
	171	Neen, Tom
248		Nehua, Wiri
	930	Neill, Jon
	951	Newall, Chris
	1034	Newton, Dave
	819	Ngataki, Shane
267		Nicholas, Tom
	1212	Nicholson, Anthony
	660	Nicholson, Dave
29*		Nicholson, L
	431	Norburn, Peter
	925	Norman, Gareth
	240	Norrey, Harold
	23	Norton, Stephen
351		Nowell, John
	433	Nuttall, Tom

RU	NU/RL	O
	508	O'Boyle, Harold
	1153	O'Brien, Gareth
	851	O'Bryan, Shaun
30*		Ogden, Bob
	985	Ogden, David
250		Ogden, George
141		Ogden, J
	1060	Ogden, Mark
264		Okell, Tom
	84	Oldfield, Tom
	1016	Oldham Stuart
	636	O'Loughlin, Kevin
	867	Olsen, Ben
	628	O'Neill, Jimmy
	761	O'Neill, Steve
	262	O'Neill, Tom
	W	Openshaw, Ralph
12		Ormrod, J
	1140	Ormsby, Gene
	402	Osmond, Frank
	810	O'Sullivan, Chris
5		Owen, John
	988	Owen, Liam
	32	Owen, Mansel

RU	NU/RL	P
	294	Paisley, William
	339	Palin, Harold
	269	Pardon, Alf

EVERY LION - IN ALPHABETICAL ORDER

RU	NU/RL	P continued
	388	Parfitt, Dennis
	170	Parker, Jack
	450	Parkinson, George
289		Parkinson, Herbert
363		Parkinson, James
335		Parlane, William
	829	Parr, Chris
178		Parr, George
	1023	Parry Ian
	788	Partington, Carl
	461	Parton, Derek
	990	Patel, Srfraz
	1127	Paterson, Lee James
	1017	Patterson, Lee Philip
	569	Pattinson, Bill
221		Paul, Arthur (AG)
	787	Peacham, Gary
	887	Pearce, Greg
296	6	Pearson, Billy
	466	Pearson, Colin
101		Pearson, F
	265	Pearson, Jack
	271	Pearson, Stan
106		Pearson, Walter
	485	Peel, Bill
	680	Peers, Mike
	1180	Peet, Jacque
	937	Peet, Kelvin
	1009	Pembroke, Mark
236		Pendlebury, T
	1131	Penny, Kevin
	746	Percival, John
	782	Peters, Barry
	641	Peters, Tony
	570	Philbin, Barry
	1182	Philbin, Joe
	558	Philbin, Mick
	427	Phillips, Owen
	297	Phillips, Syd
	608	Phythian, Steve
	766	Pickavance, Ian
	868	Pickles, Damieon
	684	Pierce, Darryl
	W	Pinnington, William
	110	Platt, Charles
243		Plumpton, Fred
	37	Pollitt, Charlie
	160	Pollitt, Jim
162		Pollitt, Sam
	63	Pomfret, Tom
	541	Potts, Cliff

RU	NU/RL	R
	621	Potts, Dave
297		Powell, B
	260	Powell, Harry
	969	Pratt, Gareth
	568	Pratt, Tony
	564	Preston, Don
	47	Preston, Jack
	360	Preston, Tom
	127	Preston, Will
	263	Price, Billy
	W	Price, David
	189	Price, Dick
	438	Price, Frank
	552	Price, Jeff
	192	Price, William
	286	Price, William (WH)
	863	Price-Jones, Gavin
	235	Priestley, Harry
	816	Prince, Glen
	465	Pritchard, Frank
	772	Pucill, Andy
	862	Purcell, Andy
RU	**NU/RL**	**R**
	791	Rabbitt, Jacent
13		Radcliffe, W
	1082	Raftery, Paul
	383	Rainsbury, Bob
	90	Ramsay, Tom
	185	Randall, Chris
	933	Randall, Craig
291		Randle, John
336		Rangeley, James
	745	Ranson, Scott
	683	Ratcliffe, Alan
	799	Ratu, Emon
307		Rawlinson, John
	221	Raynor, Frank
	1097	Reay, Sam
	311	Redmonds, Vic
	264	Rees, Billo
	530	Rees, Graham
	49	Reynolds, Jim
	544	Rhodes, Austin
	1047	Rhodes, Dean
	147	Rickers, Tom
	656	Riding, Alan
	1071	Rigby, Neil
	405	Riley, Billy
	1174	Riley, Chris
	177	Riley, Fred
	1137	Riley, Glenn
	884	Riley, Mark

RU	NU/RL	S
	208	Riley, Tom
	720	Rippon, Andy
	874	Roach, Jason
	W	Roberts, Edward
173		Roberts, Jack
277		Roberts, James (JW)
	649	Roberts, Ken jnr
	479	Roberts, Ken snr
	825	Roberts, Paul
187		Roberts, Sam
	482	Roberts, Trevor
237		Robertson, Percy
	524	Robinson, Brian
	531	Robinson, Dave
	1189	Robinson, Shaun
290		Robson
	491	Robson, Lionel
	886	Rodger, Brett
	980	Roe, Chris
	894	Rogers, Wes
	839	Rogers. Darryl
	781	Ropati, Joe
	398	Roper, Alan
	1191	Rothwell, Chris
377		Rothwell, John
189		Rothwell, Tom
	358	Roughley, Bert
	W	Rourke, Alf
	700	Rowbottom, Mark
	1193	Rowland, Jimmy
	638	Rowley, Alan
	141	Rowley, Jack
	411	Rudge, Bill
242		Russell, James
	943	Russell, Rob
	672	Rutene, Wayne
	88	Ryan, Denny
	197	Ryder, Matt
RU	**NU/RL**	**S**
211		Sabin, William
261		Sackfield, J
	309	Salmon, Hughie
	81	Samuel, Tom
	W	Sanderson, Albert
	1160	Sarsfield.Matt
	989	Saunders, Mike
121		Sawyer, Charles
122		Sawyer, J
	W	Sayers, Jim
	1028	Saywell, Andy
111		Scheele, L
	393	Schofield, Jack (JT)

EVERY LION - IN ALPHABETICAL ORDER

RU	NU/RL	S continued
	378	Schofield, John (JG)
186		Scholes, Jack
	546	Scott, Bernard
	306	Scott, Bobby
	444	Scott, Bert
	1207	Scott, Greg
	730	Scott, Terry
128		Seddon, Bob
219		Seddon, Bob - (Robert Lever)
133		Seddon, Edward
338		Seddon, James
239		Seddon, John
147		Seddon, John (JT)
	42	Selway, Jack
	441	Senior, Reg
	1056	Sharples, Adam
262		Sharples, Alf
278		Sharples, George
203		Sharples, Jacob
	29	Sharples, John
295		Sharples, W
	193	Sharples, Walter
347		Sharrocks, Richard
	320	Shaw, Billy (W)
175		Shaw, Fred
	974	Shaw, Peter
	1141	Shaw, Ryan
	316	Shaw, Tommy (TW)
	964	Shea, Alan
	732	Sheals, Mark
	1223	Shelford, Kyle
	39	Shepherd, Jim
177		Sherlock, Walter
	1221	Shorrocks, Jake
7		Shovelton, William
369		Sidebottom, James
	92	Simister, Billy
153		Simister, Charles
107		Simister, William
	624	Simkins, Colin
	527	Simpson, Barry
302		Simpson, George
	662	Simpson, Kevin
	1001	Sinfield, Ian
	744	Skeech, Ian
215		Slater, Vic
214		Slevin, Jim
174		Smethills, William
	489	Smethurst, Alex
	475	Smethurst, Peter

RU	NU/RL	
142		Smith
207		Smith, A
370		Smith, A
166		Smith, AC
	1100	Smith, Aaron
258		Smith, Arthur (AW)
	529	Smith, Colin
	764	Smith, Dennis
W		Smith, Frank
	138	Smith, Harry
	836	Smith, Ian
	180	Smith, Jim (JE) - "Nobby"
	142	Smith, Jim (JH)
	979	Smith, Kris
	1123	Smith, Mark
	1053	Smith, Mike
	920	Smith, Paul
	561	Smith, Rod
293		Smith, T
	244	Smith, Tommy - "Totty" (TL)
	490	Smith, Vince
	711	Snape, Steve
	1088	Sneyd, Carl
	1018	Southern, Paul
	1014	Speakman, Darren
	512	Speed, John
371		Spence, S
366		Spinks, John
	250	Spruce, Bob
	328	Spruce, Bob
354	14	Spruce, William
31*		Stancliffe
	718	Stapleton, John
W		Starkey, Jim
	904	Stazicker, Ryan
368		Steele, George
	106	Steele, Fred
	973	Stenhouse, Jamie
	146	Stephens, Alf
323		Stephens, James
	549	Stephens, Tony
	206	Stephenson, Ernie
	553	Stevens, John
	911	Stevens, Paul
	477	Stevenson, Jim
	1102	Stewart, Tony
	348	Stoddart, Fletcher
	321	Stoddart, Jack
	678	Stondin, Uri
	500	Stopford, Johnny

RU	NU/RL	
	448	Stott, Tommy
	1035	Stout, Mike
	794	Street, Tim
W		Stretford, Sam
	272	Strong, Miller
	798	Subritzky, Peter
311		Sudlow, Tom
	434	Sugden, Arthur
	319	Sullivan, Joe
	442	Sulway, Roy
	285	Sulway, Wilf
	251	Summerville, Wilf
355		Sunderland, Jack
164		Sutherland, Archie
	630	Sutton, Brian
	691	Sutton, Dave
	774	Sutton, Gary
134		Sutton, James
	629	Swann, John
	740	Swann, Malcolm
	547	Swanston, George
	589	Swift, Bernard
	428	Syddall, Colin
	400	Syddall, Jim
	1072	Sykes, Gary

RU	NU/RL	T
	1164	Tahraoui, Samir
	227	Talbot, Billy
	763	Tangira, Willie
	871	Tanner, Dave
	982	Tassell, Kris
249		Taylor, A
	664	Taylor, Alan
375		Taylor, Ernest
	128	Taylor, George
	394	Taylor, George
	62	Taylor, Joe
	671	Taylor, Kevin
	287	Taylor, Peter
	425	Taylor, Ron
	914	Taylor, Steve
	1205	Thackray, Tom
	169	Thomas, Gordon
369		Thomas, Hector
	387	Thomas, Jack
	53	Thomas, Jim
	129	Thomas, Llewellyn
	1165	Thomas, Mark
	426	Thomas, Rees
W		Thomas, Walter
	460	Thompson, Arnold
	462	Thompson, Chris

RU	NU/RL	T continued
	1117	Thompson, Dean
	591	Thompson, Geoff
	1128	Thompson, Warren
	721	Thomson, Ian
	1184	Thornley, Andy
	968	Thorpe, Hugh
342	12	Tickle, Bob
	532	Tighe, Ken
	860	Tinsley, Eddie
	472	Tobin, Jack
	40	Todd, Henry
	716	Tomlinson, Steve
	457	Tonge, Jack
	724	Topping, Paul
	796	Topping, Steve
	350	Town, Tony
32*		Townsend, George
	134	Townson, Richard
	156	Travis, Ellis
	77	Traynor, David
	326	Trew, Billy
	406	Tucker, Ron
	731	Tuimavave, Paddy
	771	Tupaea, Shane
	682	Turley, Norman
	981	Turner, Danny
	356	Turner, Eddie (EG)
220		Turner, Fair
	381	Turner, George
	268	Turner, Jim
	385	Turner, Ken
	702	Turner, Steve
	844	Turner, Stuart
	705	Twist, Bob
350		Tyldesley, John
	476	Tynan, Jim
	1012	Tyrell, Danny
	1073	Tyrer, Chris
	991	Tyres, Danny

RU	NU/RL	U
	257	Unsworth, Harold
	94	Unsworth, Wiliam
314		Uttley, J

RU	NU/RL	V
	80	Valentine, Albert
374	18	Valentine, Bob
170	1	Valentine, Jim
182		Valentine, Tom
	901	Veikoso, Jimmy
	936	Veivers, Phil
163		Venables, A
	392	Venn, Ken
	55	Vickers, Jim
	155	Vickers, Joe
	496	Vierod, Brian
	670	Vigo, Green
	50	Vigors, Evan
	714	Viller, Mark

RU	NU/RL	W
	840	Waddell, Hugh
	W	Wagstaff, Harold
	1086	Wainwright, Mike
	755	Wakefield, Stuart
	1048	Wakelin, Tama
	1139	Walker, Adam
	1176	Walker, Freddie
	890	Walker, Jason
	33	Walker, John
	1054	Walker, John
238		Walker, William
	W	Wall, Jim
	1013	Wallace, Andrew
	151	Wallace, Sam
	622	Wallis, Ian
	437	Walls, Tom
	68	Wallwork, Billy
	483	Wallwork, Dennis
	498	Wallwork, Frank
	351	Wallwork, Herbert
303		Walsh, Arthur
	137	Walsh, Lawrence
226		Walsh, Samuel
	696	Walsh, Steve
234		Walsh, William
190		Walton
	577	Walton, Duncan
253		Warbrick, Joseph
	859	Warburton, Steve
	1015	Warburton, Steve
318		Ward, Arthur
	57	Ward, Arthur
	619	Ward, Phil
	618	Wardle, Steve
282		Wardley, Charles
	399	Warham, Joe
	946	Waring, Phil
	1177	Warrilow, Ben
	340	Warry, Viv
	789	Waterworth, Keith
	1224	Waterworth, Luke
	653	Watkins, David
	1061	Watkins, Kash
	905	Watson, Ian
	64	Watson, Jack
	843	Welsby, Gary
	828	Welsby, Mark
	421	Welsh, Harry
	389	Wharton, Chris
	161	Wharton, Jack (JD)
	148	Wharton, Jim
	205	Wharton, Tom
	1192	White, Ben
	534	Whitehead, Derek
	211	Whitehead, Harold
225		Whitehead, Robert
	606	Whiteside, Jeff
	972	Whiteside, Mike
	818	Whitfield, Darren
	352	Whittaker, Bob
	310	Whittaker, George
	1004	Whittaker, Rob
	48	Whittingham, Stanley
	826	Whittle, Danny
	W	Whittle, Jim
	562	Whittle, Kevin
	717	Whittle, Steve
123		Wignall
169		Wilcock, Roger
120		Wild, F
	1206	Wilde, Greg
	806	Wilkinson, Chris
	26	Wilkinson, Phillip
	397	Williams, Billy
	280	Williams, Bob (RE)
	349	Williams, Cledwyn
	575	Williams, Cliff
	915	Williams, Darren
	1055	Williams, Desai
	174	Williams, Elijah
	703	Williams, Eric
	525	Williams, Graham
	W	Williams, Henry
	117	Williams, Herbert
300		Williams, J
	543	Williams, Reg
	1158	Williams, Rhys
	149	Williams, Tom
	188	Williams, Tom (TJ)
	66	Williamson, Arthur
	1059	Williamson, Ben
149		Williamson, Hugh
	W	Williamson, Joe
306		Wilson
	1098	Wilson, Dana
	665	Wilson, Danny

EVERY LION - IN ALPHABETICAL ORDER

RU	NU/RL	W continued
	58	Wilson, Harry
263		Wilson, Matthew
	965	Wingfield, Craig
	1101	Wingfield, Lee
	396	Winkworth, Ken
	579	Winnard, Dave
	214	Winstanley, Jack
233	4	Winterbottom, William
	882	Wolfgramm, Willie
	487	Wood, Dick
	556	Wood, Graham
114		Wood, H
	757	Wood, John
	1145	Wood, Paul
	1046	Wood, Phil
	312	Woodall, Stan
	361	Woodend, Vic

RU	NU/RL	
	121	Woods, Charlie
	1039	Woods, Darren
	651	Woods, Dave
	424	Woods, Les
	955	Woods, Mike
	497	Worsley, Alan
	213	Worsley, Harry
223		Worsley, Ted
	65	Worthington, Charles
159		Worthington, H
	1168	Worthington, Joe
	38	Worthington, John
	484	Worthington, Les
115		Wright, James
	305	Wright, Joe
	736	Wright, Terry
244		Wynard, William

RU	NU/RL	Y
	W	Yarwood, Billy
269		Yates
	79	Yates, Edward
33*		Yates, Henry
	363	Yates, Jim
38*		Yates, John
113		Yates, William
	82	Yates, William
	34	Yeoman, Fred
	1085	York, Dave
	230	Yorke, Jack
	300	Young, Billy
	158	Young, Eric
	566	Young, Tom

RU	NU/RL	Z
	785	Zenon, Ronel

265 Jack Pearson

749 Tommy Frodsham

475 Peter Smethurst

1147 Josh Barlow

HONOURS LIST

Swinton Lions Rugby League Club

L CHAMPIONSHIP
Winners: 1926/27, 1927/28, 1930/31, 1934/35, 1962/63, 1963/64
Runners-up: 1924/25, 1932/33, 1939/40

HALLENGE CUP
Winners: 1899/1900, 1925/26, 1927/28
Runners-up: 1926/27, 1931/32

ANCASHIRE CUP
Winners: 1925/26, 1927/28, 1939/40, 1969/70
Runners-up: 1910/11, 1923/24, 1931/32, 1960/61, 1961/62, 1962/63, 1964/65, 1972/73

ANCASHIRE LEAGUE
Winners: 1924/25, 1927/28, 1928/29, 1930/31, 1939/40, 1960/61
Runners-up: 1897/98, 1900/01, 1922/23, 1926/27, 1934/35, 1938/39, 1964/65

WESTERN DIVISION CHAMPIONSHIP
Runners-up: 1963/64

BBC2 FLOODLIT TROPHY
Runners-up: 1966/67

SECOND DIVISION
Winners: 1984/85
Runners-up: 1986/87

SECOND DIVISION PREMIERSHIP
Winners: 1986/87
Runners-up: 1988/89

CHAMPIONSHIP/LEAGUE 1 (3rd tier)
Winners: 2011
Runners-up: 1996
Play-off Winners: 2015
Play-off Runners-up: 2006

iPRO SPORT CUP
Runners-up: 2015

WIGAN SUMMER SEVENS
Winners: 1985/86

Skipper Hector Halsall, clutching the 1928 Challenge Cup, is held aloft by jubilant fans

With grateful thanks to our subscribers

GRAHAM ACTON: *In Memory of Tom Jake Dyos Acton.*

PATRICIA ARTHUR: *Wirral.*

LES ATKINSON: *Thank you to Swinton RLFC for the memories of running out at Station Road with my mates.*

DEREK BATE: *It was a great part of my life to become a Lion and to represent the Lions.*

GRACE BAYNHAM: *A 1980s Junior Blue who liked to play on the Station Road terraces! Love Dad.*

SUE BLACKMAN: *To Simon Marland, April 2017 xx.*

GRAHAM AND SUSAN BOARDMAN.

IAN BURY: *Swinton Lions means being able to share precious time with my boy, my dad and my brother-in-law.*

PETER CHAPPELL: *In memory of my father, Arthur Chappell 1910-1991, who took me to see the great 60s Lions.*

MARTYN CHENEY: *Congratulations on 150 years from everyone at Bramley Buffaloes.*

ROB DUNFORD: *Come on you Lions. Keep believing!*

DEBBIE DYSON: *To David Kozomara, with all my love to you now and forever.*

JOHN ENSER: *With thanks to all those Lions who gave me and my late father Alan Enser a treasure trove of memories.*

DICK EVANS: *I feel so proud, privileged and honoured to have been part of this great club.*

BOB FLEAY: *To all Lions' fans and players. It was an honour playing for you and playing with you.*

KAREN GOWERS: *To dad (Ken Gowers). Thanks for the wonderful memories. Simply the best. Love Karen.*

LAURA, LESLEY & MARK GOWERS: *Great memories of Ken Gowers' career with Swinton and Great Britain.*

PETER GREEN: *Third generation Swinton supporter. Sixty years and counting. Swinton 'til I die!*

SIMON GREEN: *To my wonderful Mum and Dad & every player privileged to pull on that blue and white jersey.*

CHRIS HASLAM: *Everlasting memories of the great Lions team of the 1960s.*

PAUL HICKS: *From a Leeds supporter that values the history of our game.*

NICK HILL: *With loving memories of Anne and Jack Hill, Swinton supporters for seventy years.*

NICK HILL: *A lifelong Swinton fan and a wonderful human being. Love Kim, Asti, Greg and Kate.*

ROBERT HOPE.

JOHN HUGHES: *Wilfred Hughes (Wilf) 1913-1995. John Hughes 1942-?*

STEPHEN JOHNSON: *Thanks to my father Arthur for introducing me to this fine club and the greatest game.*